FREDDY LONSDALE

Books by
FRANCES DONALDSON

★

Approach to Farming
Four Years' Harvest
Milk Without Tears
Freddy Lonsdale

FREDDY LONSDALE
from a portrait by Simon Elwes

Freddy Lonsdale

BY FRANCES DONALDSON

WILLIAM HEINEMANN LTD
MELBOURNE :: LONDON :: TORONTO

FIRST PUBLISHED 1957

PRINTED IN GREAT BRITAIN
AT THE WINDMILL PRESS
KINGSWOOD, SURREY

To
E. M.

Acknowledgments

The author would like to thank John Murray, Ltd., for permission to quote from *Stage to Stage* by Peter Daubeney, Messrs. Raymond Mander and Joe Mitchenson for information relating to the list of the works of Frederick Lonsdale on pp 247–249, and many friends for help.

Contents

Illustrations

Introduction

FREDERICK LONSDALE had his first play produced in London in 1908 and his last in 1950, and between these two he wrote twenty-four plays or musical plays which were produced in London or New York. The years of his greatest success, however, were the nineteen-twenties and early-thirties. This was the period, too, to which he seemed to have belonged. At no other time could the world have worn for him so much the aspect of his own home ground; at no other time could it have been so receptive to his talents or so enchanted by his person. So that, although he lived until 1954, and lived in a charmed circle of appreciation and love, he always seemed in later years to be a figure from the nineteen-twenties.

It was a curious period, as different from anything that preceded it as it was from the present day. It has been called the age of wealth without responsibility, and, if a label can be accepted that refers only to the upper classes, this is as good as any other. Self-regarded, it seemed the age of disillusion, and it was the expression of this that gave the peculiar flavour to the times. If there had been no great cause for disillusion it would all have been easier to understand, but there was a cause, and, looking back, it seems strange that so large a disturbance should have produced so shallow a despair.

It was, I think, the post-war boom that set the scene for a

convalescence which, if incomplete, was luxurious and indulgent, painless and light-hearted, as compared with the
struggling progress of the generation of thirty years later. The
world, or that part of it with which we are concerned, after
the First World War lay bleeding, but not, as after the second,
poverty-stricken. The earlier generation had the means to
throw off the shackles of sorrow, self-discipline and horror
which for so long had held them, and so they threw them overboard completely.

They seem to have been so innocent; but, in compensation
for any wisdom we may later have learned, they seem to have
been so robust.

In those days they danced; they danced at tea-time, right
through dinner and into the early hours of the morning.
London society moved out of the salons and the ballrooms
into the night-clubs; and these they attended so regularly that
they remained an exclusive circle, nodding and smiling to each
other across the tables and calling the waiters by name. Women
of the aristocracy boasted that they had not dined alone with
their husbands in two years, and débutantes, sidling at midnight into some crowded, dark and smoke-filled cave beneath
the streets of London, called to their elders: "Don't tell
Mummy." All that throng that permanently in England press
upwards from the middle classes to form the periphery of an
esoteric group imitated the manner of this little circle, whom
they still regarded, if not as their betters, at least as the stars of
a drama in which they were determined to furnish the chorus.
Nowadays when they meet, they sadly say to each other: "I
dined at the Savoy Grill last night. There was not one single
soul I knew."

The money that was earned in the post-war boom was spent
on the race-courses of England and in the casinos of France, on
country houses, and on the least formal but materially the most

perfected hospitality ever known. Golf, tennis and back-
gammon were taken seriously; more gin was drunk and less
wine; the daughters of rich men could get through the day
without either social work or a job in a hat shop; *The Green Hat*
(he died for purity) was a best-seller. They were not patrons of
the arts; and, when the slump came and men stood on the
streets in Jarrow, although they cut down their domestic staff,
it was not considered necessary to discuss social guilt at a
dinner party in London.

But they still felt responsible for their own personalities.
They were aware that man is born to suffer and to die, and they
felt that this knowledge might be drowned in old brandy; but
few people yet seriously believed that the whole thing could be
avoided by going to a psycho-analyst, or by a judicious use of
benzedrine. As a result they knew where they stood on all
sorts of matters which to us present difficulties. They thought
it proper to loathe homosexuals and to be bored by the clergy,
they regarded security as a thing of the past, but they still used
ridicule as a weapon to combat socialism.

In those days it was thought not merely usual but also
becoming for famous men to carry a little side; a man's position
in life could be assessed by the entrance he made into a room;
and, unless my imagination betrays me, great men cultivated
not simply a more impressive manner, but more ponderous or
more comical heads.

It was still thought nice to be rich. This was the age of Miss
Runcible and Lady Metroland, figures who, ruthlessly irresponsible, teetered to their doom, but did so with an elaborate
indifference which only wealth and rank make possible, and
with some relish. Nowadays, if they wanted to gain any
attention at all, they would have to be confined to flats in mews,
dressed in pink silk crocheted sweaters, and no ray of pleasure
could be allowed to disturb the squalid failure of their lives.

In the theatre there was a very sharp distinction between the 'West End' theatre and the 'Highbrow' theatre, represented by the Old Vic and the repertory companies, and when John Barrymore played Hamlet for a limited season at the Haymarket there was much speculation beforehand as to whether he could fill the house. In those days, boys who, on long leave from Eton, went to the opera, reported on their return to school only the visit they had made to the Coliseum.

At the head of the acting profession stood Sir Gerald du Maurier, the leader of what is now called the 'natural' drama, and despised as an inartistic and unimportant departure from tradition. He was a man of his times, and it may be true that he had no depth, or variety, or genuine emotion, or force, or sensitivity as an actor; he may have lacked the cerebral intuitions that lie behind great art, and regularly portrayed on the stage the same character he portrayed in his life. In spite of these defects he created a revolution. With studied and elegant carelessness, he destroyed overnight the whole school of what Mr. Harold Hobson calls 'rumbustious' acting, and put the modern meaning into the theatre word 'ham'. On any historical view he must be seen to have paved the way for the finely perceptive performances we receive to-day. It takes a man of quality to create an artistic revolution, a man of genuine talent to act even as a stepping-stone, and I think myself that du Maurier deserved greater respect than the more priggish of our dramatic critics are nowadays apt to give him.

He was a great director too, and the actors and actresses who, having played with him, still remain with us remember him as amongst the best they have known. They themselves are much sought after on the rare occasions when it comes to high comedy. Du Maurier was at all events a great personality, about as natural on or off the stage as *canard sauvage au bourgogne* or a wild mink coat.

The dramatists of the day were professional and many were very successful. It is sometimes said now that they wrote only good bad plays, but it has yet to be proved that this is a lesser achievement than writing bad good plays, that entertainment is not the natural business of the theatre, or that squeamishness, unless backed by exceptional talent, produces a finer tradition. The theatre of that day may stand low in the annals of culture, but it depended much less on brilliantly acted revivals, on the French and on the Americans.

It was at this time, for these actors and for this public, that Frederick Lonsdale wrote his best plays. Whether he will be remembered as a playwright or not, it is impossible at the moment to say. At the height of his popularity it could truthfully be said of him that he was amongst the most successful dramatists that ever lived, and he was often compared in his life-time to Congreve and to Sheridan. It has been said that his plays, particularly the third act of *The Last of Mrs. Cheyney*, should be taken by all students of the dramatic art as a model of how to write dialogue which, though not lifelike, is apparently lifelike. Lately, however, some people have begun to decry him; to say that he was never a great playwright, merely a weaver of frivolous trifles, or, much more surprisingly, an Edwardian embroiderer of artificial plots with leisurely and rounded phrases.

However, contemporary criticism of any playwright over fifty can often be ignored. The critics, in their inevitable struggle for modernity for themselves, are abnormally sensitive to outmodedness in other people. Quite frequently they dismiss plays as out-of-date nonsense to which the public, both old and young, continue to flock for many months to come. And, while the public may not be highly considered for their æsthetic judgments, they must surely be allowed some part in decisions on fashion.

There is another reason why contemporary judgments of writers of comedy are not an entirely safe guide. Once, after the production of a Lonsdale play which received bad notices, Mr. W. Somerset Maugham wrote a letter to the author which simply said: "Dear Freddy, Always remember the English hate wit. Yours, Willy." While it may not be true that the English hate wit, it is certainly true that they despise it and regard it as one of the minor arts. It is extremely unusual for a member of the theatrical profession who specialises in comedy, whether a writer, or an actor or actress, to receive the highest honours. These are reserved for the tragedians.

Comedy is thought of not simply as a different art, but as an easier one. (That it is not so is apparent to anyone who has had the difficult task of casting a Lonsdale play.) The critics are a solemn body of men, always looking for merit; but they look for it in those plays which set a problem in human relationships, even if this is then solved in terms which, outside the dramatic convention, would be totally unacceptable. Fantasy keeps them suspicious—it is always possible here that it is one's own dull imagination that is to blame. But the merest sucklings from Oxford can see at a glance that comedy is a craft any stage carpenter can contrive.

Yet if a member of the public were to be asked to name a list of playwrights, since the Shakespearian era, whose plays had survived, in the sense of being regularly performed, even twenty years, he would almost inevitably begin: "Congreve, Sheridan, Wilde . . . who else?"

And Mr. Ashton Stevens wrote this of Frederick Lonsdale:

"I hope he never deserts the Comic Spirit for the Significant, the Propagandic, the Uplifting. I hope the persons in his plays continue to inhabit the pedigreed Valhalla of Society. That scene was made for his fun, even as it was made for the fun of Henry James. . . .

"I wish Bernard Shaw would write about *The Last of Mrs. Cheyney* as he wrote about *The Importance of Being Earnest* when smaller critics were saying that anybody light-minded enough to do so could toss off an *Importance*. Shaw Saturday-Reviewed: 'I am the only person in London who cannot sit down and write an Oscar Wilde play at will.'

"No author of my experience can write a Frederick Lonsdale play at will. There are times when Freddy himself cannot do it."

This was written in the *Chicago Herald-American* in 1947. Mr. Stevens went on to say:

"I don't think there will ever be the last of *Mrs. Cheyney*. Its gem-like flame is as spontaneous as a poem. Or, for another figure, it is like the champagne whose slow processes of maturation in the mellowing vault, where it stands on its head like an epigram, are forgotten in the brightness of its bubbles.

"Some twenty years ago I offered this bet on the durability of *Mrs. Cheyney*—and it still goes: 'I have a fertile dollar to hazard (in escrow) that it will be everybody's play when the dateline on this journal reads Jan 2, 2027.' "

Nevertheless, all one can say for certain is that very few playwrights are remembered.

But, as long as there is anyone left alive who knew him, Freddy Lonsdale will be remembered for his irresistible charm and his unique personality. In America, France and England, people will suddenly pause in conversation, and, placing the four fingers of the right hand vertically along the bridge of the nose and the thumb between the nostrils, say: "My dear fellow! My dear fellow! . . ." in tones of great excitement, and with the accent equally on the first three syllables of the four.

His family name was Leonard, and he was christened Lionel

Frederick. It is not certain that the change of his surname was made simply to achieve euphony for the theatre.

According to one story which he sometimes told himself, being as a young man already afflicted with the costly tastes which later in life so distinguished him, he was at one time heavily in debt. He was walking along a London street one day with a young companion and explaining to him his difficulties. The other young man told him that what he should do was temporarily to change his name, so that his creditors would be unable to find him. Struck by the audacious simplicity of this idea, he looked up and read the name of the street in which they happened to be walking. This was Lonsdale Road, and at that moment Frederick Lonsdale was born.

There is nothing in the facts of this story to make it seem highly improbable. He was lucky, if it is true, to find, with so little thought, a name that combined so gracefully with Freddy.

He had an odd appearance. His face was the colour of a bright, new cricket ball, and it was marked in early youth by the use of a faulty vaccine—or so it was thought at the time. Modern science is more inclined to attribute it to an allergy to the vaccine, a thing which is occasionally known. In any case, although this gave him an unusual appearance, it was not in the least unattractive. His hair, which was very fair, remained thick and practically unchanged in colour to the end of his life. His eyes were a very vivid blue and were his most attractive feature. They could look quizzically gay and a little expectant; or sad, with the blankly bewildered sadness of a child who has unintentionally provoked wrath. This last look frequently appeared on his face; whenever, in fact, he seemed not to be getting his way about something, and it was a great help to him, and accounted, as much as anything else, for the fact that, all through his life, he nearly always did get his way when it was in the power of other people to give it to him.

His clothes were slightly eccentric. He normally wore a suit that was well cut and well pressed but more suitable to the country than to the town; he always wore white socks and a white scarf; and he wore a rather broad-brimmed hat with an edge that turned up. This hat, although it must sometimes have been renewed, was never seen to be new. It was always old and battered and not even particularly clean. In all the most expensive restaurants in the world, head waiters would, without the movement of an eyelid, take this shattering hat and the white scarf from his hands, as he made his way to a table for lunch, and hand them to a page, who would receive them with equal aplomb.

He was born of the simplest parents in a two-roomed cottage in the island of Jersey. Many years later he showed me this cottage with the greatest possible pride from the seat of an open Bentley car. His father was a tobacconist in the local town of St. Helier, and his mother a Jersey woman of whom he always spoke with extreme respect. He appears to have been a villainous and undisciplined child who refused to attend the only schooling that was open to him. As a result of this he was always totally uneducated. He knew how to spell but his ideas of grammar would have been thought astonishing by a preparatory school boy. In the whole of his life he was very seldom angry with me, but one of the few occasions I remember was when, as a child of about nine, I asked him to help me with my homework. He struggled hard for about five minutes and then he threw the book at my head and went out of the room in a rage.

He was also without taste or culture. He once told me, again when I was a child, that composers of opera were people who, having finished the score, "went down to the country for a

month to take out all the tunes." He almost never read anything, but about once a year he found a book that he enjoyed.
He would then read and re-read it, recommend it to other
people both in conversation and by letter, quote from it at
length, and carry it round in his personal luggage until he found
another. At the time that Madame Nijinsky published the book
about her husband that had such a success, he read it, and it
became his book for that year.

I said to him: "Did you never see Nijinsky dance?"

"Yes," he replied, with a snort of laughter. "Yes, I did see
him. But I just thought it was funny."

Even more curious was the fact that he almost never, in the
whole of his life, sat right through a play by any other playwright. A few years ago he went to see Sir Laurence and Lady
Olivier in Shaw's *Cæsar and Cleopatra*, and he spoke of this performance with great enthusiasm. As far as I am concerned,
this is the only time I remember his going to a play. He was
very individual and he seldom enjoyed other people's work. If
this took a form which he did not understand, he simply
thought it was bad, and he was always quite impenitent about
this attitude. Towards the end of his life, my sister, Mab, asked
him why a friend of his was going to South Africa.

"He's afraid," he replied, "that, if he stays in England,
sooner or later some woman will get hold of him and take him
to *The Living Room*."

In spite of his birth and his extraordinary upbringing, he
spoke with the accent and manner of Eton and Oxford; and
that is something that I have never been able to understand.
People who knew him in his youth say that he never spoke
differently; but how a Jersey urchin, completely without
education or background, acquired not merely the speech, but
also the confident, easy manner of the English upper classes,
is a matter which, as he would have said, beats me. The

personality which he presented to the world was a work of genius beside which his plays might easily be inferior.

He was famed, of course, for his wit; but I have never been absolutely clear that this was as great in ordinary conversation as people, dazzled by his reputation, thought it to be. P. G. Wodehouse once said to me: "Of course, Freddy is bound to live, because he will appear in every book of memoirs of the period." Curiously enough, this does not seem to be true. He appears, of course, in all those books which are written to catch a small public for a short time, and which consist largely of one anecdote strung to another, mostly wrongly attributed or at the very least taken out of context. But Arnold Bennett, for instance, in his diaries, says only this: "An enchanting evening at the Garrick. Freddy told us the funniest stories."

I think the reason is this. He was a good conversationalist and an amusing companion. Good conversation does not really consist to any very great degree of epigrams or quotable stories. The unexpected phrase, the amusing intonation, or even the successful thrust in ordinary life do not lend themselves to repetition in print in the way that is normally assumed. It is the dryer, lonelier figures who, speaking seldom and only to the point, are such a god-send to the biographer. Charm and originality, those qualities so vastly more difficult to get down on paper, were what for fifty years made Freddy Lonsdale beloved in England and America.

To people he liked he was ingenuously admiring and devoted. If you were not "one of the bloodiest bores in the world" (a thing it was only too easy to become at any moment) you were "brilliant, charming, intelligent, a very able fellow", or, highest praise of all, "a tramp". All his geese were swans, and from this quality I myself suffered a great deal. He was always exceptionally fond of me and all his life he used to praise me to his friends in terms which no human being could live up to.

Added to this, he always made use of me for his own purposes in the following way. Lying, for instance, in his bath, he would think of something amusing to say. He could not go down to dinner and begin his conversation by saying: "As I was lying in my bath, I thought . . ."; and so he would say instead: "I was talking to my daughter, Frankie, the other day, and she said . . ."

As a result, I spent my life meeting people who said to me: "I have been longing to meet you for years. Freddy has told me so many amusing things about you." I never have succeeded in evolving a technique for dealing with this opening and so I am usually left looking what Freddy would have described as "a bloody fool". And I only remember one amusing variant on this conversation.

At the time that I first met Harold Talbott he had been a friend of my father's for years. I was to sit next to him at dinner and I was warned that if he did not like people he could be difficult. However, he is an attractive personality, and I found no trouble in talking to him. Half-way through dinner he said to me:

"Have you got a mother?"

I replied that I had.

"Have you any sisters?"

I said that, yes, I had two.

"Freddy," he said with a sigh, "has only one daughter; and for years I've been so bored by her that I've always dreaded meeting her."

So much of Freddy's life was spent in hotels that it is in the restaurant of a hotel one mostly thinks of him. I can see now a picture of him standing in the entrance to some restaurant, pulling at his nose, and looking dejected and as though waiting for something. He never waited long. As the waiters sprang to attention, chairs would scrape back all over the room and half a dozen voices call out: "Freddy." Immediately his appearance changed. His hand would leave his nose and go out in a gesture of pleasure. "My dear fellow, my dear fellow . . ."

Afterwards seated at our table I would say to him:

"Who was that man you spoke to by the window?"

And, according to his mood, he would reply: "That, my dear, is the greatest power in the motion picture world to-day." Or: "God knows, some bloody bore."

He was often thought to be a snob; but this was partly because he usually wrote about dukes in his plays and partly because in his rise to fame he left many people behind him. The truth was that he went where he found it amusing, and he often found it amusing in the drawing-rooms of London society. But he was no respecter of persons, and to the end of his life he really thought the only people of any importance were writers, lawyers, and actors and actresses. He thought that a duke was a man who had inherited a position which was useful but unimportant, and any duke he knew had to be also an original and eccentric figure before he would privately allow him even equality.

He never at any time in his life wanted to meet people simply for their position in the world. On one occasion a woman friend of his telephoned to him and said:

"Freddy, will you come to a *very* small party I am giving? The Prince of Wales and Mrs. Simpson will be there."

"No, ducky," he replied instantaneously. "Ask me when you are giving a large party."

I must make it clear that he meant no disrespect for His Royal Highness, who afterwards, as Duke of Windsor, did him the honour of his friendship. It was simply that he did not know him and had no desire to go to this kind of an occasion.

But, although he was not a snob, he loved the aristocracy.

In this society he found a kind of negligent conviction of superiority which for him expressed the dignity of mankind. He had no time for humility, for the nervousness which often accompanies it, for keeping up appearances, or for the sad small points which go with these things. Amongst the aristocracy he enjoyed, as much as any, the stupid ones, or those who were sufficiently self-conscious to affect stupidity. For, although in spirit he was with them, he knew enough of life to have his sense of humour ravished by their assumptions. If he could find a blue-eyed, red-faced man who, speaking in a slightly hoarse voice which recalled the racecourses, would begin his sentences: "This damn fellow said to me . . ." he would sit contentedly all night listening to him, and never tire of this demonstration of the triumph of matter over mind.

When he came to England from America after the last war, he went to stay in one of the great houses of England, where his host, not a fool, nevertheless shared his predilections.

"Do we," Freddy asked on the first evening, with an affectation of nervousness, "do we still have those sausages for breakfast?"

"By God, I should hope so!" was the indignant reply. And, to Freddy, this was to come home at last. For here, in this land of welfare workers, of queue formers, of bottles of baby food, here was a man.

Nevertheless, he had friends in absolutely every walk of life, and I think he must occasionally have surprised some of his more fashionable acquaintances. Walking back to his hotel at night with someone with whom he had been dining, he would say:

"Come in a minute and I will introduce you to a very interesting fellow."

Marching across the foyer of the hotel, he would lean on the reception desk and speak to the man on night duty.

"Now," he would say, wagging his forefinger in the air, "tell this gentleman that story you told me last night."

He was always on very friendly terms with the servants in the hotels where he stayed.

"Ah." he would say, to the waiter, who brought him the menu. "You're back."

Then he would turn to me.

"This fellow has a garden. And he is a complete bloody bore about it. Now," wagging the finger, "tell my daughter about your garden."

He always chose his waiters well, and the man, aware that some joke had been made which he did not understand, but conscious also of the friendliness of the tone, would reply simply and enthusiastically. This meant, among other things, that for the rest of my stay in the hotel I was on garden terms with this waiter, and consequently got every possible attention.

Freddy was aware, of course, of the material benefits to be had from good manners to people who serve you, but he also had a genuine desire to be courteous. In the last year of his life I went over to Le Touquet to stay with him. He met me at the airport in his car and drove me back to the hotel. On the way into the hotel, he stopped me in the garden.

"By the way," he said, pushing his hat to the back of his head, "we Frenchmen shake hands when we meet."

He then took me into the hotel, where he introduced me to madame the proprietress, the hall porter and the head waiter, and obediently I shook hands with all three.

But, although he was friendly, he never accepted, and indeed seldom received, either familiarity of an impertinent kind, or any lapse in the highest standards of service. The Carol Reeds told me once that they were sitting with him late one night in Claridge's Hotel, when something went wrong. He summoned as many of the staff as were still awake and proceeded to harangue them.

"If this kind of thing goes on," he said, "in one year from now this place will be a boarding-house."

He was also very much loved by the servants in the houses where he stayed. Mrs. Cowdin, with whom he stayed a great deal in America, told me that on one occasion her maid came to her and complained that the house was too full.

"Mr. Lonsdale doesn't like all these people," she said, "it stops him working and makes him feel very unhappy."

However, it was not all done by charm. He was a very formidable and a terrifying character. He was never pleasant when he felt unpleasant, and he was never pleasant if he was crossed in any way. The smiles and jokes of the evening could turn to some very unexpected snarls in the morning.

The manager of the hotel in Paris where he used to stay for weeks at a time was talking to me soon after his death.

"He was a very charming man," he said, "a very charming man. He knew everybody. The Duchess of ——, Lord ——, all the Americans, they all came here to ask for Mr. Lonsdale."

He paused and then he said: "He was a very charming man, but he was also a very nasty man."

Since he was speaking of a respected client who had died less than a month before, I thought that probably his English had let him down.

"Difficult?" I queried.

"No, not difficult," he replied firmly, "nasty. Listen now to this. Lately Mr. Lonsdale had this idea that the franc was going to fall, and so he does not wish to change his money, which is in dollars, into francs. So he will not pay his bill. I get frightened even to mention the subject, he is so nasty when I talk about it. In the end I think to myself: Something has to be done. So I go to him and I say: 'Mr. Lonsdale, what about your bill?' So he says to me: 'Now listen to me, my dear fellow. If you ask me to pay my bill, I will not stay in your hotel.' "

At this point he shrugged his shoulders with a real stage gesture.

"*Quoi faire?*"

Mr. Lonsdale was not only nasty, he was incalculable. Things that pleased him one day irritated him the next, and it was absolutely impossible to predict his reaction to any event. His dearest friends of one day were his enemies of the next and vice versa. He had a very unpleasant habit of swearing on my life that he would never speak to someone again, whereas the next time one saw him he would be sitting in a restaurant with this very same person, drinking champagne and in the highest good humour. But the truth is that when people disliked him it was usually because he had not troubled to make them like him. He had an extraordinary natural charm and he knew how to use it.

He always made people feel that he found them intelligent and amusing, and he did this by a mixture of open flattery and a kind of rough, verbal shaking, which caused them, in fact, to behave with less restraint than was normal to them and, consequently, actually to be more entertaining than they usually were.

"For a woman as intelligent as you are," he would say to someone he had only met five minutes before, "that was a bloody silly remark."

It was almost exactly the same technique that Winston Churchill used in his famous broadcasts during the war, when he used to tell the British people that the situation was a great deal worse than they could possibly have known it to be, but that, as they could be counted on to keep their heads and their courage, all would be well. After the bad news, people unaccountably felt better.

Freddy had the most extraordinarily subtle methods of finding out anything he wanted to know.

"I'm sorry to hear," he would say, rubbing his nose, "that your friend So-and-so is unhappy with that man she married."

"How on earth did you know that?" one would reply; only to realise in a flash that he had not known it, had not known anything at all; that it was merely a prospective shot in the dark.

Another method was by praise.

"So you're working for So-and-so. They tell me he is a most charming man. A genial, kindly fellow and pleasant to work for."

"He may be," his provoked hearer would reply, "but that didn't stop him trying to do me out of £400 last week."

"You don't mean that!" in tones of surprise, and carefully controlling his eagerness. "Tell me more about that. I'm amazed to hear it."

This technique was known to his friends as 'bouncing'.

"So-and-so and so-and-so," people would say, "but for God's sake don't let Freddy bounce you."

People who knew him well chose their confidants, not for their honour, but for their wits. But no one was ever seriously crimed for failing to keep a secret.

"I'm most terribly sorry," one would say, "he simply bounced me."

And, although this might not be immediately forgiven, it was always understood.

In the same way, however badly he behaved, it was always impossible to remain angry with him for very long. I only remember having one serious row with him after I was grown up, but this was a very bad one. It was at a time when things were not going very well for him and he was in a nervous and profoundly irritable mood. I was living alone with him and I went into the drawing-room one day after luncheon, to be met, quite unexpectedly, with a scene of towering rage. Every kind of unbelievable charge was levelled at me and every kind of impossible suggestion made. When he wished to be vile, he had no difficulty at all.

This scene lasted about twenty minutes, and I was so flabbergasted I hardly answered at all. Before leaving the room I did, however, manage to tell him what I thought of him and to convey that on the following morning I would be removing my unwanted and practically criminal person from his house. I then went up to my room.

I had been up very late the night before, and lack of sleep combined with this extraordinary scene had exhausted me. I went to bed and slept for about three hours.

I opened my eyes to see him standing with his back to the door of my bedroom. He looked shrunken with unhappiness and his blue eyes were as vivid as the Jersey sea where he was born.

"I never could have believed," he said, "that you could have said such beastly things to me."

I knew then as well as I have ever known anything that he had waited downstairs expecting me to come back and either continue the scene or make things up. When at the end of three hours I had still not appeared, he got seriously frightened, and had thought that perhaps he would have to do something about it himself. But the act was so good that, like a scene on the stage, it touched all the surface springs of emotion, self-pity and sentimentality. An hour or two later we were sharing a bottle of champagne in a restaurant.

He always cheated in personal relationships in this way, but people always seemed to forgive him both the initial crime and the cheating. No one that I ever knew had the heart to undeceive so skilled a self-deceiver. Secondly, these imaginatively conceived and brilliantly performed acts he put on were not unflattering as a form of apology.

Such dishonesties were necessary to him. He was extremely affectionate and very dependent on people whom he loved, but he was a profound and absolute egotist. He was a man who never, if he could possibly help it, did anything he did not want to do. Only the people who knew him well realised this about him, because he was so alert to find reasons why what he wanted to do would also be the best for everyone else.

In the last year of his life when I went to Le Touquet he had told me to fly there direct by Lympne. I then discovered that without a car it is practically impossible to get to Lympne, so I sent him a wire telling him I was coming by sea to Boulogne. The night before I was to leave I came into the house and was told by my husband that Freddy had telephoned from Le Touquet and said I was to hire a car from London to Lympne because, as I was going for such a short time, the boat journey would be too tiring for me.

"But I told him," said Jack, "that you didn't really mind it a bit and were actually looking forward to the boat."

"You are an idiot," I replied. "You don't suppose he gives a damn about me. He's got some reason why he doesn't want to motor to Boulogne to fetch me."

"Oh!" said Jack. "Do you think so? I never thought of that."

"It doesn't matter," I said, "he'll ring up again."

About half an hour later the telephone rang and it was Freddy.

"Look here, Frankie," he said, "you're to hire a car from London and go to Lympne."

"It'll be very expensive," I replied.

"I can't help that," he said excitedly. "They tell me the road is up between here and Boulogne, and I'm not damn well going to motor forty miles on a bloody French road that's up."

It was because of these abominable characteristics, rather than in spite of them, that those who knew him best loved him best. One needed to be able to see the workings to appreciate the show. We used to sit goggle-eyed with joy watching him get out of any difficult situation. And, of course, like many people who regularly imposed upon others, he had some of the qualities of the ostrich. It was very often possible to see his purpose about half a mile off, and then, although obstruction was no weapon to use against him, he could very often be defeated by distraction.

He saw life so largely in terms of his own imagination that it was never possible to trust what he said about anything. This applied both to the version of any day-to-day incident that he related to you and to his renderings of established facts. Hardly anyone ever realised the extent of his imaginings, partly because he so often sincerely believed what he said himself, but chiefly because much of his invention was, from the view of anyone else, too pointless to arouse suspicion. There usually was some point, but this would often be very obscure, and only occasionally discernible by someone with a deep knowledge of his character, because these departures from the truth were usually instinctively inspired and not deliberately calculated. For the most part, of course, the intention was simply to amuse, but there might be other, more subtle and complex, motives. A game I have always enjoyed is the attempt to understand his reasons when I have known sufficient of the truth to realise that he was embroidering or distorting it; but, as did everyone else, I often accepted complete fabrications because my suspicions were not even aroused.

One of the difficulties with excessively imaginative people is that one cannot by rule merely discount everything they say.

Their powers of invention are stirred into action by deeply intuitive impulses of their own. When the truth is bizarre and immediately unlikely, it may content them; as equally where one humdrum occurrence may seem to require embellishment, some other may be left alone. Because most of Freddy's daily imaginings were uncalculated, irrational, and harmless, they were usually believed. Much force was then lent them by repetition. Any biographer without access to original sources would, for instance, be forced to conclude that in his early youth he left his home to join a circus, because this is a fact included in the biographical material under his name in every newspaper office in London. As the real facts of his youth are already sufficiently startling, there is no reason to suspect that in the case of this story, which has been so often repeated as to be unquestioningly accepted, there is neither truth nor any authority other than Freddy's word.

In the same way his version of his relationship with some other person, or his part in some episode, would frequently receive the backing of people who did not even know him, and only someone sufficiently interested to give the matter real thought would realise that this independent evidence might really stem, like a sentence passed round a whispering circle and heard at fourth or fifth remove, from some statement originating with him. His relationship with Lord Beaverbrook remains a mystery. These two men were lifelong friends and they were genuinely fond of each other. Towards the end of Freddy's life his financial position was a source of worry to those of his friends who realised that, in the event of his living to an old age, he was unlikely to be able to do so in the style on which he insisted. Someone once told him that, this subject having been discussed in Lord Beaverbrook's presence, he had remarked: "Freddy will never have to worry about money as long as I am alive." Although he would very much have disliked to have had to take advantage of this generosity, the remark lived in Freddy's heart, and could be made to engender warmth on even his most despondent days. He returned the affection that inspired it. Nevertheless, when talking of Lord Beaverbrook, he frequently spoke of quarrels between them: "God! the rows I've had with that man," he would say; or tell of times when for months at a time Lord Beaverbrook had refused to speak to him. This version of their acquaintance was confirmed to me only the other day by someone who is closer to Lord Beaverbrook than ever he was to Freddy, and who described their relationship as that of "friendly enemies" or "inimical friends". Yet Lord Beaverbrook himself cannot remember any of this. He was amused when I asked him about it, but he also seemed surprised.

"I don't recall any quarrel," he said. "There were times when we were ranged together in an argument and we made other people very angry, but I don't recall any quarrel with Freddy."

For my part, I know that it would have been essential to Freddy to quarrel with Lord Beaverbrook. It would have seemed to him that, if one were going to remain throughout a lifetime on terms of great friendship with a man so powerful and so capricious, then it was absolutely necessary occasionally to have a row with him—just to show that everything was, as it were, on the level. It may have been difficult. These two men were very fond of one another; they had no business dealings; and they did not see enough of each other to get on one another's nerves. Freddy may have been forced to invent these quarrels. In passing, he would do his friend all justice, and, in fact, his picture of Lord Beaverbrook was of a powerful, eccentric, impatient man—who allowed his chosen friends to quarrel with him.

Freddy loved making mischief between other people. The

easiest game was husband and wife. Some quite every-day discussion would begin, and by ganging up with the husband
against the wife he would soon have things at white heat. At
this point he would switch and take the side of the wife.

"Come, come," he would say, "that's going a bit far. After
all you told me yourself the other day . . ." and then would
come out a remark which, though not exactly a confidence, and
only of minor importance, was something he knew quite well
the man would prefer his wife not to hear. After this he would
retire, since his intervention was no longer needed.

After I was married he often tried this game on me; but I had
watched the sport too often to be taken in, and though he
frequently, in fact, drove me nearly to boiling point, he never
once had the satisfaction of knowing it. This was one of the
reasons why he looked on Jack and me as almost beings from
another world. He had never before met a husband and wife
who could not quite easily be inflamed against each other.

He was devoted to Jack, but since the war Jack was a gift for
him, because he is a Socialist. He has never in fact stood for
Parliament or played any part in politics larger than chairman
of the village Labour Party. But during the period of the 1945
Government, the lunatic fringe of Conservatism (most of whom
were Freddy's friends) felt so emotionally on the subject of
politics that they would make the most absurd and base charges
against almost anyone who was known to be even pink.
Freddy would wait until a large party of men and women were
gathered together and then he would somehow introduce the
name 'Jack Donaldson'. If he had any luck at all, someone
would immediately say something really base about Jack.
Freddy would then stoke the conversation by defending Jack
only as much as was necessary.

"Surely," he would say, "that's going a little far," or: "How
do you know that's so?"

When he had got the other man to say as much as he thought he was likely to, Freddy would proceed to play some cards he could not have held without a fairly intimate knowledge of Jack.

"How do you know so much about him?" the other man would ask suspiciously.

"You see," Freddy would answer happily, "he's my son-in-law."

If one ever remonstrated with him for these tricks, he would take a high moral tone.

"I'm surprised at you, Frankie," half-closing his eyes and speaking very deliberately. "This fellow said unpardonable things about Jack. To *me*." With a satisfied shake of his head. "He deserved it."

These were his minor eccentricities. His major eccentricities were even more individual.

He was immensely hypochondriacal. He actually had for most of his life a kidney disease. This did not worry him very much until the last years of his life when it got very bad. But for fifty years he thought he had cancer. He never had a spot on his tongue from smoking, or a mark on his hand, without hurrying off nervously to a specialist. His doctors had to be chosen with extreme care for their persuasiveness. Otherwise he would come back from these visits and say:

"Of course, that bloody fellow tells me there is nothing wrong with me. But that's what they always say to people who are incurable. I didn't at all like the look he gave the nurse when he said it."

Then there is this story which is told of one of his visits to a doctor. He went, it is said, into the consulting-room of one of the most famous of London's physicians, and he explained that he had a very odd pain.

"I want to ask you one question, Sir Charles," he then said.

B

"If, when you have examined me, you find I have cancer, will you tell me the truth?"

The great man looked at him steadily.

"Yes," he replied, "I most certainly will."

"Thank you," Freddy said, "that was what I wanted to know."

He rose to his feet, and he tied his white scarf round his neck, and he picked up his hat.

"Good-morning," he said, as he left the room.

He always thought he had every sort of minor disease, and no one who knew him well would ever consent to tell him what were the symptoms of any particular illness. If one did, it took him about one hour to produce them all.

He suffered a great deal from liver, but this was caused entirely by boredom. If he was staying somewhere and wished to get away, he would show you a tongue like a pastry cook's hand. Half an hour later, driving away in the car, he would stick his tongue out at you and it would be bright pink. He only gave up having cancer and liver when the disease he really had became worse, and when, at about the same time, some doctor told him his blood pressure was high. Then he concentrated either on the reality or on a stroke.

But the oddest thing of all the odd things about him was that, after the age of forty, he was completely unable to stay for any length of time in any one place. This caused him to do the most extraordinary things. He would go to America meaning to stay for six months (at a cost of about £500 return) and leave for England on the first boat that sailed after his arrival. On one occasion he sailed for America and got off the ship at Cherbourg and returned to England. He would arrive to stay a week with someone and leave the same night. He was always in London when people thought him in Paris and in Paris when he should have been in London. His excuses were legion—

film magnates suddenly required his presence, he developed pains in his back and his legs, he had cancer, his children had unexpected operations—but half the time he did not bother to make excuses at all. All his friends were quite used to telephoning to tell him what time he was expected for dinner, only to be answered by a servant who said: "Oh! but, madam, Mr. Lonsdale left for New York this morning."

Nobody ever minded. There is one absolute rule of life. If you do the same thing often enough and establish a reputation for eccentricity firmly enough, you can get away with almost anything. Sometimes he got paid in his own coin. On one occasion he asked ten people to lunch at the Colony Restaurant in New York. Arriving early, he chose the table and ordered the food. Then he sat down to wait. Not one of his guests had believed that he would remember the invitation or would by then even be in New York. He waited an hour and then he ate a solitary lunch and left.

It was very difficult to understand the reason for this perpetual movement, but I think it was the occupational disease of the successful writer at its most advanced. When a writer is a young man, and before he has achieved success, he usually marries, because, more than anyone else in the world, he needs the faith in his power and the encouragement which only a wife can give. Then, like any normal person, he has some children. Often many years pass while life is simply a struggle to maintain this family. Then success comes, and with it, or so it was in the days before the level of income tax prevented this, comes an unexpectedly large income. All men find it necessary at times to assert their independence, but the writer is upheld in this desire by the belief that only by moving out into the world can he find the raw material for his trade. And he is immensely strengthened in this idea by society. A new name on the literary scene is a great attraction to society, but if there is one

thing in the world that dulls this allure, it is his wife. This
again is understandable, because there is no reason at all why
she should have any of the qualities which are attractive in
him. So gradually he begins to make himself independent of
his family, and to cast off all except financial responsibilities.
Presently he can live where he likes, go where he likes, eat
when he likes, and see whom he likes. Probably he works only
for a few months in the year and when he is working it is
usually only for two or three hours a day. So, with all the
the defences down, the way is open for boredom, and life can
become a wasteland that can only be irrigated by constant
change, and where much luck is needed if even the smallest
plants are to root deep.

Freddy lived in Birchington until the age of forty, and he
almost never went to London except when he was forced to go
on business. He lived as any other family man, except that he
did not go to an office every day, and he sometimes had money
and at other times he had not. Then he began to achieve great
success and, soon after, to cast off all ties. From that time
onward he found it impossible to stay in one place for more
than a few weeks at a time. He was undoubtedly looking for
something, but he was very simple and he never knew what it
was. He always believed that his unhappiness was caused by
his present circumstances, and that if he could alter the circumstances all would be well.

He was incredibly wearying about it. He would discuss for
hours and hours on end whether he should go to Paris, Le
Touquet or to Jersey—or whether perhaps it would be better
after all to go to New York. Should he take a house, a flat, or
stay in a hotel? The conversation was robbed of any interest it
might conceivably have had by the fact that no decision was
possible, since any place agreed upon began to bore him in
advance. Eventually he moved off under some inward com-

pulsion to whichever of these places seemed at the moment the least distasteful.

He had so few resources. The only things he cared for were life itself as it went on around him, good conversation, amusing people, gaiety and courage. And these are so difficult to find—particularly if, as he did, you look for them in the wrong places. He could only live in the most expensive hotels and dine in the most expensive restaurants, though in them he was as likely as not to order two boiled eggs or a slice of cold chicken.

His inability to live anything but the *de luxe* kind of life was deeply bound up with his neuroses. He did not believe that he could be certain anywhere else of cleanliness. If he could be persuaded to stay for a night or two in some smaller hotel, he soon made discoveries in the bathroom that upset him so much he had to move. The beds would also be insufficiently comfortable and the noise too great, though, provided the hotel had charged him enough, they could have put him to sleep on boards, and run railway trains up and down all night without his noticing it, because he had a very strong constitution and slept like a child. He got used, too, to the type of service given in the bigger hotels and anything less polished upset him.

All of this was all very well in the nineteen-twenties, when the whole of his world moved from place to place with him, but good conversation is not easily found amongst rich retired Americans and English people domiciled on the Riviera to avoid income tax.

Towards the end of his life he blamed it all on other people (although he was so gregarious that if there was no one else around he would talk to the page boy).

"There are very few people I care to see," he would say, while dressing to go and drink a cocktail with the nearest stranger.

And:

"Actors," he said to Ronald Squire once, "I hate them. Listen to me," and he thumped his fist on the table. "They *drove* me into society, and that is a thing I will never forgive."

With this two-edged sentence he denied practically every friend he had, though it is safe to say that any member of either of these two worlds who had entered the room would have been assured of an enthusiastic welcome.

So, under it all, he was often very lonely and unhappy. Towards the end of his life his difficulties were also increased by the fact that he was forced to pay some regard to money. His attitude to money was different from other people's. Having started life without any, he found it difficult to make the distinction between capital and income that other people do. In the nineteen-twenties he invested a large capital sum in trust for my mother, but, having insured her future, he thereafter simply made money and spent it. He was enormously generous. Ronald Squire told the story after his death of how, on being told that a fellow-playwright was ill and without money, he immediately wrote a cheque for £250, saying to Ronnie: "Now, Master Squire, let it never be known who gave you this." He would always have behaved in this way when he could afford it, and he lent during the course of his lifetime vast sums, which as often as not were not repaid. Then he was a natural payer. I have often seen him in a restaurant, when there was some doubt to whom the bill should go, take the plate from the waiter who brought it and, covering it with his left hand, search in his pocket with his right for a pencil with which to sign it. During the time it took him to do this, he would talk so earnestly and so unceasingly to his companion that it was impossible to interrupt him. He intended to pay, and he intended to do it with grace and without argument. For years he could afford all this, but towards the end of his life it became apparent, even to him, that, given the combination of his own laziness and the standard of income tax, his money might one day run out. This only served to worry him, because he was completely incapable of living in any other way. Any attempt at economy only meant paying first for the cheaper thing and later for the more expensive. He was the only person I have ever known who had gold tops on his Parker pens at extra cost, and these he would have bought because of the higher price without enquiring in what way they were superior.

Jack and I went to stay with him for about four years running in Cannes. The first year we were there, we induced him to come to all the smaller restaurants by making him understand they were more amusing. He enjoyed this very much for a time, but then the head waiter in his hotel, who was a good business man, told him that the food in these restaurants was not fresh.

"They take what we leave," he said.

That finished it; we could never again move him outside the hotel.

Another time when we were staying with him, we went for a walk and took a picnic lunch, while he went to some friends. When we got back we told him that we had had a delicious lunch and a bottle of wine for about 500 francs, and suggested we should all three do the same thing the next day. He was tremendously pleased, partly regarding it as an adventure, but chiefly as a splendid way to save money.

The next day when we started out, Jack and I made automatically for the little shop where we had bought our food the day before. But he would have none of that.

"You can't trust the food in those places," he said, and went off to a sort of Fortnum and Mason's of a place in the middle of the Rue d'Antibes. Here I presently came upon him buying an enormous jar of Strasbourg *pâté de foie gras*.

"You're absolutely mad to buy that stuff," I said.

"Why?"

"It's so expensive."

He looked surprised.

"Not too expensive for a picnic," he protested.

It was all dust and ashes, because the only things his money bought which he enjoyed were the company of other people and champagne; and he could have had both of these in cheaper and pleasanter places, if it had not been for his restlessness and his hypochondria.

He used to come sometimes to stay with us in our farm-house and he was happier here than almost anywhere else. He used to arrive with enough food for a week and cases of Louis Roederer non-vintage champagne. We have no servants except daily women, and he thought this ideal.

About six o'clock in the evening he would call for champagne and start talking. As we get up very early and take a great deal of exercise, Jack and I like to go to bed early. So I used to hiss at Jack:

"Only one bottle."

However, at about a quarter to eight, when I was hoping for dinner, he would turn to me and say:

"Tell that mean fellow you married to open another bottle."

About ten o'clock we would have dinner, with Freddy saying happily:

"This is the life. This spoils me for anything else. You see, we do what we like. We eat when we like."

As I do the cooking we always have meals in the kitchen. This, of course, might be considered odd by many of the people that Freddy knew. To him it was an instance of original thought combined with audacious and independent action, and it aroused in him the deepest admiration. He used to say to me:

"When So-and-so came to see you, where did you have lunch?"

"In the kitchen."

"Ha!" he would say with the greatest satisfaction. "That made her sit up."

I forbore to tell him that at least half the people I know nowadays have their meals in the kitchen.

He was a great source of amusement to his friends. There was always a new 'Freddy' story. On one occasion he took a villa in Grasse for the whole winter, and moved out into a hotel after a week. Soon after, Jack was having his hair cut at Trumper's, when a friend of Freddy's, catching sight of him, crossed the room, wagging his finger, and said, without any previous salutation:

"My dear fellow! My dear fellow! No more bloody villas!"

On the last occasion that I ever saw Freddy, Jack and I went to stay with him in Cannes. He wrote to me two days before we were due to leave England and said that, as it would be expensive for so many people to stay at the Carlton Hotel, he was moving into a furnished villa at Mougins. We met some friends of his at dinner on the train and we told them this. The next morning as we were leaving it, one of them said to me:

"So you're going to stay at Mougins."

"Well," I replied, "you can never be quite sure."

At that moment we caught sight of a well-known figure walking down the platform, complete with white scarf and white socks. As it was about eight o'clock in the morning, I was very much surprised and rather touched.

"Have you got a car?" I asked him presently.

"A car," he said, "why do we want a car? We'll go in the hotel bus."

He had moved back to the Carlton at four o'clock on the previous afternoon, after two nights at the villa. On his

B*

way to bed that night he had gone to talk to the hall porter.

"I want to be called very early tomorrow," he said, "as I have to go to the station at eight o'clock to meet my daughter. If I'm not there to tell her she'll go to Mougins."

"How do you know, sir," the man asked him, "that by eight o'clock to-morrow morning you won't be in Mougins?"

The only times in his life when he was seriously disliked was in wars. His peculiar views in both the Great Wars, which I shall attempt later to explain, were emotional in origin and were a result of his complex and unusual temperament. Roughly speaking, he thought on both occasions that the whole thing ought to be called off; and this is a view which, at a time of serious stress, is open to misinterpretation. He himself believed the stand he took to be not merely enlightened but very far-seeing, and he believed, too, that the courage with which he stated his views was his most important contribution to modern life. Those of us who knew him well were unable to take him very seriously, but many people not only took him seriously but believed him to be pro-German. A pro-German is a person on the side of the Germans who wishes them to win. This he never was. He was only a miserable man, out of joint with the times until the war was over, and one who all his life was unable to keep in step with the majority. In peace this last quality could make him very irritating; in the stress and strain of war many people found it unendurable.

During the First World War there were reasons why it would have been difficult for him to join the Army. If he had forced his way through these, it would have been only to spend the period of the war in the then equivalent of the 'glass-house'. He was constitutionally incapable of standing army life, and he would have been permanently in revolt and under detention. By the time of the Second War, he would have been turned over to the psychiatrists.

In 1939 he was in America, and he seriously offended the Americans. His views reached England at second hand, and here too he made people very angry.

It speaks for his charm that so soon after 1945 most of the people who had vowed never again to speak to him easily forgave him. Dear Freddy was back, and how could one ever have taken him seriously? But although his war record affected very few of his friendships, it permanently coloured his political opinions. Unfortunately he was seriously interested in international politics and he used to talk a brand of nonsense which was not only highly irritating but difficult to counter, because, provided you changed some basic facts to suit his opinions, it made a sort of sense in the middle distance. If you challenged his facts, he employed a technique he used all his life when floored in argument, and said that someone in a position of high authority, known to him but not to you, had told him the inside history. My sister and my brother-in-law, Rodney Ackland, invented a character called Mr. Green. If one said to them:

"But why does Freddy think that?", they would reply: "Mr. Green told him."

The other thing that was a sadness to my family was that when he came back from America after the war he never really resumed his place in the theatre. He found everything changed from the days when he and Gerald du Maurier were the natural kings of the walk. He neither liked nor understood this new, more serious, more aspiring, but in some ways less virile theatre that had grown up in his absence, and, what was worse, he had a suspicion that they would not like or understand him. He had always had plenty of enemies because of his vicious tongue and a certain off-handedness; but in his youth this had not mattered because he could always succeed in making peace when he chose. All his life, before, his natural friendliness had made him very considerate and understanding to other people, and his egotism had never stood in his way, since, like some jolly snake, he wished to charm people for his own purposes. But now, feeling for the first time for many years insecure, his knowledge of human nature suddenly deserted him, and he turned in on himself and thought only of what he wanted for himself or for his play.

"The man," he said to me once, coming back from rehearsal, "is nothing but a bottle of Mellin's Food. I said to him: 'You're terrible. Simply terrible. Has it ever occurred to you to take up some other profession?' " He paused and pulled his nose reflectively. "Now if I'd said that to Gerald, he would have been so angry he would have given the performance of his life. But this fellow went off the stage weeping."

Whether these appalling things were ever actually said it was impossible to know, because none of his family were ever allowed at rehearsal, but the rumours that came out of the theatre made one fear the worst.

It was a great sorrow to us, because, although he spent so much of his life in other places, it was in the theatre he really belonged. Nothing ever pleased him so much as the success of his first plays; he was never so happy as when he used to trot backwards and forwards between the Garrick Club and the players' dressing-rooms; and he never loved anyone so much as he loved Gerald du Maurier and Seymour Hicks.

He died of an aneurism as he was walking from Claridge's to Hill Street, where he was staying with some friends. He had always been frightened of death, not with the vague uneasy fear we all have, but with terror, as of a man who wakes from a nightmare and sweats. He thought, of course, too much about himself, and he had a powerful imagination. In addition, I think he had no spiritual life of any sort. He was what I believe the Catholics call 'invincibly ignorant'. There was simply no pore through which religious feeling could enter. My husband is a convinced churchman and this was a matter of amazement to Freddy.

"Does Jack really believe all that stuff?" he used to ask me. When I replied that he did, he would walk away, murmuring to himself: "How a man of that intelligence . . ."

When I heard that he had died without pain or foreknowledge, I felt that his luck had held out to the end.

Two years before he died he decided to write his life. In an interview with a *Daily Express* reporter he told him this, and on being asked what would be the title of his book, he replied:

"It will be called *The Last of Mr. Lonsdale.*"

Then he found it too difficult (he was not, of course, very diligent), and he asked me if I would like to do it for him.

"But you must tell the truth," he said, "none of that business of daughters praising their fathers."

"It was all I . . . I . . . I . . ." he then told the *Daily Express* reporter. "So my daughter is going to do it. And she is very truthful."

He was a man who was not on any terms with truth; but he somehow respected it. He always valued me because he thought I told him the truth. This was, of course, not so. I had merely learned from him a little of the art of appearing to do one thing while you are really doing something quite different. But here I have tried to do as he told me. There may be people who knew him and who feel that I have here and there been unjust. I shall be sorry if that is so, but this is a matter between him and me, and I am satisfied that, when he told me to speak the truth, he meant me to do it. He was a man of immense faults, but he was vivid, defiant, affectionate, generous and gay. He was more loved than anyone else I ever knew. I often wake with a start of pain and horror, because he was walking along a street one night and he died.

CHAPTER ONE

Jersey

THE island of Jersey has changed so much in the last thirty years that, to the first glance of the returned traveller, it offers no welcome at all. It seems in the interval to have exhausted its charm for the benefit of the British holiday-maker.

It is a small island of wide sandy bays, and it is exceptionally lavish. Always a little warmer than England, it is bounded on its south coast by a sea of Mediterranean blue, by bathing pools and by sheltered coves; but on its west coast the breakers of the Atlantic sea roll in, making surf bathing possible for those tired of the gentler shore. In Jersey tomatoes grow out of doors, and early potatoes are one of the main exports. A little cow lives there, whose extraordinary production of butter fat brings buyers from all over the world to bargain with the patois-speaking natives for a bull calf in a dark pen, or a couple of heifers tethered to a bank. The sand of the shore is studded with red rocks, standing off from the mainland, and a net, drawn through the pools that lie between these rocks, is lifted out heavy with prawns. The lobster-pots are emptied daily to provide a meal in the inns that lie along the coast; and on warm nights the fisherman will take you out to look for sand eels.

It is inevitable that the tourist trade should be one of the two main industries. No effort has been spared to meet the requirements of the visitors, and all along the south coast the little houses, garages and cafés stand in ranks shoulder to shoulder, so that, nowadays, as one drives from St. Helier through St. Clement's Bay and Grouville to Gorey, there is for long stretches no break on the land side through which one might survey the country. In the summer these bays are black with people all day, and in the evening only the sea could wash away the blanket of paper that has been left behind them. So that one's first impression of the island would be of a beautiful, ravished but utterly willing little Blackpool, were it not for its strongly French appearance and its slightly medieval air. The inns and warehouses that stand in the squares and on the jetties of the bays are painted in light gay colours, and the bigger houses that can still occasionally be seen standing back from the roads are grey, many-windowed and shuttered. Sometimes they have a small tower at one end, or a cupola on the roof, and in their gardens sun-loving trees and shrubs are grown. French names abound. There is a Woolworth's in St. Helier and also a Burton's, but Woolworth's stands next to Voisin's and Burton's to Filleul's. Opposite these there is a large covered-in market, where the flowers are both more plentiful and far more brilliant than anything that can be seen in England, and where the butchers' stalls display meat to people interested in food. Most of the streets in St. Helier have two names; Hill Street, for instance, is also La Rue des Trois Pigeons, and Rose-ville Street, that will later come into this story, is Le Long Bouet—although I must admit that this particular place seems much more to me like Roseville Street than like Le Long Bouet.

The suggestion of the medieval is contributed, as much as anything, by the rocks that guard the shore; for these, although a rust-red and very beautiful, have much the appearance of fortifications. Then it is only in recent years that Castle Elizabeth, which stands out to sea and at high tide is separated

from the mainland, has ceased to hold a garrison on watch
above the island.

The second of Jersey's two main industries is agriculture,
and, because of this, the first impression it gives, of being
heartlessly and greedily abandoned to the tourist, is, even in
the summer, untrue. As is so often the case in small com-
munities, the laws are strong and well administered, and no
man may build on agricultural land. So that as one proceeds
from St. Helier, in the south, into the middle of the island, and
also to the north, the scene is changed, and here the lavishness
of the island is equalled by the thrift of the natives. Every acre
of land, on steep banks and in the smallest plots, is cultivated,
and once again one is reminded of France, because, although
the little holdings are not unfenced, but usually divided by low
banks, the trees on which have been pollarded with all the side
branches lopped to prevent even the land they shade from
remaining unproductive, the whole country is stripped like a
patchwork quilt to provide a living for all its inhabitants. Here
the houses are of the native red granite, and they are customarily
built with a wing one-half the size of the main building attached
to it. This smaller wing is the dower house, and is built to
comply with the law of Jersey that on the death of a man his
widow shall inherit one-third of his estate. There is an air on
these farms of great prosperity.

In this part of Jersey, a post-war development makes a
further contribution to its sophistication. There have always
been a few of the larger manorial type of houses, surrounded
by their own gardens and well set back from the road. These
houses are now richly inhabited, the gardens exotically planted,
and large motor-cars roll up to the doors. Nowadays, Jersey
shares with Jamaica and Bermuda the honour of sheltering the
incomes of English gentlemen from the tax. For this reason,
too, there are to be found, dotted about the island, small

restaurants where the food and the wine would not, in another setting, preclude their inclusion in the Guide Bleu.

So it is to-day. In the 1880's it was very different—much simpler, and, of course, much sweeter. It lay like an unmined gem in the balmy sea. The population of those days seems to have been roughly divided into three classes. There was a small aristocracy, descended in a straight line from the Normans, with names like Lempriere, le Gallais and le Cornu. There was a peasant class, also of Norman descent, who farmed the agricultural land, and who spoke a patois which is in fact Norman, but which sounds to the English ear like a kind of Anglicised French. It was quite common in those days to meet peasants in the countryside who had never been as far as St. Helier, a few miles away, and who spoke of it as of a great city of unknown hazards. The third class was the townspeople of St. Helier. These consisted partly of Jerseymen of Norman descent, but also of families descended from some Englishman who had settled here. Most of these people spoke English, and many of them could not understand the patois.

The other residents included Englishmen living in Jersey for some special purpose, the regiments which garrisoned Castle Elizabeth and Fort Regent and their wives, and the officers and their wives of a gunboat which lay in the harbour. These, with the local inhabitants, formed a quite tolerable society.

Jersey is only forty miles square, but it has always had an impressive exportation of men who have made their mark on the outside world. Famous golfers, singers, actors, writers, men of law and at least one famous beauty have grown up in the island, later to depart for lands of greater opportunity. In the later years of the last century there were several children unnoticed in Jersey who were later to receive the attention of London and New York.

In the 1880's there lived in St. Helier a Jerseyman, probably of English descent, named Frederick Leonard. In 1881, when his third and youngest son was born, he was an assistant in a tobacconist's shop belonging to his father-in-law, James Belford. At this time he was not at all well-off and he lived in a small cottage somewhere on the sea front. Later he was to open a shop of his own in Beresford Street, and then the family moved to live over this shop. Belford's shop still exists to-day, and is presided over by my first cousin once removed, but Leonard's shop has been pulled down, entirely rebuilt, and is now occupied by a tailor named Hector Powe.

Frederick Leonard's wife, Susan Belford, belonged to a family the founder of which, it seems probable, arrived in Jersey in the following way. During the wars against the French, he was taken by the press-gang in Southampton and shipped to France. There he escaped in a small boat, meaning to cross to England, but he drifted on to the Jersey shores, where he remained to marry and settle down. But I am in a difficulty about the exact lineage of my grandmother. Freddy always told me that she was an Irishwoman, and, until lately, I had no reason to question this. However, when I visited my cousins Belford in Jersey, they rejected this suggestion entirely, and said that Susan came of a family whose only known relatives were Jerseymen. I am at a loss to account for this discrepancy. It is not that I would, with any confidence, doubt that something Freddy said might be a pure invention, but I can think of no possible reason for this particular use of his imaginative powers.

The young Leonard and his wife had three sons—James, called Jim, who was the brilliant one, George, who was the good one, and Frederick, called Freddy, who, as soon as he could stagger about the room and speak a few incoherent words, made it perfectly plain to his parents' anxious hearts that he was destined for the black sheep.

I think Jim must have been brilliant, because, although he died of drink while under the age of thirty, he did so without diminishing in any way the glory of his memory. He fell, it appears, from a bus, and did some damage to his hip. He seems, like his younger brother, to have been deficient in that sense, normal to human nature, that little in life is so unendurable that it cannot somehow be borne. While confined in a small room because of his hip injuries, he tied together two sheets of his bed, and, hooking them round the window-ledge, started to lower himself to the road below. The sheets were rotten and, when they took his full weight, they parted and let him fall with a crash to the street. Neither of these accidents killed him, but he died, nevertheless, soon afterwards, revered and missed. When Freddy's first plays were produced in London, it was held in his family that, since Freddy could not have written them, Jim must have done so and Freddy found them somewhere after his death.

George, the good one, lived, as far as I know, a respectable and uneventful life. He seems to have shared only one quality with his two brothers—a fierce and incorruptible independence. He strongly disapproved of Freddy as a young man, but in later years he stubbornly refused to know either him or his family, on the grounds that it would not be suitable. "He has moved into a different world," he is reported to have said, "and it wouldn't be right."

Freddy was a heart-breakingly wilful child. From his earliest years it was accepted by his parents and in all their circle that he was a very bad boy. But his badness consisted only in this. He had to do what he wanted to do. He was not malicious, or insolent, or dull, or slow-witted; he was not rude, or insensitive, or in any way vile. But he never would, and no one could make him, accept the necessity to perform the routine duties of his life.

His family lived a simple, poverty-stricken life. But in Jersey every family had the sea and the sands and the pools in the rocks, the flower-strewn hills called cotils, and the small but heroic landscape. All through the summer the women used to form parties to take their children picnicking. In those days a little railway line ran from St. Helier round the coast, and people used bicycles. Freddy, like all the other children, used to be taken on these parties. A few wisps of stories remain in the memories of the men who were children with him, and they are all blown in the same direction.

On one occasion the children were fishing for crabs. Freddy caught two, and, on being taken back to the house of one of the women of the party, he expressed the intention of cooking them. The opportunity to do this was indignantly denied him. Later, while the older children were at tea, one of the women took a saucepan of milk off the stove, and, filling a bottle from it, gave this to the baby of the party to suck. She then returned the saucepan to the heat, leaving the milk that remained in it to simmer. Later still she went again to the stove, and poured the milk from the saucepan into a jug. It is inevitable that the two crabs should now plop out, but it is nice that they did so after the baby had drunk the milk in which they had been cooked.

Another time a party was given for his birthday. His mother, having occasion to leave the room for a few minutes, was recalled to it by the pandemonium which broke out. Freddy, having been bitterly disappointed in the present which one of his guests had brought him, was engaged in beating up the donor.

The only person he seriously respected was his elder brother Jim. This influence hardly made for good, however, because it led to his trailing his brother round the streets of St. Helier into all sorts of places quite unsuitable to his years. He refused to go to school. One day he would spend trotting round the town on his own devices; the next day he would be trapped and dragged to school. There he was always beaten. On the next day he would be absent again. To anyone who knew him in later years, and knew how much he hated and feared discomfort or physical pain, it is incredible that day after day for years he stood these beatings, always to follow on the next day the impulse of the moment. Nowadays, he would simply come into the category of a delinquent, and stronger forces than any his parents or school teachers could provide would be used to deal with him. It is a matter of interesting speculation to me what the psychiatrists might have made of him. He always carried with him the conviction that the world lay in front of him and that he had the power to win from it that which he wanted; but the one great difference between him and the ordinary delinquent was that, in his case, he was right.

But neither of his parents, nor anyone in their circle, realised this. Because they could not control or understand him, his parents seem to have lost quite early that feeling of apprehension about his future which would have been natural to them, and which normally increases protective love. "He is a bad boy," they said, "and he will come to a bad end." And they seem to have accepted this as a fate that had already come upon them, against which it was no longer any use to strive. Everyone in that closed, conventional and humble society was too modest to believe that talent might be the ally of this unnaturally wilful child. For this reason, very little is remembered about him. No one regarded him with the courage or the imagination to see him. He was simply unaccountable, alien, undisciplined and impossible—a cross that had to be borne.

At adolescence he was probably at his least attractive. His

developing wit was still callow and led him into impertinences. However, he was already very popular with other boys of his own age. He went about not so much with a gang as with a few chosen cronies, chosen for their high spirits and audacity. Quite early he began to rove the town not merely in the day-time, but also in the evenings. His father was a strict man, a man of principle, and also, it seems, a fool. He could neither control Freddy nor influence him, but he could still use certain gross material sanctions against him, and this he did. He took to locking the doors of his house at ten o'clock at night, so that if his son had not come in by then he could not enter at all. It was singularly ineffective, because Freddy merely returned to the house of one of his young companions. He seems often to have gone home with a young man named Guitans, whose mother would find him asleep on the sofa in her sitting-room when she came down the following morning. Mrs. Guitans was fond of him and she looked after him with an amused and affectionate care.

There is no sign that he was put to work particularly early, though he was sometimes seen in his father's shop, serving tobacco. When the Leonards opened this shop they must have become rather better off, because they now employed a maid. She would not have been considered quite in this light, because she would have been a person of much the same class as her employers—a friend. Her name was Miss Grimshaw but she was known as Aunt Kitty, although she was no relation. She was kind to Freddy, and in return he supported her for the last twenty years of her life. I remember being taken to see her, when I was about twelve, in what seemed to me a dank and noisome little cottage. She was stone deaf and Freddy yelled at her while she told him the latest news of people of whom I had never heard.

"Who was that?" my mother asked him.

"I haven't the faintest idea," he replied in his normal speaking tone.

He must always have longed to leave home because, as soon as he was old enough, at seventeen or eighteen, he joined the Army as a private. It seems, given his temperament, an incredible move. His parents must have felt with relief that the army discipline might succeed where theirs had failed, though this, I think, was a lax and optimistic view, which greater affection would have shown them could never be true.

He was immediately miserable, and the letters he wrote to his mother wrung her heart. He could have been bought out if any member of the family had had the necessary sum of money, but, as it was, he seemed doomed to stay in the Army for seven years.

To anyone who knew Freddy in later years there are in this situation two impossibilities. It seems impossible, given the circumstances, that he could get out of the Army, but equally impossible that he should stay in it. By no effort can one imagine him polishing his buttons and brasses, blancoing his belt, drilling, going on parade, living in a barrack-room; all this for seven years. There is no way in which he could have survived this experience and remained sane enough not to commit crime; no way in which he could have accepted this discipline and become the man one knew in after years. So there is no surprise to those who know him to learn that he did get out.

He was discharged with a medical certificate showing he had valvular disease of the heart. This is an established fact, and it is interesting because at no other time was it ever suggested that there was anything wrong with his heart. The question then remains how he managed it. Until a very few years ago I believed implicitly the story that he told my mother when he first met her a few years later, and which he continued to tell

for most of his life. He said that he had made a friend of the
medical officer, and that this man realised that he was utterly
unsuited to the life, had other talents, and that, consequently,
wishing to befriend him, he gave him this certificate in order to
secure his release.

I never found any difficulty in believing this story. The
certificate has to be explained in some way and what explanation
would be any more probable? It has to be remembered that
this was no ordinary private. At the age of eight no one had
been able to force him to attend school regularly; at the age of
twenty-seven his plays were filling London theatres; all his life
he got practically everything he ever wanted from other people
by a mixture of force and charm. In later years psychiatrists
were employed in the Army, and I think that they would have
recognised Freddy immediately as a type who was unsuited to
the life and in all probability a danger to the morale of the
regiment. I never found it impossible to believe that, without
the aid of modern sciences to help him, the doctor should have
recognised the situation as charged with frustration and
difficulty, and taken unorthodox steps to reach a conclusion
which £40 could have bought.

However, in the later years of his life, from things that other
people told me, I began to suspect that Freddy had changed his
story. Since his death, Mr. Robert Rubin of New York has been
unremittingly kind in attempting to get me information about
his life in America. Among the things that Mr. Rubin turned
up was the fact that there was a good story about Freddy's discharge from the Army. He therefore wrote to Mr. Brian Aherne,
who was said to know it, for details. Since the letter that Mr.
Aherne wrote him in reply to his enquiry left me breathless, in
spite of a lifelong acquaintance with my hero, I think I cannot
do better than to quote from it here.

"His regiment was down at Aldershot," Mr. Aherne wrote,

"when a notice was put on the board announcing the annual regimental entertainment and asking anyone who had any suitable material to submit it. As a lark, Freddy sat down and wrote a sketch lampooning the General, a fire-eating character, and other officers in the outfit.

"The sketch was a hilarious success, much to his surprise, and had the regiment rolling in the aisles. The next day, however, he was called on the carpet, given a sharp reprimand, and confined to barracks for having shown disrespect for his superior officers. Shortly after this, he was taken ill, and spent a dreary time in the army hospital, very bored and fed up. One day he looked up and found a strange lady standing by his bedside. 'Are you Private Lonsdale?' she asked. 'I am General Blank's wife, and I have so wanted to meet you, because I saw your sketch, and I thought it was just brilliant! I have laughed ever since!' Then she proceeded to tell him that she thought he had a genuine talent for play-writing and asked if he had ever thought of writing anything else. Freddy admitted that he had several ideas, but he didn't feel he could work on them while he was in the army, and he still had some years to go. 'Well,' she said, 'if I can get you out of the army, will you promise me to write plays?' Freddy said he would gladly, but he didn't think it possible to get out.

"She then explained that the head medico was a close friend of hers, and she thought she could persuade him to certify that Freddy's illness was a great deal more serious than it really was, and so get him a medical discharge. So Freddy promised, and she worked the trick, and he was discharged, but the General was never to know!

"Well, he wrote his play—I forget the name of it—and it was immediately accepted, and was a great London success.

"Many years later, he told the story to Gerald du Maurier, who was enchanted with it and wanted to know more about the lady. Freddy told him they were still very good friends, that she lived up in Norfolk, and always lunched with him when she came on one of her rare visits to town. Du Maurier insisted that he bring her to lunch with him at his house in Hampstead soon after. They had a delightful and amusing lunch together and got along famously. As she was leaving, she happened to look at the hat-stand in the hall and said: 'Oh, what a lovely umbrella!' As soon as she was gone, du Maurier ran to the phone, called up the airport at Hendon, hired a plane, and sent the umbrella off to Norfolk, so that when she walked into her home a few hours later she was astonished to see it reposing in her own hat-stand."

"Freddy," Mr. Aherne adds, "was a wonderful character, and I miss him very much."

So all that is known is that Freddy now returned to Jersey, where he entered the office of the London and South-Western Railway at 6, Bond Street, St. Helier. He sat there in a small room on a round stool, and his job was to attend all day to the requirements of customers who came to make enquiries about travelling facilities. He was not very good at his job and he was unable to take it seriously. He is remembered as quick-witted and gay, but totally irresponsible. In this office, for the first time in Jersey, he made, on at least one person, an impression that caused him to be regarded not only with love but with intense admiration. One of the older men in the office was from this time to be unshaken in his belief that Freddy had qualities not to be found in the ordinary man. He had, at first, a hard time in maintaining his case, and it is said that a few years later he went in triumph to the office, because he had read one of Freddy's first plays. The clerks received this announcement with gales of laughter, and said that it was really not possible for the story to be true.

"It is in his handwriting," Freddy's friend protested.

But this merely served to increase the merriment, and it was pointed out that this would hardly do, since even Freddy was capable of copying out someone else's work.

It may have been the influence of this man which kept Freddy in this office for some months, in spite of his ineptitude at the job. At the end of this time his restiveness exceeded his caution, and on being given an instruction one morning he replied with an exercise of his wit too youthful and cheap to be repeated, and received what he had deserved for some time.

A few days later, a young man named Le Brun applied at the London and South-Western offices for a job. On leaving the building after his interview he was accosted in the street by one of the company's employees, who introduced himself as Leonard.

"Are you coming to work here?" this young man asked him.

Le Brun replied that he hoped to.

"Don't be a fool," Leonard said excitedly, "I'm leaving."

It was not a very attractive remark from a young man who carried so strongly about him the suggestion of having just been fired, and Le Brun passed on unheeding. I do not think, however, that it was inspired by anger at having been dismissed. I think Freddy was filled at the same time with relief that soon he would leave that stool for ever, and with fear about what he should do instead. He was in a mood of exaltation, in which he felt that life was not meant to be lived in the office of the South-Western Railway. If the other young man had responded at all to this mood, he would have welcomed him with joy and friendship as a comrade-in-arms against the tedious waste of the whole of their hopeful youth. But he failed to communicate his message, chiefly because, for the other young man, it was of doubtful truth. And so, spoiling for adventure, he walked on alone.

Freddy was determined on adventure, and so he did not

wait for it to come to him, but rather he precipitated it.

He had lately been mixed up in an affair which, though in fact it was fairly harmless, had caused at first a nine days' wonder, and later more important repercussions. There was an academy for young ladies in Jersey, and at this there attended two young ladies from Canada who, having a relation in Jersey, had come there in order to learn French. These young ladies were well-bred, well brought up and subject to all the conventions this implied. One can therefore imagine the horror that was caused when it was learned that they had gone for two days to Southampton, where they had lived in style, and that they had been accompanied there by young Leonard, the tobacconist's son, and another young man who was a friend of his.

One knows from the novels of Henry James that at this date American young ladies had much freer ideas about the conventions than would have been possible for girls brought up in Europe, and probably the same was true of Canadians. But that these two girls should have travelled to Southampton and back, unchaperoned, with any two young men, would have aroused the whole island to amazement and disapproval. One can imagine, then, what was felt when it was learned that their companion had been Freddy Leonard, the wild son of a local tradesman. That he was wild would be bad enough, that he was quite clearly not of the right class would, in those days, have been much, much worse.

The guardian of these girls wrote the horrible news to Canada, and on receipt of it their father travelled immediately to the island, and made all preparations to return them to their home.

At this point Freddy conceived himself to be in love. Nothing so certainly adds romance to a young lady as to be forbidden her company. Simply to be denied the sight of her vests her with excitement and glamour, and makes her infinitely more attractive than she has ever been felt to be before. The moment at which the Canadian young lady achieved this heightened desirability seems to have coincided with the moment at which Freddy lost his job. As has already been seen, he did not particularly mind losing his job, but he would have felt it necessary to lose it with style. He determined that if the young lady of his heart was going to Canada he would go there too.

Given the audacity to arrive at this decision, it was not very difficult to carry it out. St. Helier is a port, and the inhabitants of Jersey are accustomed to the idea that if they wish to see anything of the world they must cross the sea to do so. Freddy simply travelled to Southampton and got a job as a steward on a liner crossing to Canada.

I think he probably enjoyed this job, and performed it more to his employers' satisfaction than he had his previous employment. He would have been interested in the clothes, the manners and the life of the passengers, and by wit and originality he would have charmed large tips out of the people he served. He would have enjoyed almost equally the company of the rest of the crew.

Arriving in Canada soon after the young lady who had inspired this long journey, his only aim was to follow her, and this for some time he succeeded in doing. He would have had some money, I suppose, earned on the way over, and at this period of his life he used to fall back on odd jobs to keep himself alive. However, the father of the two girls seems to have been aware of his presence in the rear. When Freddy tapped one evening on the window of the room in which his beloved slept, it was thrown up, but the head and shoulders which leaned through were those of her father, and the hand that advanced towards him held a gun.

The passion of love in Freddy's heart died instantaneously. Murmuring a few courteous words, he passed out of the lives of these people, never to reappear.

All this is plausible enough. Freddy had for some time been suffering from a desire to break out of the island and his former life. He believed that the world that lay away from its shores was full of opportunities for him. He never failed in courage, and almost any reason at this time would have been good enough to serve as an impetus to start him on his travels. The fact that he thought himself in love was as good as any other. There was nothing unusual either in a boy of his class taking a job as a steward; he might easily have remained one all his life. Up to this point too the story is known to be substantially true. Since he had persuaded himself that the Canadian young lady was the reason for his voyage, and, since he certainly had no other conscious purpose, it is most likely that, arrived in Canada, he would have followed this family to their home. Nor did it need any great imagination on the part of the father of the girls to realise that the sight of a gun and the belligerent reception that would go with it might easily shake off this impossible eighteen-year-old suitor, where all ordinary methods had failed. After this, however, the story begins to assume altogether taller proportions.

Freddy was now presented with a new difficulty. Whether he had been seriously in love with this girl, it is impossible to say. But she had served as the point of his intentions for some weeks past. Now he found himself alone in Canada with no purpose and no obvious means of earning a living. Nothing seems to have happened to attract him to this country, and no opportunity to have arisen to cause him to want to stay. He had only one idea, therefore, and that was to get back to his known surroundings as soon as he could. Since he had no money, it was not easy to do.

I have only his word for what happened next and I give the story exactly as he used to tell it to me.

He said that he was in a small town in Canada one evening when he fell in with another young Englishman who was in the same case as himself—that is to say he was alone in Canada, without money and wishing to return home. This other young man suggested to Freddy a plan which appealed to him very much, and they decided together to put it into operation. The following day therefore they announced in the appropriate quarters that they intended to run a football match in aid of the funds of the local hospital. They then put a good deal of work into the arrangements, raised two teams, found a ground and advertised the match throughout the town. It was a small town where not much occurred to amuse the inhabitants and great interest was aroused in this event. When the day came, Freddy and his friend stood at the gates and collected the money from the townspeople as they passed on to the ground. The whole town turned out, and most of the local police arranged to be on duty controlling the crowds inside the ground. As the last man entered the gates, Freddy and his friend departed for England.

One of the features of this story was that Freddy always described his companion as a man of great intelligence, personality and charm. It was inevitable then that one should ask at this point:

"But what became of this man? Did you never see him again?"

He always made exactly the same reply.

"Yes," he said, "I did see him. It was really very sad."

"But why? What happened?"

"I met him," he would reply ruminatively, "twenty years later at a dinner I went to in Liverpool with Lord Derby."

He then said that his friend had reached a position of some

eminence in London but he would never say what this position was, and he could never be trapped into giving a name.

"I went up to him," he said, "and, tapping him on the back, I said: 'You're wanted by the police in A . . .' He jumped round and flung his hands in the air, and then he saw who it was. 'Never,' he said to me, 'never do that again. I don't want to be reminded of any of that.'"

Freddy would pause and pull his nose reflectively.

"A great pity, a great pity. Not a good fellow after all."

It is impossible to say whether or not this incident, as it was told, ever took place. I have found that, in dealing with people of imagination, one is no more likely to reach the truth by entirely discounting tall stories than by swallowing them completely. Occasionally the whole thing is a work of art, but more often there has been some small fire to lend force to inventiveness. Freddy never had that mischievous desire *pour épater les bourgeois* which is often a source of inspiration to imaginative minds. He was insufficiently interested in *les bourgeois*. But two qualities that often caused him to obscure the truth may have been at work here. In the first place he was brought up in a world where too great a regard for the conventional social virtues would have confined him for ever to a humble, obscure and humdrum life. It takes great audacity to break out of the lower social groups in England. Freddy never failed in this quality, and he admired it more, both in himself and in other people, than any of the gentler virtues. If he was aware that any of his youthful actions might call for apology in some quarters, he showed it only by the deliberate use of unrepentant overstatement, never by any attempt to gloss the facts. In the second place, he preferred, as in fact most people do, a neat, dramatic story to one made clumsy in the telling by the unfortunate diffusion of real life. It was always therefore a safe bet that, in anything he told one, the original contours

c

had been rounded, the wandering path made straight. This polishing and pruning of the truth often buries it more completely than has ever been the intention. I have no means of checking the facts of his return from Canada at this time, and my opinion is that, allowing for some exaggeration and possibly for an aggrandisement of the whole enterprise, the story he told may be true. In any case, these two young men certainly acquired enough money to return to England and to travel as passengers.

When he arrived in Southampton, Freddy seems to have decided against returning to Jersey. I have been unable to trace his life in much detail for the next two or three years. Certainly for much of the time he was performing odd jobs on the Southampton docks. There is a suggestion that during this period he visited America, crossing the ocean in a cattle ship. I can find no real evidence for this, and he himself never told me of it. I think it most probable that this journey, which some people believe to have been made, was in fact the journey to Canada of which I have told, and that the cattle ship version was thrown off by Freddy to add colour to some dull occasion of after years.

He must, however, have been doing something besides odd jobs on Southampton docks during this time, because in 1903 he reappeared in Jersey with plenty of money in his pockets. He did not then go to live, as might have been expected, in his parents' house. He took a room instead at the Grand Hotel.

CHAPTER TWO

Miss Hoggan

In the 1890's there came to live in Jersey a Mrs. Hoggan with her two young daughters. Mrs. Hoggan was the wife of a regular soldier, at that time in command of a regiment of the Royal Artillery stationed in India. Almost the whole of the married life of Colonel and Mrs. Hoggan had been passed abroad. Hoggan had nothing to live on except his pay, and in those days there was an arrangement in the Army by which rich men who wished to serve in England could negotiate an exchange with other officers when their regiments were ordered abroad. Since the living expenses in the Empire were a great deal lower than in England, this was an arrangement which benefited the poorer officers, and of which Colonel Hoggan had constantly taken advantage. At this date, however, Mrs. Hoggan's health began to fail, and she was advised that she could no longer live in a hot climate. She had a sister living in Jersey, with two sons, on the pension of the widow of an Indian Army officer, and from her she had learned that money could be made to go much further in this island than anywhere on the mainland. The Colonel at this time intended to stay with his regiment, and so, as the expenses of two homes would be great, Mrs. Hoggan decided to make the second one in Jersey.

These were good, respectable people, occupying a position

in life high enough to make them conscious of its advantages and merits, but not sufficiently high to give them that boundless confidence in their own superiority, and that certainty of the correctness of any behaviour they choose to adopt, which so distinguishes the highest ranks of English society. In the Hoggans' world, class was spoken of a great deal, and many rules were laid down for the wives and daughters of gentlemen who had the honour to serve in Her Majesty's Forces.

When Mrs. Hoggan first came to Jersey, she went with her two well-behaved little daughters to live in rooms let by a Mrs. Aitchison. This was a cheaper arrangement than taking a house would have been, and, in any case, Mrs. Hoggan preferred to have time to look around her before finally settling down. The two little girls were put to school, and Mrs. Hoggan found herself quite happy in her new surroundings. She was a woman of character and self-confidence, and she was not at a loss to run her life without her husband.

Mrs. Aitchison, whose rooms were comfortable, was a pleasant woman, with whom, in a distant way, Mrs. Hoggan made friends. One evening, when these two women were discussing the various children of their two families, Mrs. Aitchison asked her guest whether she would care to hear her husband's two little nieces play the piano. She said that these children were rather remarkable. On Mrs. Hoggan's replying that it would give her much pleasure, two little girls, not much more than about eight years old, were brought into the room, dressed in cotton frocks and with their hair tied up in pigtails. These proceeded to perform a duet on the piano in a manner which did indeed show skill quite out of the ordinary. Later one of these two children was known in London as Miss Ivy St. Helier, and a tune she wrote called 'Coal Black Mammy' was hummed all over the Western world.

In spite of the comparative cheapness of life in Jersey, the maintenance of two homes soon began to appear too great a strain on the income of Colonel Hoggan. For this reason, he now wrote to his wife and said that he had decided that he would do better to retire and to come to join his family in Jersey, where he hoped to be able to supplement his pension by cramming young gentlemen who wished to take the entrance examinations into the Army. He instructed his wife to find a house in which they could all settle down, and he himself proceeded to hand in his papers.

Mrs. Hoggan found without much difficulty a house in Roseville Street. As you walk down this street towards the sea, the house is on your right. It is one of two, detached from the other buildings in the street, at that time called Tanglyn, but nowadays with the name Ainsdale painted on its door. It has a gloomy aspect, much like any other Victorian house built in a row, and it looks very small. This, however, is deceptive, for inside it had rooms for all this family, and provided them with a home which suited them and which they grew to love.

Colonel Hoggan settled easily into the life of the island. He was a man of some intellect, having passed out of Woolwich with honours, with a considerable knowledge of mathematics, and having passed the highest grade in Hindustani, in those days a useful accomplishment for an army officer. In company therefore with a Mr. Arthur Le Sueur, who was equally gifted in European languages and in history, he opened his cramming school. This had an immediate success, the teaching being thoroughly competent and the fees much lower than at an equivalent school in England, and young gentlemen from the mother country wishing to join the Army came over to Jersey to be forced through the entrance examination.

The Colonel was a strict man and a man of principle. He soon found his place in the local society, and easily settled down into a daily routine. After his labours were over, he used to

walk every day right round the harbour, and end up in Beresford Street, where he had joined a club. On his way to his club
he used often to stop at Leonard's shop to buy his tobacco. He
formed a liking for Leonard, whom he found a competent and
respectful tradesman and one who grew to know his requirements.

There were other shops in this area where the Colonel
stopped occasionally, du Parcq's, where he bought his stationery,
and Lander's, where he bought his boots. If it had happened
one day, when the Colonel went out to do his shopping, that
the owners of these three businesses had decided to go together
on an outing, leaving their three sons in charge of their shops,
he would have bought his pencils from the future Lord Justice
du Parcq, his boot-laces from John Helier Lander, who was
later to paint a portrait of King George V, and his tobacco
from the future Frederick Lonsdale. The Colonel, however,
knew none of these things, and if he had I do not think he
would have been much concerned. It would not have occurred
to him that talent and achievement could give a man either the
position or the responsibilities in life that belong to a man
born and brought up to a settled place in society.

The two little Hoggan girls grew up happily in the island.
Not five minutes' walk from their house was the great Jersey
bathing-pool, built into the sea and one of the largest and finest
in the world. They had made friends at school, and with these
they used to bathe all summer long in this pool every morning,
and in the afternoons they took picnics, and went round the
coast to some different bay every day. They found that, if they
mounted their bicycles at St. Helier, they could ride to almost
any point in the island and come back to their starting place,
seldom having done more than about twelve miles. There was
the little railway too, and sometimes they used to take this as
far as Bouley Bay and walk on from there.

Leslie, the elder, is the one with whom we are concerned. As she grew up she began to be a very pretty girl. She had very beautiful curling auburn hair, blue eyes and a good complexion. Once, when she was about fifteen, walking down Beresford Street she was extremely annoyed to receive a boldly admiring glance from a fair-haired boy, who leant against the door of the tobacconist's shop. In the world in which she had been brought up, it was an impertinence and a source of humiliation for a cat to look at a queen.

Soon after, however, she began to receive attentions from more suitable young men. There was a Mr. Allardyce. She became tentatively engaged to him. She herself would have made the engagement official, but her father was strongly against the match. Mr. Allardyce was a tea-planter in India, who had come home on a holiday to Jersey, and, although Colonel Hoggan could not actively disapprove of him, he did not consider him an adequate match for his eldest daughter. Besides, Leslie was at this time only seventeen, and so it was easy to delay this engagement on the grounds of her age. Her father therefore said that if she still felt the same after one year, she might then become engaged; and Mr. Allardyce returned to India to plant tea.

During this year, however, a Mr. Featherstone appeared in Jersey, in a militia regiment, and later attended at Colonel Hoggan's school to be crammed for entrance to the Regular Army. All through a wonderful hot summer he accompanied Miss Hoggan on picnics, to bathe and even on moonlight bicycle rides. He was more interesting and more worldly than Mr. Allardyce, and Miss Hoggan lost her heart. When Mr. Allardyce reappeared in Jersey at the end of the year, he was met at the station by Mrs. Hoggan, who broke to him the news that her daughter no longer loved him.

Mr. Featherstone's greater worldliness, however, allowed

him to be persuaded by his family that to marry so young would be to handicap his career, and he in his turn left the island, but without, in his case, having committed himself; and he left behind an almost broken heart.

Leslie now began to go, however, into the great world. She went to London, where she visited the theatre and saw Miss Marie Tempest. Then she went to visit an aunt in Scotland. Here she found a very gay and fashionable society. Her uncle-in-law was a solicitor, but he was also an officer in the Glasgow Highlanders, a militia regiment which had as its honorary head the Duke of Argyll. Here the entertainment was lavish, and many balls were given. Miss Hoggan had a dress made in the island and shoes from Lander's, but these were favourably compared with the dresses of ladies who shopped in Paris. She visited this aunt several times, and always with great success. One thing, however, was noticed about her: although she received the attentions of all men with equal pleasure, she never seemed to like any one better than another. No one understood that the faithless Mr. Featherstone still reigned in her youthful heart, and her seeming indifference to all her suitors became a source of misunderstanding.

Among the gentlemen who were attracted to her, a Mr. Bertie Greig soon began to make his attentions most pronounced. Mr. Greig was a very rich man indeed, one who could give his wife everything that most women would desire. When he asked Leslie to marry him, great pressure was put on her to accept him. The fact that she did not love him was not allowed to weigh with her kindly but ambitious aunt, for she had shown herself so clearly indifferent to all men. After much persuasion, then, she returned to Jersey, engaged to be married and with a very noble ring to mark the event. This time the marriage was again to be delayed a year because, although Mr. Greig was by then a gentleman in his thirties, his mother was so devoted to him that she begged for one last year alone with her son.

Back in Jersey, only Colonel Hoggan, who loved his daughter, was not entirely satisfied with the engagement.

Leslie resumed her normal life in the island, in which there was plenty of amusement for a young girl. Presently Mr. Greig visited her there, and to her shame she found him a source of some embarrassment. In Scotland, although she had not loved him, his position had been known and admired. In Jersey, where he was not properly appreciated, she found her engagement to him more difficult to explain.

About this time Leslie went to a fortune-teller. This woman began by telling her all the normal things about journeys she would make, etc. Then she said:

"In a year from now you will be married."

Leslie replied that it was true she was engaged.

The fortune-teller looked at her.

"There is a man in your life at the moment," she said, "a small dark man. It's not him that you'll marry. It's another man; fair and quite different."

Soon after this a minor sensation occurred in Jersey. It began with two words which occupied quite a large space in the advertising columns of the local newspaper, and which simply said: "Who's Hamilton?" The following week this advertisement was repeated, but in the third it was explained that *Who's Hamilton?* was the name of a play by a young Jersey playwright named Lonsdale, which would be performed by a touring company at the St. Helier theatre.

The Hoggans had heard that young Leonard was back in the island because there was much gossip about him. It was said that he had written two plays and sold them under the name of Lonsdale, and that these were being performed by a touring company in the provincial towns of England and the suburbs

c*

of London. He was staying at the Grand Hotel, and he seemed to have plenty of money, but he had not mended his ways. It was said that he drank too much, that his friends were all the wildest youths in the island, and that he was boastful and conceited. It was, consequently, all the more irritating to some people that he seemed to have had some genuine success and, in addition, one great piece of luck. Clement Scott, one of the famous London critics, had been travelling to his home one night by Tube. When he got off the train, he was met by a tremendous storm of rain and, simply in order to get shelter, he had crossed the road and entered the local theatre. Afterwards he wrote of the play he saw there. It was written, he said, by a young man named Lonsdale, and it was a very bad play. One day, he predicted, however, Mr. Lonsdale should write a very good play.

When *Who's Hamilton?* opened at the Jersey theatre, the house was very naturally packed. Before the curtain went up, an announcement was made. Owing, it was said, to the sudden illness of the leading man, he was unable to appear. For this performance, therefore, the author himself would take his place.

I think this was the only time Freddy ever appeared on the stage. He had a kind of aggressive masculinity (he shared, in fact, more qualities than would have been thought possible with Colonel Hoggan) which prevented him from even putting powder on his face after shaving. For him, grease paint and 'fancy dress' were things which only women used. But I think he was probably very good. He was a natural actor, at any rate of his own lines, and in later life he often coached his leading man. I can think of one film in particular where, if one had closed one's eyes whenever the star appeared, one might have thought it was Freddy himself who spoke the lines.

After the triumphant performance of this play, a split occurred in Jersey society. There were those who took to knowing the young Leonard, and who spoke of him as a brilliant young man with a great future; and there were others for whom he still remained the black sheep son of the local tobacconist, and for whom his pretentious behaviour served to make matters worse.

Among the former was a Miss Blanche Peyton. Miss Peyton ran the Jersey Amateur Dramatic Society, and this was a very serious business. It later became known as the Green-Room Club, under which name it exists to-day. It has always had much support and given performances of some merit. Miss Peyton met Freddy Leonard during the run of *Who's Hamilton?*, and was much taken with him. Her own company was performing at the time and she persuaded him to come to see it. Afterwards she took him backstage and introduced him to the company. At this performance a niece of Miss Peyton's played the lead, but Leslie Hoggan figured in a tableau and also performed a dance sketch.

A few weeks after young Leonard attended this performance of the Amateur Dramatic Society, a great surprise occurred to the Hoggan family. Mrs. Hoggan received a letter from Miss Blanche Peyton, in which she said that Mr. Leonard had written a one-act play, and that he had been good enough to say that her company might give it its first performance. He would only allow this, however, if Miss Leslie Hoggan would play the female lead. Would Mrs. Hoggan therefore be good enough to come to tea, bringing her daughter with her, in order that they might meet the playwright?

Miss Hoggan was at this time due to visit her fiancé in Scotland, and Colonel Hoggan would have wished the invitation simply refused. But this was too much for the ladies of the family, and, in spite of the fact that Miss Hoggan would not be able to take part in the play, she attended at Miss Peyton's house to give the answer in person.

Until this moment, Miss Hoggan had thought very little about Mr. Leonard, merely accepting the orthodox view that he was the impertinent, uncontrollable, wastrel son of the local tobacconist. With this new proof, however, of his discrimination, she was forced at least to look at him. She found his looks, later described as "no greater than those of Fred Astaire, who might be his younger brother", not beautiful or noble as Mr. Featherstone's had been, but not unattractive. She was surprised at his good manners and his formal tone. She refused, however, to play in his play.

She did allow him that evening to see her to her home, where he appears to have made a conquest of Mrs. Hoggan, but to have aroused the deepest suspicions of the Colonel. In any case, two or three days later, when the news came from Scotland that Mr. Greig's sister was ill with diphtheria and that it would therefore be impossible for Leslie to visit them, her father insisted that she should go instead to visit some friends in Bournemouth.

Here she went, not unwillingly and without regrets for Jersey. Nevertheless, whenever in the next few weeks she received less attention than she considered her due, or whenever her friends conspired to irritate her, she thought of the young playwright who, with so little to go upon, had shown so much perception.

CHAPTER THREE

Marriage

When Miss Hoggan had been staying for some weeks in Bournemouth, she was surprised one day to receive a message that a young man had called to see her and awaited her in the drawing-room downstairs. Hurrying down to this room, she was even more surprised to find Mr. Leonard waiting there. He explained that business had brought him to Bournemouth, and that, being there, he had thought it right to call upon her. Miss Hoggan was rather taken aback and not quite certain how to deal with the situation. However, she introduced him to her hosts and, since these found him one of the most charming young men they had ever met, the matter was from then on taken out of her hands. Mr. Leonard was invited frequently to visit the house, and accompanied them when they set forth on some entertainment. He paid no marked attention to Miss Hoggan, but seemed to be equally pleased with all his new friends.

Presently, hearing from Scotland that the diphtheria case was now recovered, Miss Hoggan decided to undertake the journey to visit her fiancé. She left Bournemouth, however, with a slight feeling of irritation that her friends would now enjoy alone the pleasure of Mr. Leonard's company.

They seem not to have enjoyed it for long. In Scotland, Miss Hoggan began to receive letters from her mother in Jersey which made it plain that Freddy Leonard was now a constant caller at her house. Mrs. Hoggan slightly despised her husband, quite why is not plain, for he seems to have been the finer character; but, for this reason, while she would not openly defy him, she had no great qualms in going behind his back. Her letters gave her daughter to understand that, although Freddy was a frequent visitor, he called only when the Colonel was out. Miss Hoggan wrote to remonstrate with her mother, pointing out how angry her father would be if this ever came to be known.

In dealing with innocent and unworldly people, a bad reputation can be a great advantage. Their inexperience leads them to believe that someone whom they have not met, but about whom they have heard gossip which has shocked them, must be not merely the possessor of faults, but a different species of human being—someone whose difference is instantly repellent and who must necessarily inspire horror, like a drunk met when alone on a dark night. When the person about whom this view has been formed turns out to have nothing about him of horror, but to be, on the contrary, warmly human, vivid, affectionate and gay, even if occasionally rash, there are only two possible explanations. One, that this charming and unfortunate creature has, owing to the circumstances of his background, never been given a chance; the other, that he is the object of lying rumours, inspired by jealousy and malice. Mrs. Hoggan adopted both these views about Freddy, and they endeared him to her. She determined to befriend him.

She ignored her daughter's opinions and rebuked her for her hardness and lack of charity and, when this young lady returned home, she continued to receive the young man. The house in Roseville Street in which the family lived has bay windows to the two main rooms. There are, both up and downstairs, a big window in the front, and a smaller one on either side. As you walk down Roseville Street towards the sea, you look quite straight at the left hand window of the main sitting-room. Freddy used to walk down this street, and as he walked he used to whistle a tune called 'Bedelia' from a popular musical comedy. If the Colonel was at home, the window of the Hoggans' house would have a normal appearance, and Freddy would go whistling on towards the sea. If the Colonel was out, the blind of the window Freddy looked at would be pulled half-way down at his signal, and then he would turn in at the gate and enter the house.

He and Leslie now made friends. They saw each other nearly every day, and they used to walk on the beach together. Freddy never at this time made love to her, but he did ask her one day why she was going to marry this man with whom she was so clearly not in love. She replied that it was true she did not love him, but she had engaged herself to him and she would never go back on her word.

Freddy looked at her then, and pushed his hat to the back of his head.

"How would you like to take a bet," he asked, "that in six months' time you won't be married to me?"

In those days Freddy used to entertain the Hoggan ladies with tremendous tales. He told them of how, when he had been in America (I can find no evidence that he ever was), he had been on familiar terms with the stars of musical comedy, and he told them once that on his return to England he had been met on Southampton docks by an official of the railway company, who had guided him away from the crowds and through the Customs.

Mrs. Hoggan listened with pride and admiration to these tales, but Leslie always knew that he lied. She did not hold this against him, because by now she was beginning to come under his spell, and she believed, as he did, that he was merely juggling with time. All these things would be true one day, so why not, if it passed an evening, tell them now? Amongst the people who loved Freddy, there were, all his life, those who did so without understanding him, and those who understood but loved him none the less. Right from the start, Leslie knew how much to believe.

However, this pleasant time was soon to come to an end. It was true that Freddy had received a comparatively large sum of money for the sale of his two plays in England, but his behaviour since the receipt of this sum had conformed to a pattern he was to follow all his life. In the first place he was constitutionally lazy, and he never worked unless driven to it by the need for money; in the second, whenever he had money he always spent it with reckless generosity, both on himself and on other people. Just as he would almost certainly have got into serious trouble in life but for his talent, so, if he had been born the son of a rich man, he would almost equally certainly never have worked at all. In his youth, as in his old age, he enjoyed only the company of other people, good conversation and life itself as it went on around him, and he only enjoyed these in an atmosphere where the cares of money did not arise. For the last few months in Jersey, he had been living not merely as a gentleman of wealth, but of leisure, and now the ordinary facts of life were beginning to catch up with him. Freddy, so he told Mrs. Hoggan, had not only got no money, he had a great many debts. Mrs. Hoggan did all that she could to help him, lending him money to pay the most pressing of his creditors. It nevertheless became plain that he must go back to England and attempt once more to seek his fortune.

He left with the maximum of fuss; he had, so he said, several very odd pains in very peculiar places. By now his mother and the brother he loved were both dead, while his father and his other brother felt for him only bitter disapproval. He had

passed a lonely and completely self-reliant youth, and it seems
probable that with the Hoggans he enjoyed, for the first time
in his life, the ordinary affections and comfort normal in a
family. After he had been gone a week, he suddenly reappeared
at their house. But they drove him off again, and this time he
remained in England.

It seems possible that this friendship might have ended here,
had not Mrs. Hoggan sent her daughter, on her way to visit
Scotland, one day early to Southampton, to deliver some parcel
to Freddy, who was living there. The two young people spent
a sad day walking the streets of the town; she sad because she
must leave this man she was beginning to love to visit another
she did not care for, and he sad because, owing to his unfortunate circumstances, he must let her go. They promised
then to write to each other.

The Greig family had taken that summer a house in Auchterarder, a tiny village near a wonderful golf-course called
Gleneagles. Later a big hotel was built there and the place
became fashionable, but in those days it was a simple Scottish
village, with no particular attractions other than the links. The
family consisted at this time of Bertie, the fiancé, his brother
Gerald, two sisters, and Mrs. Greig, their mother. They were
exceptionally devoted, demonstratively affectionate to each
other, and there is no doubt that, although they were always
kind, they had difficulty in not regarding Leslie as an inter-
loper. Mrs. Greig, in particular, was very much attached to
her son, and found it difficult to share him with another woman.
Nevertheless, they did all they could to welcome Leslie into the
family, and, with the golf, and the fashionable people who lived
in the other big houses of the neighbourhood, the holiday
should have passed pleasantly enough. It had hardly begun,
however, before it began to be disrupted, even though this was
not immediately plain to all the members of the household.

Leslie received one morning a letter in Freddy Leonard's hand-writing, with the postmark Glasgow, and this informed her that he was, at the time of writing, in that town, but would arrive in Auchterarder that very afternoon. He would be going to the village inn, where she must make it possible for him to meet her.

At luncheon that day, Leslie said that she had a headache and did not feel like playing golf. She would be happier to remain by herself in the garden. Bertie was much distressed and offered to stay with her, but she assured him that she would recover better alone. As soon as the rest of the party had gone to the golf links, she left the garden and went down to the station.

She was in great fear. Guests to the other houses in the village arrived constantly at the station, and household stores were also often fetched. There was much danger that she would be seen. She was alone, as it happened, on the platform when Freddy Leonard stepped off the train.

He was delighted to see her; the only difficulty he had antici-pated was in achieving a meeting with her; and he was in a mood of complete certainty and confidence in his plan. He said that it was absurd that she should continue with this farce of being engaged to Greig, and that he had come to persuade her to tell her fiancé immediately that she could not marry him. After she had done this, she must go home and, as soon as he had earned some money to support her, he would marry her himself.

Leslie refused at first to think of this. During the next few days, however, her headache unaccountably persisted, and she accompanied the Greigs very seldom to the links. She was immensely disturbed. She could not reconcile herself to break with the man who had treated her with so much kindness and affection, but she continued to see this other man who was most devilishly armed with the weapons of persuasion. She might have resisted his infectious confidence, but, when she did so, her heart was wrung by the ease with which he could be deflated. His blue eyes then dominated a face grown withdrawn, wistful and pathetic; he said little, but his whole bearing indicated that the world was very disappointing and he felt very much alone. He had, of course, too, the advantage of some right on his side. It is extremely doubtful whether a marriage between Leslie Hoggan and Bertie Greig could have brought much happiness to either. She had been persuaded into the engagement in the first place by older people, who had acted from the best but only the most worldly motives, and there had been no time at which she had fancied herself in love. Even so, it is impossible to know what might have happened, had there been anyone there with any wisdom to guide her.

One night she broke down, when alone with Bertie Greig, and told him the truth. That night he was very gentle with her, and asked her not yet to tell the rest of his family; but the next morning her breakfast was brought to her room on a tray, with a message that she should wait there until Mrs. Greig came to see her. Leslie was terribly frightened, alone and still uncertain how to behave. When Mrs. Greig came to her room, she did so in a formidable mood, and she made every obvious mistake. She spoke contemptuously and coldly, from a distance at which no relationship any longer existed between them, and she said that Leslie was known to have been seeing some strange young man. She told her that she had telegraphed to that aunt and uncle with whom Leslie had frequently stayed, and that she was to remain in her room until they came. Finally she spoke slightingly and with disapproval of Mrs. Hoggan.

All that day Leslie stayed alone in her bedroom, for the first time in her life in deepest disgrace, and with no one she could trust to help or advise her. That night, when the family sat at dinner, she opened the door of her bedroom and, dressed in a spotted muslin summer frock and a blue motoring cap, she ran silently down the stairs and out of the house. Once away from the house, she made for the inn where Freddy stayed.

Freddy behaved with decision and sent immediately for the local pastor to marry them. On their being questioned, however, it appeared that neither of them had resided fifteen days in Scotland, and so it was impossible for the marriage to be performed.

During the evening Leslie's absence was discovered at the Greigs' house and several messages were sent to her asking her to come back. One of the servants, the groom, who was fond of her, came in person to beg her on his own account not to pursue this dangerous course. But Leslie was by now too frightened to go back, and her emotions had become fast involved with Freddy and against the Greigs. The inn in which they were was kept by two old ladies, and these had their sympathies much engaged by this romantic pair. They now arranged a room for Leslie to sleep in. They escorted her themselves to bed, and, once she was inside the room, they placed across the outside of the door the kind of heavy wooden bar that is used to keep bulls inside a pen. This they secured with a padlock, and then went themselves to bed, happy in the knowledge that no temptation could disturb Freddy's rest.

Next morning, having sent a message to the Greigs' house asking for Leslie's luggage to be sent on to Glasgow, the young couple left Auchterarder and started on a journey to England. They left the train at Glasgow and sat on the platform to await the arrival of the luggage. At some time during the day a train drew in, and Leslie's aunt and uncle, accompanied by Gerald, Bertie Greig's brother, stepped out of it. There now took place a long scene in which the older couple and Gerald Greig attempted to persuade Leslie to return with them. But, tired

and over-excited, she had made up her mind. She refused out-
right to accompany them, and nothing they said or did could
make her change her ground. All the time that she talked to
them, Freddy stood by her, but he did not speak a word. Later,
when she asked him why he had not supported her, he replied:

"It was a decision only you could make."

All day they waited on that platform, but in the evening the
luggage had still not come. Tired and discouraged, they crossed
then to the station from which the south-bound trains depart,
and they spent the last of the money they had on tickets to
Weymouth. The homing instinct was taking these two poor
little birds to Jersey.

All night long, on a crowded and dirty journey through the
length of England, little Miss Hoggan, exhausted and hungry,
and dressed still in the muslin dress and the blue motoring cap,
sat bolt upright. Freddy's sense of behaviour would not allow
her to rest her head on his shoulder.

The next day, August 4th, 1904, they were married in
Weymouth. It was necessary in order to do this to get a special
licence, and neither of them had any money with which to pay
for this. Having abducted his bride from her fiancé's house,
Freddy now had to persuade the vicar of the parish to pay for
his special licence. No one was present at the interview and no
one knows what he said. But I do not find it very difficult to
imagine. He would have started by giving that version of the
facts he thought most suitable to the vicar's ears, and he would
have made it very plain that Leslie was entirely alone with
him.

"Surely," I can then hear him say, "surely you are the last
man in the world who would wish this young girl to remain
unmarried and alone with me."

He would have said this with the utmost gravity, but his

eyes would have been sufficiently quizzical to assure the vicar he was not a man it would be safe to trust.

That night Mrs. Hoggan arrived from Jersey and all three of them went to an hotel. The next day Leslie went home with her mother to make her peace with her father.

The Colonel now revealed himself as a man of noble character. One can imagine the shock he must have received, since this was the first time he had been told that his wife and daughter were more than slightly acquainted with the son of his local tobacconist, but immediately the news had come from Scotland he had telegraphed the Greigs that his daughter's luggage was not to be retained. He now told Leslie that he only desired her happiness, and, since she was married to Freddy, he would do everything he could to help them.

Not so the Leonards.

"You never ought to have done it, Leslie," Mr. Leonard wailed. "You never ought to have done it."

And George merely remarked:

"You'll come to a bad end and you'll have only yourself to blame."

CHAPTER FOUR

Early Married Life

Freddy and Leslie were married in the name of Leonard and they kept this name in private life until 1908. Then it became apparent that the difficulties of two names, one in the theatre and one in private, were great, and their name was changed by deed poll to Lonsdale.

The most difficult thing in the whole of this history is to explain how for the first four years of their married life they kept alive at all. Immediately after the marriage in Weymouth, Leslie went back to Jersey to stay with her parents, because Freddy had no money with which to support her in England. Freddy himself was unable to go, because of the Jersey law in relation to debtors which, at the discretion of the creditor, allows a man to be imprisoned for debt. Freddy could not now return to Jersey because, if he had, he would have been clapped into gaol. At all times during the next four years that they had any money, Leslie joined Freddy in England, but when this was nearing its end, the last of the cash was used to send Leslie back to her parents, while Freddy remained to fend for himself as best he could.

The first of their separations was ended with good news. Freddy wrote to say that he had sold a play called *The Follies of the Foolish* to Willie Edouin, the famous comedian. He received £500 for this and Leslie went immediately to Weymouth to

join him. It was a fairly large sum of money for those days,
and it might, with careful management, have lasted several
years. But there were two things that made life permanently
hazardous until Freddy earned a large and more regular income. Whenever he received a considerable sum down, he
was already heavily in debt and so he was forced to pay much
of it away; and that part of any payment that he kept for
himself he spent with the lack of thought he was to exhibit all
his life.

He had bad luck over *The Follies of the Foolish*. If Edouin had
put it on, it might have attracted the attention of other managements and led to an earlier success. But Edouin died soon after
he bought the play and it was never performed. Freddy tried
to induce the dead man's executors to return the play to him,
since it was of doubtful value as part of the estate. This, however, they refused to do. In the long run their refusal may
have made him money, because many years later he re-wrote
this play and produced it under the title *On Approval*.

The whole of this part of the Lonsdales' life was spent in
lodgings—in Weymouth, in Bexhill, at one time in Herne Hill,
near London, and later in Harrow. They were often completely broke and they relied for weeks at a time on the good
will of their landladies. When Freddy died, on thinking about
his early life I realised that, although I knew a certain amount
about it, it lived in my mind as a series of anecdotes, most of
them about the scrapes the two of them got in and out of
through having no money.

There was the story, for instance, of when Freddy went out
for the day, and, coming back late in the evening, found Leslie
sitting on their luggage in the hall of the house in which they
were living. The landlady had made up her mind during his
absence to throw them out. Freddy went up to see her. No
one knows what he said to her, but less than ten minutes later

he returned in her company and she assisted him herself to carry their luggage back to their rooms.

Then there was the time when he went to London to see a theatre manager named Bingham. Bingham was at this time interested in Freddy. He does not seem ever to have produced a play for him but he occasionally advanced him small sums of money. On this occasion the Lonsdales had so little money that they could only find enough for a single fare to London. Freddy departed telling Leslie that, if he sent her a telegram to meet him at the station, she would somehow have to get enough money to pay for his return ticket when he arrived on their platform. During the day she received this telegram telling her to meet him, and giving her the time of his train. In despair, she searched through their belongings, and could only find left of any value a silver frame which held the photograph of that Mr. Featherstone to whom she had earlier lost her heart. Rushing with this to the pawnbroker, she received enough money to pay the fare. On the platform, however, Freddy waved the proffered money aside.

"It's quite all right," he said, "I've got a ticket, and I've got a lobster too."

Bingham had given him £10 after he had sent the telegram, and he had decided to celebrate this with the most luxurious dinner he could think of.

Dinner that night was, in spite of this, not a success. A cold silence fell over the table. Finally Leslie, looking at his granite face, asked:

"What on earth is the matter?"

"I go to London to try to earn our living," he replied in an outraged voice, "and, while I'm away, you," and he pointed at the unframed photograph of Mr. Featherstone which stood on the mantelpiece, "you spend the day gazing at your lover."

There was the time too when Leslie, having pawned Freddy's

winter coat because it would not be wanted for a few months, felt on the way home an irresistible urge to spend the money on strawberries and cream.

None of these episodes goes far to explain, however, how they managed to live without any regular income for four years until Freddy had his first plays produced.

I consulted my mother.

"I don't really know," she replied, "I can't remember. When we had no money at all I used to go over to Jersey."

"I know. But this was a period of four years. You spent a great deal of it in England. What money, besides the £500 for *Follies of the Foolish*, did you ever have?"

"Bingham sometimes gave Freddy £10."

"But you couldn't live for four years, during the last two of which you had two children, on Bingham sometimes giving Freddy £10. Did Frank Curzon give him an advance after he had decided to do his plays?"

"I don't know," she replied, "I simply can't remember. I expect he did.

"You have to realise," she added after some seconds' thought, and as though solving everything, "we were always quite sure Freddy would be a success."

It was after this conversation I realised how different is the attitude to money of people used to a regular income, however small, from those who, like my parents, live on hopes. Freddy and Leslie seem simply to have lived from day to day like birds, dining well when the dinner was good, otherwise not dining at all. But they were not consumed by worry, they did not wake at night and sweat in case things should go wrong, they did not fear the dun at the door, or the bailiff in the hall. They thought it was all rather funny, and they "were sure Freddy would be a success". And it is quite clear, when one thinks about it, that if Leslie had had a different temperament, she would have married Mr. Greig, and if Freddy had had a different temperament, he would have kept his job in the Jersey office of the South-Western Railway. But I still do not know exactly how they managed to live.

Once, at least, they were nearly starving, and I have two versions of what happened then. My mother says they ate porridge for breakfast, porridge for luncheon and porridge for supper. She says that the landlady worried about this and constantly asked them why they did not eat meat, to which they replied that it was because they preferred porridge. Freddy's story was different. They were in Herne Hill at the time, and he said that one day he went into a butcher's shop. Down the side of one wall of this shop there was a marble slab and on this slab were displayed pieces of meat. There were several people in the shop at the time and only one man to serve them. Freddy carried a newspaper under his arm, not rolled, but folded once. He stood behind the other people in the shop, and, as though absent-mindedly, he dropped his newspaper on to the slab by the side wall. Presently the man who was serving turned away to fetch something for one of the other customers, and, with a gesture of impatience, Freddy picked up his newspaper and left the shop. He walked steadily away from the shop until he turned a corner and then he ran like hell. Inside the folds of his newspaper there was a beefsteak.

Years later, according to this story, Freddy drove through Herne Hill in a great Bentley car. He drew up at this shop and went inside it, leaving his chauffeur at the wheel. The man who served was alone in the shop on this occasion, and Freddy fell into conversation with him. Presently he told in detail what he had done all those years before. The man had great difficulty in believing him, but, on being persuaded, he regarded it as a great joke, and he and Freddy laughed together on the best of terms.

"But what would you have done if you had caught me at the time?" Freddy asked him.

"Oh!" he said, and all the merriment left his face, "Oh! I should have put you in gaol."

In spite of all their difficulties, Freddy and Leslie seem to have enjoyed their lives. They always quarrelled a great deal (no one could live with Freddy without quarrelling), but when they had any money at all they amused themselves with the rather cheap entertainments usual to young people without much background or wealth. At Bexhill they used to visit the Kursaal, which the then Lord De La Warr managed with the same personal interest his son was later to give to the hotel at Cooden Beach. They seem always to have had friends amongst people of their own age.

From the start of their marriage Freddy always assumed a completely independent attitude in his comings and goings. He once asked Leslie if she would mind crossing the street and walking on the other side, as there was a girl coming towards them whom he rather fancied.

"I don't want her to know I'm married to you," he said.

And Leslie obligingly did as he asked.

Quite early in their married life he taught her not to worry about him when he returned home late at night. They had been in the bar of some hotel one evening, and he had sent her home before him, saying that he had a man he wished to see and would follow her shortly. At two o'clock that morning he had still not returned, and Leslie, who had been unable to sleep for worrying about him, sat in an overcoat on the balcony of their bedroom watching the street. At last she saw him turn the corner, and she noticed that he tacked slowly and quite steadily from right to left, from left to right. Furious that all her anxiety should have been for this, she jumped back into bed and awaited his entrance to tell him what she thought of him.

Presently the door of their bedroom opened and only his head appeared.

"You . . . " he said, "you . . . " and he seemed choked with indignation, "you go home to your mother in the morning."

He then entered the room, slowly undressed, and got into bed, refusing to answer any question. He fell instantly asleep, but Leslie stayed awake for hours wondering what she could have done to provoke this outburst.

The next morning, fresh and gay, he explained that he had not wanted to be "nagged" all night.

In 1905, a year after their marriage, their finances were so bad that Leslie tried to earn some money. Her father had some acquaintance with a man named William Greet, who produced musical plays. Leslie went to him with a letter of introduction and asked for a job in his chorus. In those days at an audition it was only necessary to pass a visual test, because if a girl could look beautiful on the stage and walk with ease, nothing much else was required of her, and Leslie got the job. She had only been rehearsing for a few weeks, however, before she had to go to Mr. Greet and tell him she was going to have a baby. She begged him to let her keep her job for a few weeks, but he refused.

"Where is your husband?" he asked her.

"He's walking up and down outside waiting for me," she replied.

Mr. Greet seemed surprised.

"What does he do for a living?"

"He writes plays," she replied.

"Oh!" said Mr. Greet. And then, "Well, you'd better tell him to send me a play to read."

Freddy sent Mr. Greet two plays, and Leslie went home to her parents, where she remained until her child was born.

Mr. Greet wrote without much delay and he said that he had

read the plays, and that, although they were not the kind of thing he himself produced, he thought they might be of interest to a Mr. Frank Curzon, and he had therefore sent them on to him.

This, I believe, is the true story of how Freddy first made his entrance into the London theatre. He himself never liked it. It offended his sense of the dramatic to have owed his introduction to his chorus-girl wife. He preferred an invention of his own, in which he sat all day on the stairs outside Frank Curzon's office, until the impresario, tired of tripping over him, asked him in.

Curzon gave him a contract for both these plays, and he finally produced them and two more. Nevertheless, none were produced until nearly three years later, by which time two children were born and a third on the way. However, in spite of the fact that my mother cannot remember it, I have ascertained from Miss Gertrude Butler that, from the time that he first read the plays until they were produced, Frank Curzon did make Freddy an allowance. Miss Butler says it was very small and she thinks it was £3 a week.

Freddy was right from the start an affectionate and responsible family man. When his first child cried in the night he would get up and make her bottle. But if she continued to cry while he was doing this, he would say to my mother:

"Can't the bloody fool see I'm getting it?"

When he first saw me, lying on the foot of the bed, he looked at me for a long time and then said to my mother:

"There is something very sweet about this baby. I think I shall love her all my life."

While they were living in Harrow, Freddy brought home one day for luncheon a young actor, who was beginning to make a name for himself, called Gerald du Maurier. Du Maurier was elegant, insouciant, rather mannered, and often very witty. While he was at luncheon he told them a story of how a great London hostess had asked him by himself to dine.

"I replied," he said, "that I couldn't dine with her that night because I was dining with my wife."

When he left, Freddy asked Leslie whether she did not think him a charming fellow. But she replied that, no, she had thought him patronising and conceited. Life must often have been hard for her in those days. She could not, for instance, have been very satisfied with the luncheon she was able to offer the young celebrity in their rooms in Harrow.

At that time, too, an extra burden was added to their already sufficiently great difficulties. Colonel Hoggan, failing in health, found himself unable to continue with his school. The Hoggans therefore left Jersey and came to live near their daughter in Harrow. But they had now only the army pension, and on this it was almost impossible to live. Freddy added to this income as best he could from now on, and, when his father-in-law died, he returned Mrs. Hoggan's trust and kindness to him by looking after her financially until she died in 1930.

If he had been less thriftless and less confident, it would have been impossible for him to survive this period as a playwright. Harassed by debt, uncertain from one day to the next how he would feed his family, in one small room in lodgings, amidst the cries of newly-born babies, he wrote four plays. Later, in comfortable surroundings, with the whole household hushed for fear of disturbing him, without worry and with every management in London competing for his work, he often found it impossible to write a word until the spur of poverty once more pricked him on.

CHAPTER FIVE

Success as a Playwright

On September 3rd, 1908, Frank Curzon produced *The King of Cadonia* at the Prince of Wales Theatre. On September 7th, the following Monday, he produced *The Early Worm* at Wyndham's Theatre. On August 5th, 1909, he followed *The Early Worm* with *The Best People* at Wyndham's, and in February, 1910, he presented *The Balkan Princess* at the Prince of Wales. These four plays had one quality in common, which they shared with almost every play that Frederick Lonsdale wrote—they were very successful.

The King of Cadonia was a musical comedy with lyrics by Adrian Ross and music by Sidney Jones. It was given a popular caste with Bertram Wallis, a well known young tenor, in the male lead, Isabel Jay, in private life Mrs. Frank Curzon, as the heroine, and Huntley Wright to provide the comedy, and it was exceptionally well staged and dressed. It had a riotous first night, and settled down to a long run.

The story of the play is roughly as follows. Cadonia, a Ruritanian country, peopled largely, it seems, by anarchists, has lost so many kings in the last few months that it is found necessary to protect the reigning King by keeping him under guard at the Palace, and, in order to secure the succession, a marriage is arranged between the Sovereign and Princess Marie, daughter of the Duke of Alasia, unwilling heir-apparent

Picture Post

The Early Worm. A. E. Matthews and Muriel Beaumont

Frederick Lonsdale   Frank Curzon

BLATZ:
"Do you know
this man?"

MAGDA:
"Do I know him?
He's my husband."

Blatz - Mr. LAURI DE FRECE   Henri - Mr. JAMES BLAKELEY

The Balkan Princess. Left to right: Lauri de Frece, Mabel Sealby and James
Blakeley; a page from *Play Pictorial*

to a perilous throne. The Princess objects to the marriage, because she disapproves of the King and thinks that he fails in his duty towards the people. The King objects both to marriage and to being kept prisoner in the Palace, and so he breaks out, having first disguised himself by shaving off his beard. While under an assumed identity, he meets his future bride, falls in love with her at first sight, is taught his responsibility to his people by words she innocently lets fall, and so returns, having won his bride, to do his duty to the nation, and to a triumphant finale entitled 'There's a King in the Land Today'.

This production was on the whole very well received by the critics and it was considered that Mr. Frank Curzon had 'hit the right nail on the head'.

The *Daily Graphic* had this to say the following morning:

"Some little while ago, Mr. Frank Curzon caused quite a flutter among the dovecotes in the musical comedy world by announcing that he proposed producing a musical play with a 'straight' story—a story, that is to say, which begins at the beginning, goes straight on to the end and then stops. The average musical comedy is, of course, quite incapable of performing such a feat. Hardly has it been launched upon its way before it takes the wrong turning, whence it occasionally peeps out, but without making any serious attempt to resume its journey. Mr. Frederick Lonsdale, however, who is responsible for the libretto of *The King of Cadonia*, which was presented at the Prince of Wales Theatre last night, has, with Mr. Frank Curzon's connivance, treated his plot more firmly. It is never allowed to get out of hand, but it is made to progress steadily and straightforwardly from the rise to the fall of the curtain. It is true that it has frequently made the journey before, and may therefore be presumed to know its way, for it is none other than our old friend the story of a young couple who have been betrothed against their wills before they have met,

D

and who fall in love without being aware of each other's identity . . ." (One famous London critic, on being asked whether he had liked *The King of Cadonia*, is said to have replied: "I like it very much. But then I always have. I liked it when it was *The Prisoner of Zenda*.") "The story is exceedingly pleasantly told by Mr. Frederick Lonsdale. . . . Altogether the new musical play seems cut out for success."

The Balkan Princess was also a musical comedy. The music this time was by Mr. Paul Rubens and the lyrics by Mr. Arthur Wimperis. Mr. Bertram Wallis and Miss Isabel Jay were again in the leads, but Mr. Huntley Wright was replaced by Mr. Lauri de Frece, and Miss Mabel Sealby, who had a long career before her as a Lonsdale soubrette, was this time in the caste. Again an uproarious first night was succeeded by notices from the critics which were on the whole excellent, and by a long run.

The story this time was of the Princess Stephanie who must marry or abdicate. Her choice of a husband must be between six Balarian Dukes, all of whom are summoned to the Palace. Only five obey the summons, and so the Princess, in disguise and incognito, goes in search of the sixth, amongst the Bohemian haunts which he is known to frequent. They fall in love at first sight, but later the Duke gives the treasonable toast "Down with the Princess," and Her Highness gives him over to her guard. He thus reaches the Palace by force, where he captivates everyone and finally wins the Princess's hand.

It is to be hoped that the critic who approved of *The King of Cadonia* and likewise of *The Prisoner of Zenda*, also enjoyed *The Balkan Princess*. It would be disappointing if he were a man who baulked simply at a change of sex among the leading roles.

However, it is easy to poke fun at musical comedies from the heights of a succeeding generation, or, for that matter, from anywhere at all. Years after the production of these plays, Freddy went to see Ivor Novello in his dressing-room when the latter was playing in a great success called *King's Rhapsody*.

"You know what this play is based on?" Ivor said to him. "When I was quite young I was taken to see *The King of Cadonia*, and I thought then: 'This is how a musical comedy should be written. One day I will write one like this myself.'"

What I have been interested to discover, in tracing the history of these early Lonsdale successes, is two things. The first, what were their merits? In terms of the sophisticated world he was writing for and about, Freddy can be said at this time to have been nowhere, met no one, and seen nothing. Since he was also incapable of reading a book, he received his inspiration from the air. The other thing I wanted to find was support for a claim he sometimes staked, at any rate in the privacy of his own family, to have made theatrical history at this time by writing musical comedies with plots. Specifically, he simply said, with a quite usual and becoming modesty: "I taught them how to do it."

It is not easy to reach a decision on either of these two points. All one has to turn to now is the opinion of the dramatic critics of that date. While the conventions of musical comedy may sometimes change, it is safe to say that critics never do. Their opinion, taken collectively, is therefore equivocal, contrary and often flatly contradictory.

"Wherein," the critic of the *Morning Post* begins a notice, "does *The King of Cadonia*, produced at the Prince of Wales Theatre last night with every sign of success, differ from preceding musical plays?" and, after several rather derogatory sentences, he concludes that it does not.

The critic of the *Morning Post* says, however: "There is an element of freshness in *The King of Cadonia* . . . that is certainly very attractive. We were, truth to tell, getting a little tired of the apparently unending succession of 'Girls' who have of recent years been wending their way across the musical comedy stage . . . and we were pining for a change for the better. That Mr. Curzon's latest production deserves to come into this category cannot be questioned, and we sincerely trust that other managers will follow his excellent lead and branch out into musical plays with *plots*." (My italics.)

"There is no wit," complains the critic of *The Times*, while the *Daily Graphic* congratulates the author on his story being "exceedingly pleasantly told," and *The Stage* admires the humorous second act.

However, when the critics are speaking of plays for which the public's support was never for a moment in doubt, and of an author who goes on to become one of the most successful in the world, it is reasonable, I think, to give more weight to those opinions which support the writer's own than to those which quarrel with it.

On these grounds, I think there is plenty of evidence to show that, although these two musical comedies were written round an old theme, they were written with wit and charm, and that the fact of a properly and tightly constructed plot was, in those days, an innovation. I have already quoted enough of the notices of *Cadonia* to show that there were people of this opinion. Here is what the critic of the *Daily Telegraph* had to say of *The Balkan Princess*:

"When a new musical play, differing in degree but not in kind from many others, is welcomed on production with a good deal more than ordinary enthusiasm, as was the sumptuous entertainment offered to the public on Saturday night by Mr. Frank Curzon, one is tempted to seek the chief factor in success."

He then goes on to say that in *Miss Hook of Holland* this was to be found in the personality of the chief comedian, in *The Merry Widow* in the interest of the story and the charm of the underlying sentiment, etc., and he then continues of *The Balkan Princess*:

"After giving full credit to all the collaborators mentioned individually and collectively, making full allowance for the cleverness of the artistes concerned, and taking other considerations into account, we incline to the opinion that it was the 'straight' story and the pretty thread of sentiment running through it that captivated Saturday's audience, and carried *The Balkan Princess* shoulder-high to a popular verdict, the sincerity of which was never for a moment in doubt."

Another critic said:

"A charmingly consistent story is what we have in *The Balkan Princess*, and that in a large measure was the reason for the splendid applause and the unqualified success which greeted its unfolding on Saturday night at the Prince of Wales Theatre."

The Early Worm was described as an original farce, and *The Best People* was a comedy. Mr. Frank Curzon treated his young playwright very well in the matter of cast. The leading players in *The Early Worm* were Mr. Weedon Grossmith, Mr. A. E. Matthews and Miss Muriel Beaumont, and Mr. A. W. Baskcombe also played a part. The cast of *The Best People* included Mr. Frederick Kerr and Miss Eva Moore.

Mr. Kerr and Mr. Matthews, the latter of whom is still drawing full houses nearly fifty years later, and has been known affectionately as 'Matty' to generations of playgoers, remain two of the three actors who have best understood and best performed the Lonsdale 'lines'—the third being Mr. Ronald Squire. All three have been noted for their extraordinary polish, their exact timing, and the aristocratic negligence so suited to this author's plays, seemingly so easy and in performance so difficult to achieve. Mr. Weedon Grossmith, who with *The Diary of a Nobody* may have achieved the immortal shades, was, on the stage, a comic genius. Miss Muriel Beaumont (in private life that Mrs. du Maurier for whom Gerald refused the invitation to dine) was a beautiful and adequate heroine, and Miss Eva Moore an actress of real accomplishment. All his life Freddy was very difficult about the casting of his plays, and he often so overloaded them with the salaries of stars that they could only remain in being while playing to capacity. Looking at the list of performers in his first plays, one sees that he was spoilt from the beginning and taught at that time to expect perfection.

The Early Worm was probably the worst play he ever wrote. It was a farce—unusual for him, and I think he never wrote another—and only under this designation could the situations in it become acceptable at all. It had already, however, certain Lonsdale hallmarks. The hero was a duke, the heroine an heiress possessing £50,000 a year, and Mr. Grossmith played the part of a virtueless intriguer, a man who 'wormed' his way out of every situation. Many of the lines have a faint but unmistakable Lonsdale ring. The finale to the third act is as follows:

Miss Sybil: You are not marrying me for my money?

The Duke: No. But I'm awfully glad you've got it.

Once more, however, the public received this play with rapture and the critics at least with kindness.

"The little farce by a new writer, Mr. Frederick Lonsdale . . ." *The Daily Graphic* said, "thoroughly deserves to have a long and prosperous career, and this for several reasons. It is exceedingly amusingly written, with light and pointed dialogue, it is admirably cast, and it is beautifully played. It is a mere trifle, light as air, but for an after-dinner nine o'clock entertainment it is exactly the thing . . ."

Of Weedon Grossmith, the *Pall Mall Gazette* said:

"He has to give comic expression to a variety of the meaner qualities, such as mercenariness, cowardice, snobbishness, peevishness and a kind of comic despair; and one watches their portrayal with unbroken enjoyment. There is a scene in the last act in which, momentarily overcome by his social isolation, he leans one hand on the table, rolls his eyes up towards the gallery, smooths his hair with his other hand, turns down the corners of his mouth and moans 'Who cares for me?', with the result that the audience care for him very much and fervently hope that he may go on despairing, so that they may go on laughing."

When *Aren't We All?*, originally produced in 1923, was revived at the Haymarket Theatre by H. M. Tennent in 1953, a party of people connected with the production went on to dine at Mr. Hugh Beaumont's house after the first-night performance. Mr. Roland Culver, who had directed the play, arrived there late, and said that he had been talking to Mr. Guy Bolton in the bar of the theatre.

"He said," Culver told several members of the party, " 'This play has worn very well considering that it was written in 1908.' Surely," he continued, "it was written in 1923."

There was more than one person present who had been connected with the original production, and they all agreed that it had been written in 1923, and that Guy Bolton had made some mistake.

Two or three months later, when I saw Freddy, I told him about the conversation.

"Guy Bolton was right, wasn't he?" I asked.

"Yes," he replied, "Guy Bolton was right. *Aren't We All?* was *The Best People* re-written, and it was originally written before 1908."

The Best People was in fact *Aren't We All?* with a very much weaker third act. Nevertheless, in this play the author got really into his stride and showed all the promise of things to come.

The following three quotations are taken from the notices of critics after the 1909 production of *The Best People*, the 1923 production of *Aren't We All?* and the 1953 production of *Aren't We All?* respectively.

"Mr. Lonsdale's latest comedy reveals the writer as a shrewd and sympathetic student of man and womankind, the possessor of a nimble wit, and of no inconsiderable powers of invention. His plot is not, perhaps, strikingly new, but it is set forth with a freshness and lucidity quite delightful. . . . The situation is in essence not particularly novel, but the author's ingenuity contrives to give it a most unexpected and diverting twist. So we have an amusing re-shuffling of the matrimonial cards, each of the players being placed in a curiously false position *vis-à-vis* the others. It helps materially to confirm the belief that in Mr. Frederick Lonsdale we have a dramatist who will go far. . . . Frederick Kerr's Lord Emsworth is a model of the easy-going, cynical, cool and shrewd man of the world, whose instincts for good a selfish and self-centred life have failed wholly to dull."

"In Lord Grenham he has created a character of an extraordinarily effective and attractive type. A man of the world, a cynic without a particle of bitterness in his composition, a lover of women but singularly indulgent to their weakness, as he is an admirer of their finer qualities, he makes an incomparable stage figure. He is played by Julian Royce with a superb finish and a sympathetic understanding rarely equalled."

"Ronald Squire was born to play the foxy old boy, Lord Grenham, rejoicing in his reputation as a bad old man and regretting only the opportunities he has missed of being a worse one.

"Few actors can twirl a Lonsdale line more nimbly around their lips."

When I showed these notices to Harold Hobson, he commented: "Anyone would think the 1914 War never took place. Here have we been believing that the inter-war period was the age of cynical disillusion and the downfall of idols, when these things were written and obviously enjoyed in 1908."

What is equally surprising is that the Lonsdale jibes at the aristocracy were so often said to be a product of knowledge of the world, but here is Lord Emsworth springing fully armed with epigram and tolerant scepticism from the brain of a young man of twenty-seven who had spent his earlier years in Jersey, on the Southampton docks, or in lodgings in Weymouth or Harrow.

These four plays established Freddy Lonsdale quite firmly in the theatre. They also clearly defined the scope and brilliance of his talent. One critic, speaking of *Cadonia*, wrote:

"The author . . . has not, it is true, happened upon a pre-eminently fresh theme, but, as a decidedly accomplished writer for the stage, he has proved (as so many accomplished writers have proved before him) that the whole art of the matter lies rather in the treatment than in the theme itself."

During all his writing life, he was seldom to hit upon a very fresh theme; on occasion he appeared to make do without a theme; but he was born with an instinctive knowledge of the theatre. His construction was nearly always sound, his dialogue sparkling and often very unexpected, and his inventiveness, never great for the main plot, was inexhaustible in contriving twists to any story however slight. His third acts remind one sometimes of the compositions of some great musician. "I could end it like this," he seems to say, gathering up all the threads towards a great crescendo, "but I'm not

D*

going to," slipping off into some new theme or into a variation of an old one, "or again like that, or like that," until his audience, satiated with mirth, leave the theatre unaware that the evening has been contrived from material most people would find insufficient for a one-act play.

Mr. Leonard and George, his second son, travelled from Jersey to witness the first nights of each of these plays. They sat always in the pit, having refused the best seats in the house, and they never consented to go to the back of the stage to meet the company.

"It would not be right," Mr. Leonard said. But he was also a little frightened. He was unable to believe that Freddy had written these plays. He thought they had probably been written by Jim, but he was not even sure of this. It seemed to him there was a possibility that at some moment the true author might appear, flanked by policemen, and he was determined not to witness the hideous scene that would then ensue.

CHAPTER SIX

Westgate

After the successful production of his first plays, Freddy was able to take a house at Westgate-on-Sea. It was a small and undistinguished house, but it was a great change from lodgings. Two servants were kept, a cook and a house-parlourmaid, and the Lonsdale children, well dressed and well scrubbed, were pushed out every day in a double pram by a nanny. Freddy was very pleased by his success, but his character and behaviour were in no way altered by it. He was born completely individual and with a proper opinion of himself, and he was unmoved by other people's opinion of him. It is the essentially insecure who have difficulty in carrying their oats. He now settled down to a life that was to remain very little changed for about ten years, until he was nearly forty.

He made friends locally, gravitating as always towards the richer and more carefree houses, where he was regarded as an interesting young man—an established and very promising playwright. He was free at last of worries, and his wife was able to live very much as other ladies of the district. They began to live a life, not so unusual in those days, of leisure. They played golf and they played bridge, in the summer they bathed and played tennis, and they entertained the gentry. They took part, too, in the ordinary functions of a small country town. Freddy was at some time president of the local fire brigade.

He went very seldom to London in those days, and when he did go he never stayed for more than one night. He was firmly rooted in his own home and he seemed to have no desire to travel, or for any variety in his life. When he went to London, he used to lunch with Frank Curzon or with Gerald du Maurier, usually at the Piccadilly Hotel, sometimes at the Savoy. It was then he laid the foundations for much comfort in later life. The young waiters in London hotels are often there to learn English, and many who served Freddy then were later in big jobs all over the world. In the 1930s and '40s the head waiter of a big hotel on the Riviera would have started life at the Piccadilly, the owner of a two-star restaurant on the route there would introduce himself as the son of a chef who had been at the Savoy. No matter how many years had separated them, none of these men ever forgot Freddy, or the way he had treated them when they were underlings in London. The impression he made was never deliberate, nor was it done by over-tipping or a propitiating manner. He merely spoke to them as though they were fellow human beings and people who shared the same world as himself. For instance, having teased Frank Curzon on some minor matter practically to apoplexy, he would say to the waiter who came to change the plates:

"Be a good fellow and bring a bottle of smelling salts. Mr. Curzon is about to have a stroke."

This simple joke might be carried to the lengths where the waiters actually produced a bottle of smelling salts on a silver salver, and felt themselves to be sharing with the playwright the leg-pulling of the great theatre magnate. If he wished to complain about the food he had been served, he would send for a waiter and say to him:

"Taste this, my dear fellow."

The waiter, having hesitantly tasted it, would ask:

"What is wrong with it, sir?"

"Prussic acid. Do you imagine the chef bears me some grudge?"

Not only was his food changed without question, but twenty years later, as he was guided to the best table in the room, the *chef de restaurant* would murmur to him:

"No prussic acid to-day."

The society in Westgate was much the same as it would have been in any other seaside town, though it was very different from what it would be now, since so many people lived on unearned incomes. Most of the families were quiet and undistinguished, though here and there a name was heard that would have been known in other parts of the world. George Bancroft, who achieved a glinting fame as a playwright and again as a character in a broadcast by Max Beerbohm, lived there. He was the son of Sir Squire and Lady Bancroft, great names in the English theatre. Freddy shared with Lady Bancroft a belief in black cats. He always looked for one on his first nights, and he usually found one. On one occasion a strange black cat entered the theatre and walked right across the stage in the middle of a scene.

Living in Westgate, too, was an old and distinguished playwright named Haddon Chambers. His name is forgotten now, but he was a giant in his time, and in a play called *The Tyranny of Tears* he coined a phrase, "the long arm of coincidence", which passed into the English language. He was a noted wit. The story was told of him that, a play of his being a terrible flop on its first-night production in New York and being received with much angry noise from the house, he went on to the stage to take his bow.

"Ladies and gentlemen," he said, "there are few great men in the world to-day, but we are alive to our responsibilities."

He was quite old at this time. I think I remember him myself, looking like a polished but, nevertheless, repellent frog.

He had a manservant who was a sort of Jeeves and who controlled his life. This man had come ahead of him to Westgate to find him rooms, and, on interviewing the landlady, had explained that his master was a very difficult man, and that he had to have absolute quiet, could not be required to be punctual for meals, and slept when he felt like it.

"Oh!" said the landlady, "I see. A mental case."

"No," replied the Jeeves, "not exactly mental. Experimental."

With Haddon Chambers, Freddy enjoyed his first taste of that kind of conversation which, for him, was one of the greatest joys of life. It can only be described as a battle of wits, where no quarter is asked and none given, and where the successful thrust of an opponent gives as much pleasure as personal victory. It is a kind of talk which is difficult to repeat, for two reasons. The obvious one is that it is not always as good as it seems at the time. Life is much larger than the printed word, and conversation that in fact needs quick wits and tough good humour may seem small change when written down. The other reason is that in the excitement and exhaustion of the battle it may be only the smallest flick of the verbal wrist that brings victory, just as in a real battle the last aeroplane, or six tired men making a stand in the evening, may defeat the enemy. This conversational struggle is an entirely masculine pursuit. It reached its greatest heights in the Garrick Club in the 1920s. Then, stars of the literary, legal and theatrical worlds engaged each other ceaselessly. It is not everybody's game. Outsiders elected to the Garrick for their promise often failed to make the inner circle, and others, frightened by the tales they heard, after election never entered the Club. They indulge in this form of debate in the House of Commons too. This explains why the House is often reported as rocking with laughter at jokes which, to the amazed public, seem unworthy of a preparatory school boy. It is not that our chosen representatives are so simple-minded that they enjoy a humour that would not pass muster in the nursery. They are playing a different game—a game in which strong nerves and self-reliance often count for more than wit, and in which a quick and undismayed retort from a hard-pressed opponent brings a release of tension. It accounts too for the popularity often achieved amongst men, and so surprising to women, of some rough, aggressive bragger. He is sure to be found to be relentlessly malicious in pursuit of some selected victim, and buoyantly unyielding in defence of himself—a "good fellow".

Gerald du Maurier used sometimes to come down to stay with Freddy, and these two and Haddon Chambers would sit up all night, drinking brandy, smoking cigars and exchanging witticisms—always on the alert. I was brought up on one of the cracks that Haddon made at this time.

There was a young lady who shared his life in Westgate, in the hope, it was thought, of advancement on the stage. On one occasion Gerald made some spiteful remark about this girl, designed to make Haddon ridiculous, and Freddy immediately protested.

"Leave him to me, old boy," Haddon murmured, "leave him to me. I'll get him."

Later in the evening he was talking about his experiences in America and he told of a dinner he had attended in New York, given to a great impresario by all the actors, actresses, writers and other persons connected with his productions. At the end of the dinner a toast was given to the guest of honour, and it was expected that he would reply to it. The great man, however, was seen to be fast asleep. Nudged awake by his next-door neighbour, he had the situation explained to him, and, rising unsteadily, he placed both hands on the table.

"Ladies and gentlemen," he said, "any man who paints his face is a son of a bitch."

He then sat down and resumed his sleep.

Freddy was a rapturous audience for this stroke, because he was curiously prudish, and actually inclined to this sort of view. Haddon was not left unmolested, however. They went on to talk of the law of aliases or pen-names, and Haddon maintained there was no law to prevent a man calling himself what he liked.

"I could call myself Christ if I chose," he said.

"You do," Gerald answered bitterly, "you do."

Freddy could have continued with this pleasant, unambitious life indefinitely had he done anything to maintain it. But he did not. From the time that he finished *The Best People*, for five years he never wrote a line. He was always said to be congenitally lazy. Lazy is a comprehensive term, describing behaviour not explaining it, and during the course of his life he wrote twenty-seven plays or musical plays and at least two original films—not a bad output. A play is a difficult thing to write, even if it does not require real literary talent. It has during two acts to create absorbed interest in some problem, and in the third act it has to solve it. If a satisfactory solution is not hard to achieve, sufficient curiosity is not excited. There are many technical difficulties too. Actors have to be brought on and taken off the stage naturally and smoothly, but at the moments that suit the play and are not necessarily a consequence of the preceding action. There was a time when it was considered technically maladroit habitually to divide acts into more than one scene. Again, to-day it is desirable for a playwright to confine himself to as few settings as possible, because of the enormous cost of stage scenery.

All creative writers have recuperative periods in which the nerves and bloodstreams of their talent replenish themselves.

Some have no staying power and write themselves out with very few works. After a period of rest and peace, few can overcome their resistance to summoning once more a teasing and unmanageable muse, who can be unexpectedly generous, but often responds only to a painful expenditure of spirit, without the jab of outside circumstance. For many people the jab is given by fear of poverty—they work to fend it off. Freddy had no fear of poverty; indeed, until old age brought with it an apprehension of an actual loss of power, he never made this kind of calculation. I think he enjoyed self-expression, but not so much more than he enjoyed other things that he could be easily driven to it. He certainly enjoyed success—he often made artlessly pleased references to his—but again it did not matter enough to him to cause him to seek it. He simply reacted to different stimuli from other people, and the only jab that could certainly start him working was that of stark disaster.

In Westgate, after the success of his first plays, he only began to write once more when his money was nearly gone and his vision of the future showed almost as many hazards as had the old Weymouth life. Then he sat down and wrote a musical play called *Teresa*, and sent it to Frank Curzon.

Presently Curzon asked him to come to see him. Freddy and Leslie travelled to London together that day, and, while Freddy went to Curzon's office, my mother went to a matinée, filled with an unreasoning foreboding. When she met Freddy on the train that night she knew from his face that something had gone wrong. Curzon did not like *Teresa*, had refused to put it on and returned the script. This was a good deal more than Freddy had bargained for.

He was now very seriously up against it. He had three children to support, a house and servants, and his wife's parents also now depended to some extent on him. The fact that his life was not completely broken at this time was due to a very remarkable happening, the result of phenomenal luck combined with his unusual qualities.

In Westgate, as in most country towns, there was a club which drew its membership from the gentlemen of the surrounding district, and where these foregathered for that mixture of alcohol, cards and masculine society which draws Englishmen all over the world. One night a new member entered this club, a very rich Australian gentleman, named Conran. Mr. Conran settled himself down in a chair and called to the waiter to bring him a whisky and soda. The waiter explained to him that, owing to the licensing laws of England, no one might order a drink and pay for it until he had been a member of the club for more than twenty-four hours. At that moment there detached himself from a group of men standing together on the other side of the room a youngish, fair-haired man who crossed and spoke to Conran.

"My name," he said, "is Lonsdale. Please order yourself anything you want this evening and put it on my bill." He then spoke to the waiter: "Give this gentleman anything he wants." Afterwards he returned to the group on the other side of the room.

Mr. Conran could not fail to be interested in a man who had shown such skilful consideration for a stranger, and who had saved him from an unpleasant evening and a slightly humiliating experience. He had two daughters and a son, rather distinguished young people, noted for a kind of reckless courage which went further than a simple defiance of unintelligent convention. Their chief interest in life at that time was hunting and they only came to Westgate in the summer, and then they brought with them their favourite horses, which they used to exercise on the sands, dressed themselves in bathing dresses. They were not much younger than Freddy and Leslie, and the two families, finding in one and another the slightly unusual, made great friends.

Soon Mr. Conran learned that his new friends were on the rocks, and he must have reflected with amusement that the only man in the club that night who had offered to pay for his drinks was the one who could not afford to do so. He sent for Freddy.

"Could you write down every debt you have on a piece of paper," he asked him, "leaving out nothing at all."

Freddy did this, and Mr. Conran paid his debts to the last penny. He then made the Lonsdales an allowance of £5 every week until such time as they no longer needed it. The terms of this loan were that it should be paid back as and when it became possible.

These events took place some time in the early part of 1914. During that summer Freddy received a message asking him to go and see George Edwardes at Daly's Theatre.

Daly's was a theatre with a great and glamorous reputation. It had been built late in the nineteenth century by George Edwardes for an American called Augustine Daly. Daly brought Ada Rehan there, and during his time Duse also appeared in *La Dame aux Camélias*, and, from its opening, the theatre achieved a *réclame* it was never to lose. When Daly left London, George Edwardes himself took over the management of the theatre, and he is given the credit for introducing to London a new form of entertainment. His first production at Daly's was the opera *Hansel and Gretel*, and this was only a moderate success. Edwardes believed, quite correctly, that what London was asking for was a more popular version of the form of light opera. He produced in succession and with enormous success a series of productions known then and since as 'musical comedy'.

Looking back on it, these productions seem to have reached almost the lowest point of art of any theatrical tradition. One method employed was to take a light opera score and libretto and present these with a new book written to fit the most tuneful of the arias. Much attention was paid to the scenery and dresses, enormous choruses of beautiful girls were engaged, the leading ladies had to be young and attractive, and always there was at least one big part for a comedian. Of this type, the English production of *The Merry Widow*, in Vienna given as light opera, was the outstanding success. The other method was that of an original production written and composed in the same style by English writers and musicians. Nothing very strenuous was required of anyone but the comedians. The stars and the chorus were not expected either to dance, except in an inconsequent and graceful manner, or to be able to sing. Some of the music was charming, but little of it was of real merit. A great deal of it was derived, sometimes with acknowledgments, sometimes without, from light opera. Years after the period of which I am speaking, we had staying in our house a professor of music who liked to amuse himself on the piano by musical stunts. One evening he gave a demonstration of how the scores of musical comedies are often written, and as an instance he simply played the waltz from *The Merry Widow* and also that from *The Maid of the Mountains*, passing without transition from a phrase of one into a phrase of the other. It then became apparent that the first of these begins with a phrase of four notes played in succession and repeated, whereas the second begins with the same four notes, only in this case they are played in pairs. When I was talking to Freddy some weeks later, I asked him if he was aware of this fact.

"Oh yes," he said, "what happened was this. We all said to Fraser-Simson: 'This score's too dull. We'll never get away with it. What we want is a waltz like *The Merry Widow*.' And he went home and wrote it."

Later the Americans took hold of musical comedy, made it

harder and more athletic, introduced music from a different and less explored source, trained choruses to dance, wrote lyrics of genuine wit, found singers with an authentic if secondary talent, and turned it into a live entertainment. But in its early days in England it was simply a bastard art—and the most bastard part of all was the comedians.

In all these musical comedies there was a highly paid, much starred comedian, who spent a great deal of time on the stage. These provided light relief whenever the plot began to wear thin or the musical score to pall. One or two, such as George Robey and, I am told, W. H. Berry, possessed the real comic spirit, but all too often they only worked extremely hard. They derived from the English music-hall, but they were expected to be less broad, more sophisticated and to manage without the more outrageous jokes permitted to artistes in that sphere. In order to make up for these disadvantages, they relied to a great extent on exaggerated clothes and make-up, and for the rest on spontaneous inspiration (such was their position in the theatre that they often wrote their own lines, altered their performance nightly, and took liberties with the script and the rest of the cast that were permitted to no one else). When their inspiration flagged, they relied on holding the line that had failed of effect, while making distressed and india-rubber faces until the audience laughed from sheer embarrassment. They never succeeded in sufficiently embarrassing me. From the age of about ten I used to watch them from the stage box provided by my father, from which it is regarded as good manners to lead the applause, in cold and disapproving silence—and I believe now I was right. But they were at the time a source of great joy to everyone but myself.

All these criticisms of musical comedy have, of course, been made before, and they have been answered before. In his book on Daly's, Mr. Forbes-Winslow quotes Paul Rubens as saying:

"It is very easy to poke fun at a musical play, but there are some things which it is unfair to analyse. Few people realise the work entailed in the writing and composing of a musical play, how situations have to be altered to make room for songs, how songs have to be changed to suit situations, how music has to be sacrificed for stage effects, how scenes have to be devised to afford opportunities for this or that artist, how arrangements have to be made to enable the chorus to change their costumes for the next scene, and how actors or actresses have to make their exits early in this or that scene so as to be dressed in time for the commencement of the one that follows."

He also quotes Sir Seymour Hicks as saying to Mr. Frederick Lonsdale:

"The fellow I take off my hat to is the fellow who can write a musical play book. He has to know how much and how little story he can have, how long he can hold on to a scene and twenty more things you don't know about till you try."

Mr. Lonsdale is said to have agreed.

These two were not the only men famous in more sophisticated arts who worked in the musical comedy theatre at the time. Harry Graham, who wrote *Ruthless Rhymes*, also wrote lyrics for musical plays in London, while an even greater master of the comic art, P. G. Wodehouse, was doing the same thing in New York. P. G. Wodehouse was so highly satisfied with his productions that he thought it worth quoting some of them, without music, in a book he wrote more than thirty years later. He, like Seymour Hicks and Freddy Lonsdale, was in a position to appreciate the difficulties.

It also has to be remembered, when considering the musical plays of this period, that in order to fill a theatre in London it was necessary to attract young men. It was to this end that most of the difficulties described by Paul Rubens were undertaken. Beautiful women in beautiful dresses had to be kept

moving about the stage, light-hearted themes had to be inter-
spersed with sentimental songs, and the whole evening had to
be softly alluring and sexually titillating. At some unrecorded
point of time, the young men gave place at the stage doors to
queues of excited women, waiting with autograph book in
hand for their favourites to appear. To-day, I think I am right in
saying, most members of the theatrical profession can walk as
unmolested to and from their jobs as those who work from nine
till five. It might take much research to pinpoint the social
conditions which caused these changes, but their effect on
theatrical productions can be seen almost at a glance. It may
not be true to say we get the government we deserve; there is
no doubt we get the theatre we deserve.

In 1914 Daly's Theatre was the fountain-head of musical
comedy, and any actor, composer or writer who was engaged
to work in this theatre had reached the top of his profession.

When Freddy was sent for to go and see George Edwardes,
there was no money in the house. Mr. Conran's £5 for that
week had been spent. He went into the town and he borrowed
the fare to London from Mr. Setterfield, who kept the dairy
shop.

When he arrived at Daly's he met Mr. George Edwardes and
his theatre manager, Mr. Robert Evett. They explained to him
that they were working on an adaptation of a continental book
and score, and that the book was turning out unsatisfactorily.
Mr. Edwardes gave him a cheque for £100 and the existing
script, and explained to him that he wanted him to work on
this. It was proposed that he should read the script immediately and return to George Edwardes's office to give his
views and, if possible, to make suggestions for alterations.

Later that day Freddy returned to George Edwardes's
office. He placed the script on Edwardes's desk and then,

with a fine dramatic gesture, he tore the cheque into two pieces and placed these on the top of the script.

"Why is that?" Edwardes asked.

"Because," Freddy replied, "no man living could do anything with this story."

He then travelled back to Westgate to tell Leslie, and, one supposes, Mr. Setterfield, that he had torn up a cheque for £100.

George Edwardes never produced this piece. In August of that year war broke out against Germany, and the reason given for dropping this production was the fact that it emanated from enemy territory. This is unlikely to have been the real reason, and it is more probable that Freddy's sensational behaviour gave the *coup de grâce* to a production that was already admittedly in need of much improvement. They produced instead at Daly's a revival of a musical comedy called *The Country Girl*, and this settled into a moderately successful run; not so successful, however, as to make it unnecessary to look around immediately for a possible successor. Bereft of continental sources, some talent had to be found at home.

"Send," Mr. Edwardes said to Mr. Evett, "for the young man who tore up the cheque."

Freddy collaborated with Miss Gladys Unger to produce a musical comedy book called *Betty*. In this play they reverted to the *Cinderella* theme brought up-to-date. The music was by Paul Rubens, and great names were engaged to play in it, Mr. W. H. Berry and Mr. G. P. Huntley, both noted comedians, Miss Winifred Barnes and Mr. Donald Calthrop. It was produced on April 24th, 1915, to a war-time audience and it ran for 391 performances. As with so many other Lonsdale plays, its success was never for a moment in doubt.

A leading daily newspaper announced next morning:

"It was a triumph and a success and Daly's is provided with full houses for a long time to come."

So began a collaboration between Freddy Lonsdale and the Daly's Theatre management which was to last for many years and make fortunes for everyone concerned. Freddy now had a ready outlet for anything he chose to write, and it was to be some time before he was to break out of the musical comedy world to achieve fame as a writer of comedies.

CHAPTER SEVEN

Birchington

After the production of *Betty*, the Lonsdales left Westgate and took a house in Birchington, a village about two miles away on the coast. They lived here for seven or eight years. The first house they lived in was named Ailsa, and had a rather good walled-in garden with, I think, two tennis courts. Later they moved to 6, Beach Avenue, a semi-detached house in a row, and later still they bought a house on the sea front which they named Rozel.

In 1916 Freddy did the English version of a musical comedy originally French, named *High Jinks*. This had music by Rudolph Friml, and it was very successful, running at the Adelphi Theatre for 383 performances.

Before this, in 1915, George Edwardes had died, leaving liabilities of £80,000. He had been a great gambler, both in the theatre and on the racecourse. Robert Evett, with Edwardes's daughter, Mrs. Sherbrooke, took over the management of the estate, and with it the management of Daly's Theatre. His first production there was *A Happy Day*, with a book by Seymour Hicks. This had some success, running for about nine months, but it was soon necessary to look about for its successor. At this time Freddy offered Evett *Teresa*, the script which Frank Curzon had refused, and Evett decided to put it on. He engaged Harold Fraser-Simson to write the music and

Harry Graham to write the lyrics. Oscar Asche was put in charge of the production.

Oscar Asche immediately made one constructive suggestion. He did not like the title *Teresa*. The name that he suggested to take its place was *The Maid of the Mountains*.

The Maid of the Mountains was one of the two or three greatest successes in theatrical history. Produced for the first time in Manchester on December 23rd, 1916, it opened at Daly's on February 10th, 1917. It ran for 1,352 performances in this its first London production, and is said to have made its promoters a profit of some £300,000.

The production was anything but lavish, since this was the last chance of restoring the lost Edwardes fortunes and of paying the debts. The scenes were arranged for a small chorus, the cast of 'bandits' made possible inexpensive clothes, and Miss José Collins, who played Teresa, took a cut in her salary until the production was established.

The writers and composers of this piece owed a great deal to José Collins. She had a very beautiful voice and was ideally suited to this part. With dark and curling hair and wonderful eyes, she, nevertheless, suggested more a figure from grand opera than one of the famous 'Girls'. But the clothes in this production, gay and gypsyish, suited her to perfection, and she spoke the unusually astringent Lonsdale lines with admirable character. She made an enormous personal success. The fabulous success of the play can only be accounted for, however, by giving all credit to each and every one concerned in its production, and also, of course, to that curious element of luck in timing necessary to hit the jackpot in the theatre. Freddy was born with luck on his side.

Robert Evett cannot, nevertheless, have had an altogether easy time during rehearsals. He was dealing with at least two personalities with the artistic temperament. Miss José Collins, who claims to have gypsy blood in her veins, is reputed to have thrown a plate of Irish stew in his face when he annoyed her past all bearing, and Frederick Lonsdale, always quarrelsome in the theatre, and unwilling now, as always later, to have the smallest changes made in his work, left Daly's in a rage during rehearsals, hurling insults at Evett, and returned to Birchington, where he sulked until Evett telephoned him from Manchester to suggest that he should come and watch the audience's reception of his play. *The Maid of the Mountains* had no false starts, but from its first performance was a phenomenal success.

In his book on Daly's Mr. Forbes-Winslow, after remarking of Frederick Lonsdale that he was said to have succeeded Pinero as the most efficient of our commercial dramatists, says:

"Frank Curzon always claimed to have 'discovered' Lonsdale, but he paid him only two per cent royalty for the privilege of doing so. Lonsdale had to struggle for years before success came."

Frank Curzon did discover Lonsdale. He produced *The King of Cadonia*, *The Early Worm*, *The Best People*, and *The Balkan Princess*, over a period of about two years and before any other play by this writer had been done in London. Miss Gertrude Butler tells me that not only did he pay the normal royalties when these plays were produced, but before their production he made Freddy an allowance of something like £3 a week for over two years. He seems to have taken the most deliberate risks in backing so heavily on the talent of an unknown author. My parents were very fond of him and grateful to him, and I suffer the nickname Frankie to this day because they wished to please him.

The suggestion "Lonsdale had to struggle for years before success came" also seems to me to be untrue. The only struggle Freddy ever had after the production of *The King of Cadonia* was against his own preference for an easy life. The only play he ever wrote that was rejected by a theatre manager was *The Maid of the Mountains*, over which Frank Curzon made a colossal mistake. This play eventually made Freddy so much money that even his idleness could never again reduce him below what might be described as comfortable circumstances.

Robert Evett once showed the accounts of Daly's Theatre for this period to Ronald Squire. One of the items in the account was the sum of money it had been possible to pay each week to the Edwardes family. This began with a figure of about £2 at the beginning of the run of *The Maid of the Mountains*, and rose very slowly at first. In under two years the whole of the debt of £80,000 had been paid off and the £2 turned into an astronomical figure. If Freddy's account with Mr. Conran could have been laid beside it, the graph of the rise to solvency would have followed about the same course.

With *The Maid of the Mountains*, Freddy said good-bye to the vagrancy of his youth. He was never again to owe even the smallest sums, and although, until the halcyon days of the nineteen-twenties, his fortunes moved up and down a little, they did so only within the bounds of solvency. He paid all his early debts with money from *The Maid of the Mountains*, although he had to wait until the end of the war to settle the last of these.

In 1919 Freddy took his wife and three children to stay in Jersey for their summer holiday. It will be remembered that during his early married life he had been unable to go to the island because he owed money there, and because of the Jersey law in regard to debtors. Until the success of *The Maid of the Mountains* he had never possessed a large enough sum to pay these debts. Since this was produced in 1917, it was not until after the war he acquired sufficient money, and he entered the island in 1919 as a debtor.

On the first evening of their arrival in Jersey, the three Lonsdale children, tired and over-excited, were put early to bed in the hotel. Freddy and Leslie then went out to dine with Miss Rozel le Cornu, an old friend of Leslie's and a member of one of the most distinguished Jersey families. At some time during the course of the evening the maid entered the room to say that some officers of the law were at the door and wished to see Mr. Lonsdale.

Freddy went to the door and welcomed them in. He knew some of them and he appeared to be pleased to see them. The spokesman then rather shamefacedly explained to him that because of his debts in the island it would be necessary for him to return with them to the police court.

"Would it put the matter right if I paid you the money now?" Freddy asked them. And it was agreed that this would settle the case.

Freddy then took £400 in notes out of his pocket and handed them over, thus securing discharge of the last of his debts.

Both my father and my mother, who had enjoyed this scene, thought Miss le Cornu lacking in humour, because she now remarked that, as she lived in the island, she would have preferred it to have taken place before they came to her house.

Freddy wrote the book for four more plays at Daly's, which was bought in 1922 by 'Jimmy' White. The first of these was *The Lady of the Rose*, which was an adaptation from a book by Rudolph Schanzer and Ernest Welisch. The music was by Jean Gilbert and the lyrics by Harry Graham. Harry Welchman, Roy Royston and Phyllis Dare played the leads, and, produced on February 21st, 1922, it ran for 514 performances.

His next play there was *Madame Pompadour*, again an adaptation from an Austrian original, with music by Leo Fall and lyrics again by Harry Graham. Evelyn Laye achieved fame in this piece and, with her, Derek Oldham. Produced at Daly's

on December 20th, 1923, it ran for 469 performances. Freddy
was by this time making so much money that he was able to
give *Madame Pompadour* to my mother as a present, and to this
day she still receives small sums in royalties from it.

In September 1925, *Katja the Dancer*, another successful
Lonsdale adaptation, was transferred from the Gaiety Theatre
to Daly's, and in the two theatres this play ran for 505 performances.

Finally an original play called *Lady Mary* was produced at
Daly's on February 23rd, 1928, and this, though less successful,
ran for 181 performances.

There are too many collaborators in a musical comedy for it
ever to be possible to apportion praise, but it cannot but be
noticed how many of the most outstanding of the Daly's
successes had a book by Frederick Lonsdale.

For several years after the success of *The Maid of the Mountains*,
Freddy continued to live a very simple life. When I was about
ten he started to make me his frequent companion. There is a
place on the outskirts of Birchington called Quex Park. Anyone who walks right round this park has done about four miles.
All his life Freddy was addicted to taking his exercise on the
hard road, and we used to walk almost daily round the park
while he talked to me about life. Neither at this time nor at any
other did I ever find him entirely human. One was always on
the alert in his company, always striving to please, and, even in
those days, it seemed to me that there were whole realms of
thought and behaviour which he knew nothing about. Of
course, my impression may have been the result of my relationship to him. But I rather doubt it. I think the minds of men
with a special talent move with an extraordinary impetus and
speed down certain tracks, making impossible that dawdling in
the by-ways which enlarges the understanding of more

ordinary people. I used on those walks to strive to sustain my part in the conversation, and I soon learned the kind of attitude to life that was likely to win his approval. Occasionally I was rewarded for my efforts.

"Well, that was good. That showed courage," or, "Well, that was at least original."

But for the most part I simply provided the kind of audience he needed for the expression of his thoughts—a loving, admiring and loyal listener.

Then, after the war, two things happened which eventually caused him to change his whole mode of life. The first of these was his election to the Garrick Club. I think almost the greatest day in Freddy's life was the day on which this happened. As I have said, he always took the success of his plays quite calmly because he had never doubted it. But membership of the Garrick was for him an honour and a pleasure not beyond his dreams, but in fulfilment of them. Here and only here he met his equals in wit, confidence and colourful eccentricity. Here and only here he met a whole society which, without re-servation, he respected. They used to use the word 'authentic' at the Garrick with a shade of special meaning. Almost any quality or any sin could be forgiven someone who was sincerely, unpretentiously and vigorously himself. "Well, at least," it would be said, "he is authentic." This word, used in this way, summed up almost everything that Freddy cared for in life.

The membership of the Garrick, or that part of it with which Freddy consorted, consisted for the most part of writers, actors and lawyers. (All his life Freddy was in love with the legal profession.) It was a gathering of wits; it had its own codes of behaviour, and it was a very robust and strenuous society. The difficulty for any outsider in understanding its charm was that, although one could not fail to be impressed by the names of the participants in any story that came out of it, so few of these

Monsieur Beaucaire. Marion Green and Maggie Teyte

Madame Pompadour. Evelyn Laye and Bertram Wallis

stories re-told were understandably funny. Much of the fun of the Garrick seemed to be of an artlessly schoolboyish kind, and there is no doubt that high spirts and bonhomie, coupled with that tough, alert behaviour in conversation which I have earlier described, constituted the greater part of it. The simplest jokes presented in the right way won approval. The hunt was always up, first against bores, and secondly against people whose eccentricities differed from those accepted by the majority of members. There was one character, a Reverend Dean of a famous parish, who had managed to arouse some very deep suspicions. E. V. Lucas caused much pleasure on one occasion by the simple expedient of cutting out of a newspaper an announcement which read: "The Very Reverend Dean of . . . will hold Divine Service in the Chapel at 10 o'clock on Sunday . . ." and underlining in red ink the word divine. Freddy carried this cutting in his pocket for many days.

But the most permanently and relentlessly pursued quarry was the 'bore'. The only deadly sin in the eyes of the membership of the Garrick Club was to be a bore. Anyone who told long stories, showed too much eagerness for familiarity with famous men, mistook simple rudeness for rudeness coupled with wit, boasted of his own successes, failed gracefully to conceal malicious envy of other people's, or quailed before the onslaughts of his fellow members was ripe for massacre. The hero of these occasions was the wit who dealt the *coup de grâce*. Lord Birkenhead won pride of place on an occasion which took place, I think, in some other club, but there were many other lesser achievements. Freddy was welcomed into the Garrick because of his natural understanding of the rules and his prowess at the games.

On one occasion, he was accosted by a stranger who said to him:

"Aren't you Freddy Lonsdale?"

E

Freddy surveyed him swiftly, and replied:

"No. Not tonight."

Then on New Year's Eve one year he was asked by Seymour Hicks to make up a quarrel he had previously had with one of his fellow members.

"You must," Seymour said. "It is very unkind to be unfriendly at such a time. Go over now and wish him a happy New Year."

Freddy crossed the room and spoke to his enemy.

"I wish you a happy New Year," he said, "but only one."

This story has been told of him several times in different contexts. But it was at the Garrick Club it happened and at this time.

Freddy himself preferred the gentler wits who showed deep cynicism and a weariness of life. He loved, for instance, 'Willie' Somerset Maugham. Once these two were crossing the Atlantic together in one of the luxury liners. Freddy, installed in a chair in one of the smoking-rooms of the ship on the first afternoon out, was accosted by a theatre manager who proceeded to talk to him at great length, in an attempt to acquire one of his plays.

"It seems to me," Freddy said to him, "that, for what you want, Willie Maugham is your man. Why don't you go over and talk to him?"

"Is he here?" the man asked eagerly, and, on having pointed out to him a small figure, deep in an armchair on the other side of the room and surrounded by books and papers, he readily left Freddy in peace.

Freddy returned to his newspaper until, about ten minutes later, he became conscious that Somerset Maugham stood by his side.

Mr. Maugham stutters slightly.

"As this voyage is going to last six days," he said to Freddy, "don't you think it would be fairer if we were to share our responsibilities?"

Men who stutter are always displeased by their disability, but the truth is that the witticisms of people who stutter like Maugham, or who, like Harry Higgins, because of an injury to the vocal chords, speak in a whisper, or who, like Arnold Bennett, have a squeaky voice, gain immeasurably in the telling from an imitation of any of these infirmities.

For many years Freddy spent a great deal of his life in the Garrick Club, and the greatest compliment he could pay anyone was to propose his name for membership. In after years, when he was dissatisfied with life, he often compared it disadvantageously to "the days when the Garrick Club was an amusing place". It was here that he first met many people whom he was to love and respect for the rest of their lives.

Amongst writers he met at that time were Arnold Bennett, E. V. Lucas, A. E. W. Mason and H. G. Wells. I have always been interested in his friendship with these people. All four were men whose major interest lay in the realms of thought. They were not, it is true, poets, and their works, though excellent, were not primarily imaginative, but they all lived by and for the things of the mind. Freddy was the greatest, most unequivocal and most intractable philistine I have ever met.

It sometimes happens that people indulge in speculation on how he might have developed both as a man and as a playwright had he been born to the benefits of education. The question is not worth ten minutes of anyone's time. He turned his back on education; rejected it and mocked it; it was as though the skin and membranes of his brain were impermeable to the thought, creations and accumulations of other men. I am not thinking of the fact that, as a child, he refused to attend the only schooling available to him; there may, for all one knows, have been nothing here for the instruction of a lively mind.

But he was as capable of self-education as other brilliant men born to this necessity, and where, in the sphere of thought and manners, he attempted it, he achieved a complete and casual success. He lived by instinct and by his talents, and his talents, from beginning to end, owed as nearly nothing as is possible to the influence of other minds or the vast legacy of civilisation, except as these conditioned him in the course of his every-day life.

He told me that when he was a child he always intended to become a playwright, but it is difficult to imagine how the thought can have entered his head. He can never have seen a play. In the same way, even those critics who did not admire his work always admitted that he was a very able craftsman, with a superb knowledge of the technique of writing for the theatre. He did not learn this by watching other people's plays, nor yet by a slow struggle to improve his own work. In 1908 he jumped into the world of theatrical London fully armed.

So, because he was hard, egocentric in his personality and talents, genuine, in his presentation of himself—in the Garrick word—'authentic', although he was completely material, absolutely Philistine, he was never silly or vulgar, and he earned the respect of men who valued a heritage and a culture he was unable to absorb.

H. G. Wells, I believe, understood very well both his quality and his limitations, and sufficiently respected his quality to care little for his limitations. He used to tease him mercilessly—"I will not discuss this question with you, Freddy. You are too uneducated." But somewhere in the spirit he recognised an equal. This must have been so, or Freddy, as personally humourless in many ways as most people who try hard the humour of others, would never have accepted or forgiven the teasing.

These two used to play tennis together, and Wells used

regularly to cheat. This was a form of teasing Freddy could not endure, and in my mind I see them now, Freddy standing at the net, his hat pushed over his eyes, one hand holding his racquet, and both hands on his hips, shouting: "You goddamned blackguard. That was not out," while Wells, complacently and impishly innocent, maintained his case.

When Wells was dying, he spoke of Freddy.

"I wish he was here," he said, "he would cheer me up."

Freddy finally resigned from the Garrick Club because of the following events. A celebrated London critic wished to join the Garrick and he asked Freddy if he would put him up. Freddy agreed to do this and he asked Seymour Hicks if he would be the seconder. He then, as is usual on these occasions, enquired of the chairman and all the members of the committee whether anyone was likely to have any objection. On being assured of the contrary, he let his friend's name go forward. Exactly what happened at the election can only be known to the then members of the committee. This is the story that is told. As the result of the election, there were two black balls. The chairman, who knew that all the usual precautions against this happening had been observed, called for a second vote. This time there were three black balls.

Whether or not the whole of this story is true, it is certain that Freddy's friend was black-balled. Freddy, in a furious rage, persuaded Seymour Hicks that their only honourable course was themselves to resign from the Club, and this they proceeded to do. Their resignations were not immediately accepted, however, and in the following weeks much pressure was brought to bear on Freddy on behalf of Seymour Hicks. The Garrick Club was part of Seymour's life, and in these weeks, when he kept away from it, he was an utterly miserable man. It was unreasonable that he should make this sacrifice, since the only part he had played in the preceding events was in friendly support of Freddy. It was felt, nevertheless, that he could not withdraw his resignation unless Freddy did the same. With Seymour, then, Freddy made it known that he was prepared to forget the whole proceedings. In fact he never did; he never again frequented the Club, and several years later he once more sent in his resignation, this time to have it accepted. His behaviour was probably influenced by the fact that by this time he had many interests outside this immediate circle, many of the older members whom he had loved had died or retired, and he found it less amusing. But certainly this incident was responsible for spoiling for him the charm of the place.

The second thing that happened soon after the war to disrupt Freddy's quiet country life, was that Birchington suddenly had a period of popularity as a smart summer resort. It had certain features that made this possible, such as the sea, a good tennis club with many courts, and two rather attractive hotels. The particular kind of clientèle these hotels were to receive was much influenced by the fact that Gerald du Maurier came down to Birchington to visit Freddy, and afterwards stayed often at the Bungalow Hotel, bringing his wife and three children with him. Later, in his wake, came other theatrical stars, friends of his, and the reputation of the place was made.

Gerald was that remarkable thing, a 'star' personality. People who have this quality seem always a little larger than life, and when they enter a room other people in it fade slightly into the background. Gladys Cooper has it too, and, to this day, her entrance on to the stage has the effect of wiping out the other players. Gerald was charming, gay and witty, and people whom he liked were enchanted by him. But he was possessed of a devil, a relentlessly mocking familiar, whose presence was only forgiven him because he himself suffered as much from it as ever anyone else did.

Freddy adored him, and Gerald had an influence over him which I never remember anyone else to have had. My mother believes that it was this influence that kept Freddy writing only musical comedies for so many years. Gerald loved Freddy, but he always took up a quietly mocking attitude towards him, referring to him usually as the "muck writer".

They enjoyed each other's company, and in Birchington they still sat up all night, drinking brandy, smoking cigars and talking. We had a gramophone with a very large well, and they used to sit on one side of the room, throwing playing cards into the gramophone, which stood on the other side, betting quite large sums of money on the result, and gossiping. One evening, my mother, who often went to bed early, leaving them to each other's company, was woken by Freddy, who stood at the end of her bed.

"Could you come?" he asked politely. "Gerald wants to go home and there's a horse leaning over the front gate."

My mother looked at him in amazement.

"Gerald doesn't like horses," he explained.

So my mother got up, and, putting on her dressing gown, went out and chased the horse away. Our house, No. 6, Beach Avenue, lay in a triangle between two roads, both of which led in a matter of two or three hundred yards to Gerald's hotel. My mother now advised him to go through the back garden and go out that way. Then she returned to bed.

In a few minutes Freddy appeared again.

"I'm most awfully sorry to bother you," he said, "but that horse is leaning over the back gate now."

By day they played other games, and some of these remain in my memory as the most terrifying experiences of my whole life.

Freddy had this weakness that, although superbly confident of himself in any company, he could not stand the strain of being responsible for anyone else. In the case of his own family, this quality produced much torture both for him and for us. He used to take my sisters and myself into the most difficult and sophisticated society and he expected nothing less of us than to shine. Since he did not entirely trust us to do this, he always waited on the alert to cover up or to laugh off our mistakes. It was the laughing off that was so terrible for us. His sense of the ridiculous was so much stronger than his sense of loyalty that, even if we had shone much more brightly than we ever did, he would have been forced to mock us. He could not have allowed himself to be caught in the absurd and innocent position of a parent whose eyes are blinded by love. He could never, in the company of strangers, be for us, and so he was forced to be against us. Of course, he was quite unconscious of any of this, or, at the least, he did not know of our awareness of it. If he had known, his distaste for his own behaviour would, I think, have caused him to make great efforts to control it. As it was, unable ever to judge what conversational responses would meet with approval, what with ridicule, we grew up making, as far as humanly possible, none at all.

I remember many years later dining with Adrianne Allen, who was then married to Raymond Massey. There was a young man at dinner, as yet comparatively unknown to the public, whose name was Laurence Olivier. The next morning Adrianne told me that, after I had left the party, he had said this of me:

"That is a most extraordinary girl. She never says anything stupid."

Adrianne repeated this to me because she thought it was a compliment and would give pleasure. But I knew that it was not a compliment. Anyone who, during the course of a long and convivial evening, noticeably says nothing stupid, is sitting there meanly watching, cravenly considering, adding nothing

Play Pictorial

Betty. Mabel Sealby, Daisy Burrell and W. H. Berry

The Maid of the Mountains. José Collins

to the joy of the evening. It takes candour, courage and generosity to risk stupidity, and I possessed none of these; they are far more attractive qualities in social intercourse than carefully regulated cleverness.

In the Birchington days, when the du Mauriers came to stay the discomfiture of my sisters and myself reached its heights. Gerald was a mocker too and he never spared the three of us. There are two possible reasons why this was so. He may simply have disliked us. People of an instinctive rather than a thoughtful nature can feel an aggressive and uncontrollable antipathy to children they find unattractive, and this is a thing no skill can disguise from the children themselves. The other reason, which is not at all impossible, is that, while Gerald's sense of the ridiculous, like Freddy's, prevented his lending his own children open aid in the competitive war which constitutes much of life, he was not above covertly weakening their opponents. In any case, when he entered the room we held our breath and waited, submissively and without much hope, for the blows to fall. He was extremely clever in all he did, and it would have been difficult for any adult to realise that, as it suited him, he deliberately and steadily added to the discomposure of three children under twelve. He merely asked questions it was impossible to answer, made jokes one could not understand. None of this would have mattered very much if we could have returned his enmity with a hearty hatred. But we could not. We thought him the most important man in the world, we regarded it as an honour and even a sign of superiority that we knew him, and, although we feared and distrusted him, we would have given our souls for one word of affection or approval.

When Freddy and Gerald got bored in Birchington, they used to call in their six children, all girls, to amuse them. A series of terrifying games were invented. The worst of these

was when they decided that any child suspected of a mis-
demeanour should be tried in a properly constituted court.
The culprit became the prisoner at the bar, the other five were
forced to become counsel for the prosecution and the defence,
and witnesses on both sides. Freddy and Gerald were both
judge and jury.

Daphne du Maurier was always immensely talented. With
corn coloured hair that hung in a heavy bob and her father's
enchanting crooked face, she had the appearance of a medieval
page. She had no difficulty in abandoning at a moment's notice
the role of leader of a band of Cavaliers, who spoke lines which
were a brilliant mixture of Shakespeare and du Maurier, and
assuming that of a serious and frowning Counsel for the
Prosecution. Angela, her eldest sister, if less accomplished, was
serenely uninhibited. Only the Lonsdale children, with far less
distinguished looks, and stumped for histrionic power, were
reduced to lumpish misery.

Once a tennis match was organised, the two elder du
Mauriers against the two elder Lonsdales, and Gerald and
Freddy were said to have bet £100 on the result. My mother
told us afterwards that the bet was not serious, but at the time
we believed that this enormous sum rested on us. We should
have won the match easily, because, if lesser dramatic performers, we were far the better at games. But two of the most
noted wits of the period stood on the sidelines and barracked
us. When the game was five against us, my mother appeared
on the scene. She sized up the situation immediately, and,
muttering threats in Freddy's ear, she restored the morale of the
broken Lonsdale troops, advising us to pull ourselves together
and beat their heads off, which we then proceeded to do.

Freddy's part in this was quite innocent, if bluntly insensitive. He was simply unable to understand the effect this
adult teasing produced in us, and his attitude, when rebuked by

my mother on our account, was summed up in the sentence: "They must learn to have a sense of humour". As a result we are all deeply touchy, desperately without humour in personal relationships to this day.

All this was in the first years after the war. In later years so many other people came to Birchington that Gerald and Freddy, much to our relief, found entertainment without recourse to their children. People filled the hotels and also took furnished houses for the whole summer. Gladys Cooper came there often and one year she and her sister Doris shared a house with Ivor Novello and Bobby Andrews. The three of them, Gladys, Ivor and Bobby, walking together in those days, looked too beautiful to be human. They used to come through our garden at Rozel to reach the beach, where they spent the whole day, bathing and lying about on the sands. Many other theatre stars came also, until after two or three years their presence there caused the place to be so full they found it no longer amusing.

It was in Birchington during these years we first met P. G. Wodehouse, his wife Ethel and his step-daughter Leonora, who was to become one of my greatest friends. Plummy—P. G. Wodehouse—is a most lovable person, but he is not without his oddities. He thinks of himself as very shy, but the quality in him takes on a far more determined and complex character than it does in most other people. One of his great antipathies is to being considered capable of any intellectual conversation of any kind. At the age of twelve, I put myself out of court with him for about five years by asking him if he had read Compton Mackenzie's latest novel.

"That," he said to Leonora, "is a most terrifying girl."

Another thing he hates is even the smallest suspicion of smartness. About ten years after this period, Jack, my husband, used as a young man to play golf with Plum fairly regularly in the evenings at Addington. On one occasion, Jack took with him one of the most sought-after débutantes in London—a girl who was exceptionally charming and very pretty. This finished him with Plum. It was not until years after, when they were thrown much together because of our friendship with Leonora, that he was ever trusted again.

I went to the same boarding-school as Leonora. One Saturday afternoon, several girls, including myself, were loitering about in a classroom which was in the front of the house.

"Do come and look," somebody said, "there is the most extraordinary man coming down the drive."

We all hurried to the window. Coming down the drive on a bicycle was a broad-shouldered, red-faced man, crouched low over the handlebars. It was a hot day and on his head was a white handkerchief tied in four knots at the corners.

"That," said Leonora, "is Plum."

As we watched he did a most peculiar thing. He got off his bicycle and wheeled it into the shrubbery at the side of the drive, himself crouching low beside it under the bushes.

"What on earth is he doing?" we asked.

"He's frightened of Miss Starbuck," Leonora explained. "So when he comes to see me we have an arrangement that he hides in the shrubbery and I go out and meet him there."

Miss Starbuck was the headmistress of this school.

Ethel Wodehouse, his wife, is a natural party giver, and on occasion her inclinations are allowed to override Plum's. Once, when they had a house in Norfolk Street, Ethel gave a party, and Freddy and I went there together, arriving rather late. When we rang the bell, the front door was opened not by the butler but by Plum. He surveyed us carefully and, recognising us as friends, he put out both hands in a gesture to push us away.

"Don't come in," he said, "don't come in. You'll hate it."

But people he knows very well he likes very much, and he is always most enthusiastically on their side about everything.

Freddy and Plum were fond and appreciative of each other, but Freddy thought Plum very peculiar.

"I took him to the Garrick," he told me once, "but he wouldn't speak a word and I could never get him to come there again. The only thing that really interests him is football."

Then, in the early nineteen-twenties, Freddy, like all the rest of the world, began to dance. My sisters and I taught him to the music of records played on the gramophone. He became fascinated by it and he used to practise his steps assiduously. One day when he was alone, he swept up the rugs in the drawing-room and, turning on the gramophone, solemnly, with his hands in his pockets and his head bent, chassé-ed round the room. Presently he looked up to see a man standing in the doorway—a man with a magnificent head and a commanding presence.

"Ain't ye *ashamed* of yeself?" Lord Carson said, in his strongest brogue.

Lord and Lady Carson had recently bought Cleve Court at Minster, and Freddy adored them. He used often to go to see them and would listen for hours in a silence unusual for him while Lord Carson told stories of the law. Once he was present when Sir Edward Clark, who had defended Wilde, and Carson, who prosecuted, discussed the case. He was immensely struck by the sorrow and pity Lord Carson had felt for Wilde and the many attempts he had made in the early days of the case to let him down lightly.

In the last year in Birchington, Freddy went mad on dancing. This was the first time in his life he had had money to entertain on a large scale, and the first time in his life that he had found a great outlet for his gregarious and pleasure-loving nature. Both hotels in Birchington had dance bands all through the summer, and there were many others in Margate. Freddy and Leslie, with crowds of other people, attended these dances nearly every night, and on Sunday nights Freddy hired one of the bands and continued the party in his own house.

In 1923, having acquired a taste for society, Freddy and Leslie sold the house in Birchington and went to live in London. This was the end of the first phase of his life. From now on he was to become the restless, travelling eccentric whom most people who remember him knew.

CHAPTER EIGHT

'Aren't We All?' and *'Spring Cleaning'*

During the last years in Birchington, in spite of the dancing and the gaiety, Freddy must have done a great deal of work, because in the year 1923 he was to enter a period of fabulous output and of fabulous success. For the next seven or eight years there was to be almost no time when there was not a Lonsdale play on in London and it was quite a common thing for there to be at least two on together. At one time there were three. Some of this work was done at rehearsals, because he regularly contracted to do plays of which he had not written a single line, and, in these days when at his lightest word managers hired theatres and engaged a cast, he was often faced with the necessity to write the last act of a play during the intervals of rehearsing the first two acts. Nevertheless, a great deal of work must have been done at other times.

It is difficult to think when he did it, because all one can remember about him is his not working. He had a large and airy room at Rozel, looking on to the garden, and day after day the most stringent rules of silence and invisibility were imposed on the rest of the household, because he was known to be inside this room. But he resorted to every kind of trick to evade the real effort, and often, after we had spent the whole day walking about on tiptoe and talking in whispers, we would find that he had left the house by the balcony of his workroom quite early in the morning. At one time he decided he could work only at night, and then he used to have a light dinner, and sleep in a leather armchair until about twelve o'clock, when he awoke, or so he suggested, and did two or three hours' work. Anyone who counted the pages of completed manuscript the next morning was apt to be very disappointed.

The only reason why in the last resort he was able to deliver his plays on time was that, in fact, he composed them in great detail in his head without committing a single word to paper. He could always recite whole acts of plays of which no word had yet been written. It was very uncomfortable when he did this, because, since he was not reading from a manuscript, he was able to keep his head up and watch the smallest reaction of his audience. He used to punctuate the lines of his plays with terse questions.

"You don't think that's funny?" "I'm boring you?" "It isn't any good?"

Since one was taught by experience to expect these un-nerving interruptions, one's state of mind when listening to his lines prevented one from adequately performing the rapturous facial expressions which were the only thing that would have satisfied him.

In February 1922 *The Lady of the Rose* had been produced at Daly's and this was an enormous success, running for 514 performances; but this was musical comedy and, although it made him a great deal of money, it did no more than confirm his already established position in this branch of the theatre.

Then on April 10th, 1923, *Aren't We All?*, his first comedy since *The Best People*, was produced at the Globe Theatre with Marie Löhr, Ellis Jeffreys, Herbert Marshall and Julian Royce in the leading roles.

Curiously enough, as has already been said, *Aren't We All?* was in fact *The Best People* re-written. With the exception of

Guy Bolton, no one seems to have noticed this either at the time or later.

Freddy always believed *Aren't We All?* to be his best play. Like so many of his other plays it has an extremely light plot, but there are two reasons why it must always be considered as amongst his very best work. In the first place, starting with a rather weak and slow first act, it goes from strength to strength in the second and third act. This is not only rather uncommon in the theatre, where the reverse is too often true, but in this play Freddy's technique, which consisted always of embroidering the lightest theme with a series of twists and unexpected situations, can be seen at its most accomplished. From the end of the first act of *Aren't We All?*, all but the most simple-minded theatre goers must be aware of the inevitable end of the play, but there is no moment in the second or third acts where the route to this end can be foreseen, or where the attention of the audience is not diverted by the unexpected situations which develop.

The second reason why *Aren't We All?* must be considered, if not as his best work, as amongst his best is that, in the part of Lord Grenham, he achieved to absolute perfection his favourite character.

The story of the play is of a young wife, Margot, who, on returning unexpectedly from a holiday in Egypt, enters the room to find her husband embracing another woman. The curtain of this act goes down with Margot, bitterly hurt and disappointed, preparing to make the most of her anger against her husband Willie, who loves her, and who has been caught in an act caused by loneliness and temptation and not by in-fidelity of purpose; and with her father-in-law, Lord Grenham, perturbed at the situation but neither shocked nor deeply disturbed, considering how he can best help his son to resume his place in his wife's affections.

In the second and third acts Lord Grenham, who has discovered that Margot herself has fallen for exactly the same kind of temptation in Egypt and has left for home in a hurry only in order to avoid it, proceeds to use this knowledge in an attempt to unite the young couple by frightening Margot into a more tolerant view of her husband's peccadillo, without giving her away either to her husband or to anyone else. It is through his actions that the twists and turns in the play occur.

Lord Grenham is the character of a man of wealth and breeding, cynical but not disillusioned, worldly but extremely wise, witty but always kind, with little regard for conventional moral standards, but highly-principled according to his own lights. The play is full of the wit and epigrams for which Freddy is famous, but Lord Grenham also has some very effective scenes in which his character is revealed.

The part of Lady Frinton, played at this first performance by Ellis Jeffreys, is that of a woman of uncertain age who is determined to marry Lord Grenham. From the opening of the first act the audience is made aware that Lord Grenham is equally determined not to marry her. When Margot, later in the play, discovers Lord Grenham's intrigues against her, she takes her revenge by announcing in the columns of *The Times*, without a word to anyone, that a marriage has been arranged between the older couple. Lord Grenham knows nothing of her action when, one after the other, the characters in the play come on to the stage and mysteriously offer him congratulations. He becomes more and more bewildered until Lady Frinton herself makes her entrance.

Lady Frinton (puts arms round Grenham, kisses him): You darling! And to have done it in such a perfectly sweet way! (Turns to the others.) I give you my word of honour I hadn't the slightest idea until I read it in *The Times* this morning.

Lord Grenham: Hadn't you, Mary? May I see *The Times*?

Lady Frinton: There! (Puts her finger on a paragraph.) You angel!

Lord Grenham (reads): "A marriage has been arranged and will——"

(as he is reading Margot enters)

—"shortly take place between Lord Grenham, of Grenham Court, and Mary Frinton, widow of the late Sir John Frinton."

For a moment he looks at the notice, then raises his eyes and looks fixedly at Margot, whose face is expressionless.

Margot: I congratulate you with all my heart; you have done a very wise thing.

Lord Grenham: Thank you, Margot.

Lady Frinton: Why did you do it in that divine way?

Lord Grenham: I didn't want to take the risk of being refused, and I realised the moment it was published in the papers there was no way out for either of us!

I do not remember the 1923 performance, but when Ronald Squire spoke the last of these lines at the Haymarket in 1953, no one in the theatre could fail to be charmed by the rueful gallantry of the improvisation to cover a situation of which, until that moment, Lord Grenham had been unaware, and which he could only be presumed to regard with horror.

Later, alone with his son:

Lord Grenham: I notice you haven't congratulated me, Willie?

Willie: Frankly, I don't know why you've done it. I thought you were perfectly happy.

Lord Grenham: Evidently I wasn't.

After the first night in London, *Aren't We All?* received wonderful notices. A. B. Walkley, the dramatic critic of *The Times* opened his review as follows:

"Musical comedy doubtless has many attractions, but we

have always understood that witty dialogue is not one of them.
Indeed, amid cues for song and dance, wit might lie super-
fluous. Judge of the general surprise—and gratification—
when the distinguished author of many musical comedy
libretti writes a 'straight' comedy (if the stage jargon may be
pardoned) which is witty from end to end. One can only suppose poor Mr. Lonsdale to have long been suffering from
repressed wit and then, in desperation, to have poured out
upon us this pent-up store. Our state is the more gracious; he
has had all the previous discomfort and we now have all the
fun."

The *Daily Telegraph* said:

"When, on the fall of the curtain at the Globe last night,
Miss Marie Löhr declared it was a pleasure to welcome Mr.
Lonsdale from musical comedy to the legitimate theatre, she
obviously and indubitably voiced the feelings of everyone
present. For nothing could be more clear than that in the case of
a man capable of writing so witty, so human and so delightful a
piece as *Aren't We All?* the one right and proper place for him
to occupy is the stage of the latter. That the auddience enjoyed
every moment of the play was unmistakably proved by the
ripple of laughter, occasionally broadening into uproarious
merriment, that formed a pleasant accompaniment to the
entire performance."

Most of the other papers praised the play in similar terms.

In spite of the unqualified enthusiasm of its initial reception,
Aren't We All?, which was to be played in most of the capital
cities of the world and was to be revived again and again in
London, was not, on this its first production, to be more than a
moderate success. It ran for 110 performances.

But to anyone with experience in these things it would have
been apparent that success walked very close to Mr. Lonsdale.
All over London, agents awoke and began to write letters.

"Have you disposed of the American rights in this play?" "Could you call at my office?" Column writers found a new source of inspiration, and actors and actresses discovered an old, and unexpectedly strong affection. Most important of all, Charles B. Dillingham contracted to put the play into immediate production in New York.

The New York theatre, unlike the London, has a season. Owing to the heat in the summer it is usual for plays to be produced in the autumn and to run through the winter, while the theatres are all closed down in the height of the summer. It is unusual, and, where possible, it is avoided, for a play to be produced late in the spring, since it has then before it so short a season. When this is done and the play is successful it is sometimes taken off for the summer months but continues its run the following autumn, and, occasionally in the case of a great success, it is run right through the summer.

In the winter 1922–23 Charles B. Dillingham, one of the greatest of New York's impresarios, had had a tough season. None of his plays had had success, he had Cyril Maude under contract, and his last production with this actor, *If Winter Comes*, was failing to fill the theatre. He therefore contracted to do *Aren't We All?* immediately after its London production, and it was produced in New York on May 21st, 1923.

One evening, in Dillingham's New York offices, some members of the staff were sitting round discussing the production of this play.

"I don't know how Charlie wants me to bill it," one of them said, "Cyril Maude in *Aren't We All?*, or *Aren't We All?* by Frederick Lonsdale, with Cyril Maude."

Dillingham was out of town at the time and it was decided to telephone to get his views. That evening he sent exact instructions as to how the play was to be billed:

CHARLES B. DILLINGHAM

announces

positively his last failure for this season

AREN'T WE ALL?

In spite of this billing everyone concerned with the production was happy about the play. There is a very exciting
feeling in a theatre during rehearsals of a play in which the cast
and the management have confidence, and, on this occasion,
this feeling crossed the Atlantic. The New York first night
was awaited in London as well as in New York with unusual interest. The cast in America was excellent. Cyril
Maude wrote to Freddy during rehearsals as follows:

"The cast is fine:
"The two boys are first rate *and* English gentlemen (Willie—
Leslie Howard, John Willocks—Geoffrey Millar).
"The Parson. Harry Ashford, *excellent*.
"His wife. Marguerite St. John, *first rate*.
"Mabel Terry Lewis (Lady Frinton), perfect.
"The Vamp, fine and vampish (Roberta Beatty).
"Margot, lovely, young and natural (Alma Tell) and Ford
(the director) is a charming fellow and has produced it beauti-
fully and with great tact."

Seldom is such praise given in the theatre by one member of a
cast to the others.
On the night of May 21st, 1923, the New York audience and
critics gave *Aren't We All?* a reception which justified all the
anticipation which had preceded it, and which resounded in
London.
Heywood Broun wrote in the *New York World:*

"It is curious that Cyril Maude should have chosen to open his American season with *If Winter Comes* when he had as good a play as *Aren't We All?* available. Not only is Frederick Lonsdale's comedy first-class foolery, but it affords Mr. Maude an opportunity to appear at his very best. . . . Possibly one reservation should be made in regard to *Aren't We All?* It might easily be a better play if Frederick Lonsdale, the author, in addition to his other merits had happened to be a Frenchman. The comedy suffers, though only slightly, from the fact that it respects the Anglo-Saxon tradition which holds both hero and heroine to the strictest accountability of virtue in comedy. . . . We have no hesitation in recommending *Aren't We All?* as one of the most agreeable light comedies now to be seen in New York."

John Corbin wrote in the *New York Times*:

"Winter having come in spite of the 'If', Cyril Maude last night celebrated its going, and the advent of spring, by producing a very genuine, if very light, light comedy.

". . . In London the play was taken somewhat too seriously, to its great detriment and to the equally great loss of those who might and should have enjoyed it. The audience last night gave itself freely to Mr. Lonsdale's amiable cynicisms, chuckled deeply at his always brilliant and often richly human wit. If the occasion had any defect it was that it comes at a time when summer is at hand with no 'If' or other peradventure. Produced in October, *Aren't We All?* would safely brave the icy blast, and it may yet do so."

(*Aren't We All?* was to run right through the summer and until January 19th, 1924.)

Alan Dale in the *New York American* said:

"Nothing could be more soothing to the refractory nerves, more restful to the play-jangled mind, than the gentle, ingenuous, little comedy at the Gaiety Theatre last night. It was called *Aren't We All?* And to that I say, cryptically, of course, if we're not, we should be."

And Charles Darnton in the *New York Sun*:

"Although the situations are farcical, the dialogue makes Mr. Lonsdale's play a light comedy of high quality. . . . Coming at the end of the season, it is bright enough to make us feel like beginning playgoing all over again."

The news crossed the Atlantic in cables.

CONGRATULATIONS BRILLIANT SUCCESS MAUDE SUPERB.

'AREN'T WE ALL?' SURE SUCCESS CONTINUOUS LAUGHTER PRESS UNANIMOUSLY FAVOURABLE.

PLAY SUFFICIENTLY WELL DONE AND UNDOUBTED SUCCESS MUCH APPLAUSE AND MAUDE MADE SPEECH MENTIONING EVERYONE BUT THE AUTHOR.

SAW PLAY TONIGHT BIGGEST HIT IN ALL CITY.

Later letters followed.

> Dewar House,
> 11 Haymarket, S.W.1.

DEAR MR. LONSDALE,

My manager writes me that the Brokers have taken 271 a night for the first four weeks and it looks as if the play will run through the summer.

> Yours truly,
> CHAS. B. DILLINGHAM.

> Dewar House,
> 11 Haymarket, S.W.1.

DEAR LONSDALE,

I have had a letter from Cyril Maude in which he says you will be very unwise not to hurry out to New York as soon as possible to reap the benefit of the big success of *Aren't We All?*

Freddy Lonsdale and family at Rozel, Birchington, about 1921

"Miss 1925." Madge Mavis as Fay Collen in *Spring Cleaning*

in commissions to write plays galore and besides that he does
want you to see how it is done over there.

Yours sincerely,

J. A. MALONE.

Nothing, in the theatre, succeeds like success, and nowhere in
the world does it succeed so thumpingly as it does in New York.
Freddy was besieged with letters and cables asking him to go
out there. Many people were anxious to put him up, those who
were unable to do this offered their advice as to hotels and their
services to book him rooms. Everyone insisted that he go. It
was not until late in the summer that he went, however. He was
always curiously reluctant to be in on his own successes. He
was also extremely suspicious of them, in a kind of wood-
touching way that, for a man who in the whole course of his
career hardly ever had a failure, was inexplicable.

John Rumsey, who was to be Freddy's agent in America for
the next thirty years, and who grew to understand him as well as
anyone alive, and who loved him, told me that the first time he
met him was when Freddy went into his office when he first
landed in New York. He said he was very restless and nervous,
and he refused to sit down.

"Do you think this play is a success?" he shot at Rumsey.

John Rumsey looked at him in amazement.

"Why, of course it's a success," he said.

"What makes you say so?"

"Well, the notices and the reception."

Freddy shrugged this off.

"What else?"

"The business and the advance booking."

"I know all that," Freddy said, "but what makes you think it
will last?"

"Well," John said, "there's one thing about this play. People go to it several times. When they have seen it once, a couple of men may be dining together and they'll say after dinner: 'Let's go in and see the last act of *Aren't We All?*' "

John told me that this seemed to satisfy him.

It did satisfy him. He repeated it to me.

"Do you know what makes my plays successful?" he said. "People are always ready to see them more than once. And if they are dining together and they've got nothing to do, they'll go in in the middle of the play to listen to the dialogue."

Freddy was a natural in America. The Americans understood him much better on the whole than the English. They revelled in his eccentricities and they loved his wit. One reason for this I think was that they could better afford him. All his life Freddy broke contracts, failed to deliver plays, ran out on film studios where he had been hired to work for months, and no one could ever be certain of anything until the goods were actually delivered. In America the companies he dealt with were so rich that they could not be more than slightly flustered by anything he did, and so he amused them. Provided his behaviour tickled their humour and was utterly unexpected, the Americans were always willing to pay the price to see the show.

He did not stay very long in New York on this occasion, but he came back to England with a haul of trophies only America could provide, with an enthusiasm for everything American, a contract with the Selwyns to do *Spring Cleaning*, and a passion for Charles B. Dillingham.

Amongst the trophies were several photographs of exceedingly beautiful women, signed with flourishing phrases of affection, a card made of paper-thin gold with words engraved on it which gave the bearer two seats in any theatre of Florenz Ziegfeld's at which it was presented, and a gold octagonal watch, almost equally thin and studded on the edge with rubies.

Charles Dillingham was a man of limitless humour and good humour, and very much beloved. There are so many stories that are told of him illustrating his qualities. On one occasion, when he put on an English play, he was cabled from London: "How's it going?" and he replied: "It's gone." He spent enormous sums on the New York production of *Hassan* and then on the first night cabled London: "*Hassan* passed peacefully away at ten o'clock tonight". Freddy found him irresistible. He also found irresistible the whole of his staff, the Dillingham 'set-up', who worked with a casual and independent devotion which was a revelation to English eyes. The office was run by a girl called Vera who ruled everyone. Michael Arlen told me that when he first landed in New York he went straight to Dillingham's office, and, opening the door, he slid nervously into the room. Vera was working at a desk facing the door.

"Come right in, Mike," she said, looking up from her work, "we're expecting you."

Then there was a boy called Jack who did odd jobs in the office. During the run of *Aren't We All?* they gave him a chance in the box-office, but they had to take him out because his enthusiasm was such that when asked by an innocent play-goer for two seats he replied:

"Get to hell out of here. We're sold out for weeks."

When Freddy, a year or two later, took my sister and me to New York, it was at a period when people were nervous of taxi-drivers because several had driven their fares to the middle of Central Park, where they had robbed them and left them. When my sister and I went to a theatre that was not under Dillingham's management, Jack stationed himself at the back of the stalls throughout the performance, hovered near us in the intervals, and chose the taxi which took us home. No one had asked him to do this. He did it for love—any friend of

Dillingham's was a friend of his. The English may have every quality in the world, but when they reach New York they are astounded by the capacity for friendship, the genuine democratic feeling, the hospitality and the willingness to take trouble for other people which they find in the Americans. Freddy from this time on was to spend as much of his life in America as in England, and to have friendships as deeply rooted there as any he had here.

After November 9th, 1923, Freddy had two plays on in New York. He went back there in the autumn to produce *Spring Cleaning*.

Spring Cleaning was not really a good play. It was brilliantly executed and it pilloried in a sensational way exactly the people that audiences wished to see pilloried (Freddy's idea of pillorying people was to make them bad but clever. Almost no one would prefer to be good but dull). But now, as, in a rather striking phrase of Graham Greene's, "the dye washes off", all that is left is the pointing of a moral. Freddy was too simpleminded, too narrow-minded, to be safe with morals, too 'uneducated', as Wells would have said, to discuss these questions. The moral in *Spring Cleaning* is too obvious to be worth pointing, the moralising ingenuously trite. But, at the time, the wit and the dexterity with which the sensational plot was handled made it a certain winner. In New York it was again extremely well cast, with A. E. Matthews in the part that was to make Ronald Squire famous in London. Freddy used to tell an amusing story of 'Matty' at rehearsals. He had a line to speak as follows:

"With a charm of manner, there's a hell of a lot of fun to be had in cathedral towns."

At rehearsal Matty came on and said:

"There's a hell of a lot of fun to be had in cathedral towns."

Freddy spoke from the stalls:

"With a charm of manner, Matty."

Matty tried the line again.

"There's a hell of a lot of fun to be had in cathedral towns."

Freddy said again:

"With a charm of manner, Matty."

When this happened for the third time, Matty strode off the stage and disappeared out of the theatre and no one knew where he had gone. Freddy, who knew his haunts, went to look for him. When he found him, Matty was sitting with his elbow on his knees and his chin in his hand, glowering. Freddy said: "Matty, the line in the play is: 'With a charm of manner, there's a hell of a lot of fun to be had in cathedral towns.'"

"Oh!" said Matty, jumping up, "I thought you were criticising my acting."

Spring Cleaning was a tremendous success in New York, but, reading now the notices of the play written in New York and later in London, it is obvious that, although audiences and critics enjoyed it, many of the critics in both towns rumbled it. Where this was so in London, it was expressed with the sour and unwilling admission that "in spite of this, the play will undoubtedly attract audiences". In New York it was done more gracefully.

"Writing his comedy of *Spring Cleaning*," one critic said, "Mr. Frederick Lonsdale teems with moral saws and immoral instances. In his vineyard of the theatre, he is cousinman to the evangelist of the temple. . . . Is he not writing for the twentieth-century theatre where, if the proprieties are silver, the improprieties are also golden? . . . *Enfants du siècle*, the audience at the Plymouth last evening received both as Mr. Lonsdale intended them. When the moralities tipped the tongues of the personages, applause sometimes made approving answer. When they gave place to the immoralities—of speech rather than act—merry was the laughter . . ."

And the *New York Times* remarked:

"A curious and anomalous comedy which promises to be very popular but is otherwise only important as giving promise of solider and more significant work."

Many of the critics were more wholehearted in their praise, however, and Robert Benchley wrote in *Life*:

"The evidence of our depravity in the face of good clean fun is made only the more convincing by the fact that we enjoyed *Spring Cleaning* from beginning to end. Here is the very antithesis of good, clean fun. It is a super-sophisticated, brazen and what is known as 'frank' play. There is not one character in it who would be worth knowing in real life, unless perhaps it is the prostitute. And yet it is written with respect for the audience's intelligence and has an easy humour which brought a pleasant glow to this sin-hardened heart."

As from the success of *Spring Cleaning* in America, Freddy was, over the next year or two, to become one of the most famous playwrights in the world, and one of the best-known personalities in London and, I think, in New York.

He went back now to London, and in December of that year he had produced at Daly's Theatre the musical comedy *Madame Pompadour*. This production, with Evelyn Laye as leading lady, was to have a run of 469 performances.

Then on March 13th of the following year, 1924, his play *The Fake* was produced at the Apollo Theatre, with Godfrey Tearle in the leading role.

The Fake was a curious play, serious and melodramatic, and right outside the comedy stream of his natural talents. It was suggested to him by the situation of a woman he knew well in real life, and was concerned with the marriage, for worldly reasons, of a young girl to a man known to her father to be an alcoholic, and of her final deliverance from the misery of her married life by the altruistic and calculated murder of her husband by an old friend of her family.

In any assessment of Frederick Lonsdale's position and importance as a dramatist this play has never been taken seriously. With Godfrey Tearle as the murderer and Franklyn Bellamy as the husband, it was very well acted in London, however, and it had a success, running for 211 performances. When it was produced later in New York, the theatre-goers there refused to accept this kind of thing from one of their favourite comedy writers and the play was an unconditional flop. I re-read it the other day, and having, over the years, learned to regard it as a rather silly play, I was surprised how well it was done. The story remains melodramatic and unreal, but the construction seems excellent and the dialogue is firm and unexpectedly convincing.

At the time of its production in London, it did nothing to increase or decrease Freddy's reputation, but commercially everyone concerned with it did well out of it.

Three months after the production of *The Fake* at the Apollo Theatre, *The Street Singer*, with book by Frederick Lonsdale, and Miss Phyllis Dare in the leading role, was produced at the Lyric Theatre. With *Madame Pompadour* at Daly's, this gave Freddy three plays running in London at the same time.

The Street Singer was more uniformly praised by the critics than any other production I can remember. Said to be the "best musical comedy since *The Maid of the Mountains*", "easily the best musical comedy in town," it was, as was so often the case with musical comedies with which Freddy was connected, considerably praised for its 'book'. It ran for 360 performances.

All this time *Spring Cleaning* was eagerly awaited in London. Freddy himself was waiting for Ronald Squire.

Until that time Ronald Squire had been known to everyone interested in such matters as an exceedingly competent small-

part actor. He had had a romantic start on the stage as the boy
in the motor-car act with Harry Tate, and he had gravitated
through the ordinary channels to the West End theatre. In
Bulldog Drummond, with Gerald du Maurier, he had played one of
those young men who strolled nonchalantly about the stage
with a golf club, and he had given a faultless performance.
Freddy, who knew the difficulties of finding actors to speak his
lines, was always clever at spotting that peculiar mixture of
timing, humour, and highly-polished casualness, that disciplined avoidance of intensity, which makes the comedy actor.
He always believed that Ronald Squire would join A. E.
Matthews and Frederick Kerr as one of the great light comedy
actors of his time.

Ronald Squire—'Ronnie', as we know him—in return
appreciated Freddy probably more than any other actor living.
This was not such an easy feat as, in view of Freddy's tremendous success at this time, it sounds. Comedy always reads
badly, and Freddy's lines, when read, give to very few people
any idea of their effectiveness when spoken. All through his
career it happened that, on first nights in London, whole
chunks of his play were lost to the ears of the audience because
the actors had stopped the play with lines they had been unable
to see, refused to believe were funny, and, not expecting the
laughter, had failed to wait for it. Ronnie never fell into this
fault.

So Freddy and Ronnie were determined, with *Spring Cleaning,*
to start a partnership which was to last for many years.

By the time of the production of *Spring Cleaning* at St.
Martin's Theatre, on January 9th, 1925, a Lonsdale first night
was a great event in London. For days beforehand the press
built up the publicity, everyone who liked to be in on an
occasion fought for first-night tickets, and when the advertised
moment arrived the theatre was filled with the minks, scent,

and the wonderfully groomed persons of all that was smartest in London.

In those days, when money was being spent on a production, the programme was, compared with anything we have now, a great book, filled with little gossipy articles and shiny photographs. I have the programme of *Spring Cleaning*, and there are two little articles about Freddy, neither of them, as far as I can see, giving a recognisable picture of his character, or, after the passage of time, startling one with a vivid and living recall of his personality. One of them is by Michael Arlen, and this did give me, when I first re-read it, a genuine though faint and fast-retreating stir of that feeling which is not memory—or at any rate not in any intellectual sense—but, as it were, the re-awakening of the nerves of the living tissue at the touch of past experience. It is not to-day worth quoting at any length, but there is one very odd thing in it. It is called 'A Photograph' and written in dialogue; the scene is a restaurant; the characters Frederick Lonsdale, Michael himself, a critic and a waiter. Freddy is represented as grumbling eternally about managers and actors (which I do not remember him ever to do), Michael as talking about nothing but money (again I have no recollection of this preoccupation), and the critic as trying fitfully and unsuccessfully to break through the conversation of these two egotists in order to get some food. Thus:

Critic (to waiter): I will have some mussels, please.

Arlen: Of course, the trouble is that writers don't make enough money——

Waiter (to critic): Mussels are off, sir.

Lonsdale: Now listen! I want to tell you that of all the—and this will be a help to you, Michael, when you come to deal with these manager blokes——

Critic (to waiter): A nice grilled sole, then.

F

And later in the piece:

Lonsdale: . . . when you've gone into this playwrighting business as much as I have and you come across Guthrie—mind you, I like the man—but——

Critic (to waiter): Yes, sprouts will do.

Who in the world would believe that, in those reprehensible, slightly despised but enviably pleasure-loving days of the ninteen-twenties, a satirical photograph in a restaurant would show mussels as off, and sprouts as made to do?

Basil Dean produced *Spring Cleaning*. Edna Best, who had been known until then as a charming little *ingénue* and the mother of twins, made a great success as the Eton-cropped, corrupt young lady, Denys Blakelock succeeded equally as a pansy youth, while Ronald Squire became overnight, as both Freddy and he had thought he would, one of London's leading comedy actors.

When the curtain came down on the last act, there occurred the first of many similar incidents to take place on Lonsdale first nights. Freddy hated the necessity to perform the rather foolish entrance on to the stage of an author at his own first night and he always refused to do this. But the gallery loved him, and after cries of "Author! Author!" they would change to "Freddy! Freddy!" and actually refuse to go home until they had seen him. He would eventually therefore come on to the stage. But he was quite determined that never in his life would he be caught making the kind of little speech that begins: "We are all so happy with the reception you have given us this evening . . ." and so, when he arrived on the stage, pulling at his tie or his nose, one used to wonder how he would get out of it. On this occasion Basil Dean had recently had a public breach with Sir Alfred Butt over the direction of the productions at Drury Lane, and this had been very much featured in the newspapers. After the applause that greeted his appearance had died down, Freddy pointed at Dean and, addressing the audience, said:

"Sir Alfred Butt wishes to speak to you."

During the clamour that greeted this remark, he made his escape off the stage.

Most of the critics the next morning were unanimous in their enthusiasm for the 'wit' of this 'brilliant' play, though, as I have earlier remarked, a few were unconvinced. However, it scarcely any longer mattered, because, as one newspaper remarked, "everything that Mr. Lonsdale writes runs and runs and runs." *Spring Cleaning* was to play at St. Martin's Theatre, and at the Playhouse, to which it was transferred in the middle of the run, for a total of 262 performances.

One month later a musical comedy called *Katja the Dancer*, with a book which Freddy adapted from a continental source, was produced at the Gaiety Theatre, and there, and at Daly's, to which it was transferred, it ran and ran and ran for 505 performances.

CHAPTER NINE

The Fruits of Success

When Freddy was returning from New York after one of his earlier visits there, he met Richard and Jean Norton on the boat. Richard Norton was the son of Lord Grantley, Jean the daughter of Sir David Kinloch—children of the aristocracy. The upper classes in England are socially the most attractive people in the world; considered as a class, and not, of course, as a group, they have the most highly-developed intelligence of any class in England.

That is a statement which during the whole of my lifetime would have been very unpopular, and which to-day may be thought by many people to plumb the depths of vulgar stupidity. This is because the upper classes have for so many years had, and even now to a remarkable extent keep, so many advantages over the rest of the population that the only way the more ambitious of their social inferiors can endure them is by regarding them as half-wits accoutred by pomp and circumstance, people who know nothing of life outside the sheltered and make-believe world they inhabit, or else as no different from anyone else. None of these things is true about them, and anyone who believes that it is would be at a loss to explain how they so easily attract, why they so often corrupt.

The children of the English aristocracy are trained and, in the word of the film studios, groomed from birth to be at ease in public and private life, to entertain and be entertained by the great of all nations, to pursue diplomacy or intrigue, to control crowds, make speeches, lead regiments, dispense favours. The boys are not educated simply to do a job, but to assume a position; the girls are not brought up merely to get married, but to attract, persuade, amuse, to control great households, to meet with equanimity all personages.

If the products of this exceptional upbringing were not in most situations better equipped than the average man, much art would have been wasted. In the early stages Eton combines with an exalted home background to ensure confidence and, in spite of the British talent for debunking, a wide education. The Paris finishing schools exist only to plane off rough edges; the master tailors, great couturiers and cosmetic makers improve vastly on nature. The growing child develops in surroundings which assure him constantly of his superiority, while the cold draughts that breed suspicion, uncertainty and envy are for the most part unknown.

All this may, and often does make only for arrogance; no environment can successfully burnish the commonplace mind. But where pride and egotism are subdued in natures of genuine intelligence or sensitivity, or natural talents matured in this way, the result is the finest social creation in the world; and when the lessons of twenty years or so of schooling are used on the small change of daily intercourse, it should be as when a highly trained soprano lends her voice to the singing of some simple song. People from other worlds who meet members of this society for the first time more often than not find them irresistible, and their attractions can only be heightened by a former disbelief that they existed. Freddy found Richard and Jean Norton and all the circle that surrounded them more than irresistible, enchanting.

These two belonged to a section of society which was to grow

larger and larger. They had the training but not the employment, the position but not the responsibility. Richard would
one day inherit wealth, but in the meantime his resources were
stretched to maintain what he had been taught to regard as the
necessary background to life. Jean, who was as beautiful and as
glamorous as anyone of her day, had no wide sphere in which
to exercise her talents. Spirited and intelligent, reckless and
luxury-loving, they grew up in a world where accepted values
were crashing, where the future offered only a shadow of that
certainty known to generations of the past. Children of their
period, they used the accomplishments of an older one largely
in the pursuit of pleasure, wholly without commitments to any
great enterprise in the background. They would have served as
symbols of the spirit of the nineteen-twenties.

Richard was a nervous, restless man, with a body slightly bent
by some injury of the 1914 War. He was talented, spoilt, witty
and gay, and at this time he was not yet saddened by any
knowledge of the emptiness of rank without position, or the
inexcusable, paltry, but iron tyranny of money. He was as
conscious of his birth and social position as anyone I ever knew,
but he had a great liking for the theatre, and he sought entertainment anywhere and with anyone with whom he could find it.
He wore a monocle with equanimity, even aplomb, and he
smoked Balkan Sobranie cigarettes ceaselessly. To those of his
friends not born to his environment, his natural attractiveness
was in no way decreased by a slight formality of manner, a faintly
discernible air of patronage, and throughout the whole of his
life he made discriminating use of his earlier advantages. Years
later, after he had inherited his title but while he was working
in a film company, a characteristic story was told of him. It was
said that on the wall of one of the studios someone chalked the
words: "Richard Norton is a dirty bastard". Richard, screwing
his monocle into his eye, read this sentence carefully, and went

away to fetch some chalk. Returning, he drew a line through the words Richard Norton and substituted the words Lord Grantley.

I think this is a very good joke, showing humour as well as wit, but it is also a joke that could have occurred only to someone brought up against a formal background.

Jean was very beautiful. She had dark blue, very short-sighted eyes, and, when she needed to see, she wore horn-rimmed spectacles. In the days when everyone else's hair was bobbed, hers was grown much longer and curled up high against the back of her head. She spent a lot of time, and one remembers her, in her bedroom. The room was very glamorous with soft pink quilts and thick white rugs. She wore pink satin pyjamas with a rounded 'Peter Pan' collar, and she entertained half London sitting up in bed. Cocktails would be brought there in the evenings, and people would lie about at her feet or sit on the floor. Presently she would get up to dress for dinner and go to her dressing-table, which held face cream from Bond Street, rouge from the Institut de Beauté, enormous sprays of scent. Everything in the room was very feminine, except the pink satin pyjamas, which were severe like a man's.

Jean cared little for anyone's opinion, she swore like a trooper, and she, too, chain-smoked without rest. She was not always or only feminine. When she appeared on a golf course she wore thick, spiked shoes, woollen socks, a tweed skirt and a jersey, and she smote the ball over two hundred yards down the fairway. Later, I am told, when in the war she went to work in a factory and for the first time turned her attention to the sterner side of life, she rose to be a forewoman and a shop steward, and only left this work when her health failed.

At the time when Freddy first met them, the Nortons were the centre of a group of young people who were amongst the most attractive in the world. Of course, these people were also a trifle vulgar, but they were richly, romantically vulgar, like a piece of Empire furniture decorated with ormolu and superb architectural jokes, or a magnum of champagne, or a Rolls-Royce motor-car. One may tire of a pleasure-loving society, but at first glance it is as beguiling a piece of temptation as human nature can provide.

Freddy formed a quick and enthusiastic friendship with dozens of people, and this was his introduction to society. The aristocracy of England is a most integrated group. By marriage or by blood relationship almost everyone is everyone else's cousin, and they move through life in formation like a swarm of bees, or, to be more accurate, like a volunteer army that picks up support on the march. In their own minds they never grant equality to anyone who is not a cousin, but anyone who is known to a cousin may be known to them. Freddy's friendship with the Nortons secured him entry to many of the famous houses of England, and later by his own charm and wit, and also because of his integrity of personality, he entered others more difficult of access. Of course, he himself was a lion, London's wittiest playwright, and, as far as he permitted this kind of thing, the cousins passed him eagerly from hand to hand.

He made many other friends at this time too—Michael Arlen, who for a short time was to be much in his company, Lord Beaverbrook, who was to be a lifelong friend, Lord Castlerosse, who as long as he lived was a sorce of joy to Freddy, as to many other people. In London he was a man of the moment, sought after, spoiled, always in the news.

When my father and mother first left Birchington they spent the next few years in furnished houses in London. They had in quick succession a house in Hobart Place, one at East Sheen, one in South Eaton Place, and one in Ovington Square.

High Tide

"Surprised and expectant"
An unfinished portrait by Simon Elwes

This sort of existence really suited them both. Whether because they had had no stability in their youth or whether by temperament, neither of them was ever content to stay very long in one house. After about six months they began to think that everything that was unsatisfactory was due to present circumstances, and that if they moved to some different house the minor irritations of life would cease. However, on this occasion, after a few years of furnished houses they both believed that the minor irritations were caused by other people's furniture, and they then took a long lease of a house in Lowndes Street, which my mother furnished with the loving care that everyone spends at least once in a lifetime on the house in which they mean to live. In fact the minor irritations had a deep and developing cause.

Freddy had now passed through two phases of his life, both of which had a clear-cut beginning and end, and from which the picture that emerges of him might be of two different characters. In the first he had been the wilful, reckless, undisciplined little boy in whom no one had recognised any talent, growing into the independent, rather wild youth who had ideas that no one had ever taught him, money which he had inexplicably made for himself, debts which the money was insufficient to pay, and who frightened his family even more than had the uncontrollable child. In the second phase, from when his first plays were produced in 1908 until 1923, he appears as a successful and quickly established writer of musical comedy, living the life of a minor country gentleman—a family man with three children, a quiet background and no great ambition. The 1914 War was probably the reason why this phase lasted so long, because by the time Freddy began to make big money England was gripped by fear and grieving over the ghastly slaughter.

Now, on looking back to 1923, one can see that this second phase had really closed, and Freddy was beginning to emerge in

F*

the third of his characters—that of the vastly successful playwright, the amusing, lonely, gregarious, restless, charming and utterly eccentric man of the world. The temptation to compare him to the butterfly leaving the chrysalis is irresistible, and my parents' household was beginning to be shaken a little by this metamorphosis.

At the same time as the world scene cleared and a revulsion from the desolate past took place, my parents had, for the first time, a really considerable income. They tasted, as they had not done until now, the joys of the metropolis, the pleasures of wealth and the charm of society. They were neither of them people who took much thought for the future—had they been they could hardly have survived the first years of their married life. They were at this time both of them just over forty, and previously their life had often been hard, nearly always uncertain. They threw themselves with zest into spending the money which Freddy earned so easily. They acquired two Bentley cars, a saloon which was my mother's and an open car which Freddy drove. Two separate chauffeurs took care of these cars, though between them they had also to service an A.C. two-seater which was given to my sister and myself as soon as we were old enough to drive. Butlers and footmen replaced the one-time house-parlourmaid, and the clientèle of the Embassy Club or Ciro's would often see my mother and father lunching or dining there, together or separately.

At first they were often together. They made an attempt in all these changes to live together as married couples do, making the same friends, pursuing the same course. This was hardly possible. Freddy spent much time at the Garrick Club, much time in the theatre, he was often in America, and he was being sucked ever more strongly into that new world I have described. My mother had neither the wish nor the energy to follow him wherever he went, and although during this period of transition she was frequently irritated beyond endurance by his desire for independence, she ultimately understood it. Freddy was an impossible man to live with, egotistical and uncontrolled, and only people with youthful and strong nerves could bear to have their lives entwined with his. In Birchington the lack of opportunity had kept him becalmed and moderately well anchored, but he was not intended by nature for peace, stability, or ultimately for happiness. Looking back on his life, the thing that is surprising is that it was not until after the age of forty that his personality hardened into what it was so inevitably to become.

The first open sign of a break was when Freddy announced that it was impossible to work at home, and took a flat for this purpose. When he was in London he now slept sometimes at Lowndes Street, sometimes at his flat. This mode of existence continued for a year or two, when my mother, finding it impossible, and egged on by my sisters and myself, who had conceived a desire to own horses and to hunt, sold the lease of the house in Lowndes Street and took a furnished house in the country. From this time on, Freddy never again lived with his family. He used to visit us at week-ends and he took my sisters and myself, particularly me, about with him, but he was from now on to regard himself as a completely free agent. He remained all his life devoted to my mother, there was never any question of a formal separation, and, as long as he lived in England, he saw her often. Late in his life he only saw her infrequently, but all through the war, in America, and afterwards in France, he wrote to her regularly. There was never any doubt that he had roots here.

Some time towards the end of the Birchington period Miss Chesher came to work for Freddy as his secretary. She had been secretary to Paul Rubens until he died, and she had an intimate knowledge of the world of the theatre. When she first arrived she was very efficient, flashing off letters on the typewriter, keeping box files, marking in-coming letters with an A to show that they were answered, and making copies of her replies. She kept accounts too, and she presented Freddy with detailed lists of his takings and also of his expenditure. We watched all this with idle amusement, keeping our tongues firmly at rest in our cheeks when she told us we must be very quiet because Freddy was working. She proved surprisingly adaptable. In no time she was spending half her working day discussing with Freddy where he should go and what he should do, packing his clothes or unpacking them. She quickly got used to being asked in the morning, when she arrived with her smart new toque on her head, whether she had joined the Air Force, and in a very short time, when Freddy said he was going to work, she attached herself to parties of my sisters and myself who crept up to the window of his room to see what he was really doing. She never in all her life gave up trying to make him look at her lists of his expenditure, but this was simply cussedness on her part, because she knew it was a waste of time. All her life she was absolutely loyal to his interests. Much of his money was banked in her name, and, later in his life, when enormous sums had suddenly to be found for income tax or for one of his family, the consternation was suddenly abated by an announcement from Miss Chesher, who had seized the fees of some past production and hoarded them against just such a situation as this. She found him, as did everyone else, maddeningly irritating, fiendishly intransigent, and very boring; but he brought colour into her life, and she loved him.

From the time Freddy first lived in London until he left England for good in 1938, he always employed a chauffeur. Various men held this job for a year or two, but in 1926 or 1927 Ernest Day came to work for him. Day was soon transformed into a chauffeur-valet, and developed into a friend and companion. He had the same irritated, understanding affection for Freddy that Miss Chesher had, and he was soon very wily in anticipation of, and most crafty in response to, Freddy's vagaries. He had a more amusing time than Miss Chesher because he accompanied Freddy wherever he went, travelling often to America or the Riviera, attending racecourses armed with tips straight from the stables, and staying in houses where the entertainment in the servants' hall, or the housekeeper's room, which I believe he frequented, was as varied and almost as lavish as that in the front of the house. But he would have followed Freddy anywhere. In 1938, when Freddy went to America, Day stayed behind, because, with the danger of war, he could not leave his wife and family. When war was declared he entered a factory and rose to a position of great responsibility in which he earned a very big income. For himself, he would have been ready at any moment to give this all up and return to Freddy, and after the war, whenever Freddy was in London, Day was amongst the most regular of his visitors.

When Freddy ceased to live in a family, he never suffered the lack of the warmth that a family supplies, never wanted for all those small attentions which a large household gives, never walked into an empty flat at night, or felt alone and uncared for with a cold in his head. Miss Chesher and Day between them filled all the gaps in a life where only the humdrum virtues, the most homely affections, might have been missed.

CHAPTER TEN

'The Last of Mrs. Cheyney'

One of the greatest theatrical events of the year 1925, which had already seen the productions of *Spring Cleaning* and *Katja the Dancer*, was the first night, on September 22nd, at the St. James's Theatre, of *The Last of Mrs. Cheyney*.

Although there has never been general agreement on this point, I have always thought this to be the best play Freddy ever wrote. Opinions vary, both as to the quality of real success he achieved, and as to the merits of the different plays, according to the standpoint from which his work is regarded. In the days of his greatest success, he was highly praised as a satirist, a connoisseur of human nature, for his epigrams and for his wit. He was criticised for the most part where the critics felt that he had failed in these things. This was the "verdict at midnight", the view arrived at by people for whom the plays were the last word in modernity, and whose minds were conditioned by the same environment which inspired the author's. That it was a curious environment is made clear in much of the literature of the period, and I think no one can understand the success of certain novels and plays of that time unless he appreciates one thing. The great discovery of the nineteen-twenties was that honour and respectability are not necessarily synonymous. The generation of the 'twenties was most concerned with honour; they found, however, the unexpected principles of the conventionally disreputable far more romantic and far more exalting than the virtues that had hitherto passed under this name. It was a time for revaluation of all standards, and youth, determined to throw overboard the more inhibiting of the older ones, felt, nevertheless, an emotional need to discover a new set of morals of their own. The success, for instance, of *The Green Hat* seems to me now to have been caused by the fact that a woman who was not in the then accepted sense of the word a 'good' woman, and who proves this with a sensational bang in the first chapter, was capable of a chivalrous gallantry which led to her sacrificing her own reputation for that of her dead husband, and finally to suicide. No generation not enchanted by this new idea of honour could have overlooked the inherent absurdity of the characters in *The Green Hat*. In the same way, when Freddy invented a character who, though a cad and an utterly useless specimen of humanity, showed tolerance for other people's weaknesses and an elegant and witty gallantry in moments of defeat, the audience of the time seemed to think it had something to do with human nature—a new, especially enlightened, reckless, but exquisitely high-principled human nature.

The truth about Freddy's work, I believe, is that it never approached sufficiently closely to human nature to be regarded even as satire. It should be judged on its merits as pure comedy. The qualities that lifted it above the ruck and run of other works of this type of that time were his very great talent for the theatre and his genuine and original wit.

What makes *The Last of Mrs. Cheyney* for me the best of all his plays is that it has, if not an original, a strong plot. In consequence, the humour and the unexpected twists with which this dramatist was accustomed to embroider his plays are used to further the action, rather than to keep the play alive until the moment is reached for the dénouement. This may require less art, and the play may be less of a *tour de force* than *On Approval*, or those of his plays where the plot is so slight that they are almost an exercise in pure wit and dramatic skill, but I prefer the swifter action and dialogue which the plot of *Mrs. Cheyney* enforces on him. I have always thought that Freddy suffered as a dramatist from a rather simple mind, and from an innocence of the accumulated thought of the human race which made him believe that the tritest of his own observations were freshly unexpected. He often thought about life, but he did so with a mind so empty of the influence of other people's philosophy or moral opinions that he constantly arrived, with ingenuous pleasure, at conclusions which had occurred to other people a thousand years or so before. As a result, he could sometimes be very prosy, and he was always capable of inventing some hideously stagy character to serve as a butt to receive his freshly-conceived, epigramatically pointed, but stale moral reflections. The vicar in *Aren't We All?* is a good example of this type of character. He furthers the plot of the play in no way at all; he merely acts as a foil to Lord Grenham, and allows the author to show off his new-found belief that the more obvious of the Christian virtues may sometimes lead to narrow-mindedness, self-righteousness and intolerance! Freddy himself thought *Aren't We All?* his best play, but although, to my prejudiced mind, it had too many good qualities for me to be unable to forgive it the vicar, I think he mars it considerably. But, in my opinion, Freddy had no peer in his day as a dramatist where his very unexpected and genuine wit was used in dialogue which served only the plot of the play. In *The Last of Mrs. Cheyney* the plot keeps him briskly on the move and prevents that dawdling in the by-ways which always with him provoked the epigram, the moral attitude, or the commentary on life. But, if I am right in my views, he was consistently encouraged in his faults by the critics, who praised him continually and in glowing terms for his epigrams, and, with few exceptions, entirely failed to castigate him for his clumsier characters.

On the other hand, when I lately looked at the original notices of *Mrs. Cheyney*, I was amazed to find that these were by no means as good as those for his earlier plays. Of course, there were certain difficulties. The play had a practically all-star cast; Mr. Lonsdale, no longer a discovery, had been praised and praised and praised, and every production which bore his name had run and run and run; the first-night audience con-sisted of people who had stood on the pavement outside the theatre for twenty-four hours or so, or of other people few of whom by themselves would not have provided a paragraph for the columnists. No one was exactly longing to praise it. Nevertheless, the faults the critics found are a little unexpected.

The *Last of Mrs. Cheyney* is a melodramatic comedy and, regarded as such, it must be seen to have succeeded brilliantly. The author sticks to his last, as Wilde did in *The Importance of Being Earnest*, and is never side-tracked by the necessity to pad out a scene, or the temptation to use his play as a vehicle for reflections on matters which are strictly not his business. It is a little surprising, then, to find the critics quarrelling with the author for his morals, criticising him for thinking that women of the upper classes have more fun than shop girls, and com-plaining that his play is simply melodrama, while mostly allowing that it succeeds in being entertaining and is extremely witty. The same critics who, with few exceptions, had accepted the second-rate moralising of *Spring Cleaning*, overlooked the vicar in *Aren't We All?*, did not object to *The Fake*, which was ultimately a play written to condone, with qualifications, murder, were saddened by *The Last of Mrs. Cheyney* because it was not like life, because its author had a penchant for the upper classes, and because, although admittedly successful, the comedy was melodramatic. *The Importance of Being Earnest* is surely not valued for its verisimilitude to life, morally un-impeachable, or free of dramatic conventions. It is also about the upper classes, as are most of the Restoration comedies. (There is one thing about the upper classes, they may not have more fun than shop-girls but they have certainly provided more fun.) One critic went so far as to say of *The Last of Mrs. Cheyney* that he believed that, without the extraordinary cast, the play would have been a failure; a remark which, in view of its subsequent history with other casts, in other towns, in other languages, and later with another cast in London, was, to say the least, ill-judged.

I recently re-read this play, which is still often played in English and Continental towns, and, although some of the every-day assumptions on which it is based are now a little dated, I found it as amusing and as charming as I had remembered it. There seems to be a general belief that if a play is old-fashioned, this is a fault—surely an extremely naïve view. When a play has become old-fashioned because it was originally based on a sensationalism which is no longer sensational, or because the poetry, wit or thought no longer retains life, that is one thing; but when customs and ideas have merely altered, that is surely something quite different. If this is not so, then the whole of the theatrical heritage of the past can be seen to suffer from this fault. In the play which I am discussing, Mrs. Cheyney con-stantly adopts the view that it is insulting for an unmarried man to make love to an unmarried woman without the in-tention of marriage—an idea which I think the audiences of to-day might find a trifle ridiculous, though even so short a time ago as 1925 it passed without comment.

It is a play in three acts, with two scenes in the second act. In the first act the curtain rises on Mrs. Cheyney, a rich Australian woman, about whose past nothing is known, but who has been taken up by a smart section of London society,

entertaining many of her new friends at a concert in aid of
charity which takes place off-stage in the garden of her London
house. Mrs. Cheyney is very charming and very beautiful and
she is possessed of a butler whose demeanour, while not open
to criticism, is intriguing, and of two footmen. A large cast of
characters includes Lord Dilling, a rich and attractive, but
cynical and unreliable, young man, and Lord Elton, an older and
far more worthy character. It is clear that both these men are
attracted to Mrs. Cheyney, and that, while Lord Elton's
intentions towards her are probably honourable, Lord Dilling's
are unlikely to be. There are also present a Mrs. Ebley and
Lady Frinton. (Freddy always used the same names for certain
characters in different plays. There are several Lady Frintons,
and hardly a play without a Duke of Bristol. I think this
was simply laziness and there is no intention that they should
be thought to be actually the same people.) Both Mrs.
Ebley and Lady Frinton, it is conveyed to the audience, are
women with a past, and, in the case of Mrs. Ebley, her past has
left her with several strings of pearls worth a fortune, a house in
the country, and, in consequence of these, a position which, by
all but the most particular, is extremely respected.

At the close of the first act, after her guests have all left and
Mrs. Cheyney is free to relax, the audience are surprised by the
fact that Charles, the butler, a cigar in his mouth, and the two
footmen, casual in attire and in manner, are unselfconsciously
prepared to relax with her. It then becomes clear that Mrs.
Cheyney is a member of a gang of crooks, of which Charles is
the leader, and the footmen fellow members.

In the second act, Mrs. Cheyney is planted in the country
house of the rich Mrs. Ebley, who is also entertaining the whole
cast of characters who have appeared in the first act, with a view
to stealing her pearls. It is made plain, in the first scene of this
act, that this deed is to be done that night by Mrs. Cheyney

entering Mrs. Ebley's bedroom after that lady is asleep. During this scene Charles appears with a message for Mrs. Cheyney, and he is dressed, not in butler's uniform, but in an ordinary suit. Lord Dilling, who by now is seriously in love with Mrs. Cheyney, recognises him, when he sees him for the first time in the clothes in which he has known him before, as a man whom he has seen shown up as a crook in the past. In consequence, he opens the message which the butler has left for his mistress, and recognises immediately what is planned for the night. He then employs a subterfuge to make his hostess change her bedroom with his.

The second scene of this act is set in Mrs. Ebley's bedroom, but when Mrs. Cheyney later enters to steal the pearls, she finds in the room not her hostess, but Lord Dilling, who is awake and awaiting her arrival. There then follows a scene in which Lord Dilling, having first ensured the safety of the pearls by putting them in his pocket, and having also locked the door of the bedroom, offers Mrs. Cheyney complete cover for her secret and the opportunity for herself and her gang to make a getaway in return for her honour. Mrs. Cheyney refuses, and, when Lord Dilling will not unlock the door, she finally rings the bell and arouses the whole household. Forced by the clamour outside to unlock the door, Lord Dilling lies to protect Mrs. Cheyney, and assumes the blame for their presence behind the locked door in Mrs. Ebley's bedroom. Mrs. Cheyney, however, herself tells the truth, and, as the curtain goes down, she leaves the stage, a self-confessed thief.

This scene, which is, perhaps, too unashamedly melodramatic, is redeemed both by the excellence of the dialogue and by the brilliance of the third act which follows it. In this scene the characters of the play, with the exception of Mrs. Cheyney and her gang, gradually assemble at breakfast on the following morning. They are all of them shocked and surprised, and they discuss what they should do with Mrs. Cheyney and the rest of her gang. It is then that Lord Elton discloses to his hostess and his fellow guests that, being very much in love with Mrs. Cheyney and wishing to marry her, he has written a letter making his proposal. He goes on to say that, as Mrs. Cheyney is an Australian woman, without knowledge of English society, he felt it his duty to explain to her in this letter that, in the event of her becoming his wife, there were many people in London she might know, but others he felt it would be better for her not to know. Covered with embarrassment, he confesses that the whole of the present company are included among those it would be better for her not to know, and that, in justice to himself, he has given her his reasons in each case for his feeling about them, reasons which, if published, would expose his fellow guests to ignominy or ridicule. Mrs. Cheyney is, consequently, in possession of a strong card for negotiation. When Charles and Mrs. Cheyney come on to the scene, they use this card with much wit and with a skill that forces the rest of the company to abandon any idea of sending for the police and instead to offer £10,000 in return for the letter.

As this play is a comedy, not like life and without any moral, it is essential that it should be given a happy ending. The author achieves this by making Mrs. Cheyney, on receipt of the cheque for £10,000, tear it up as, she tells the assembled company, she had already torn up the letter that morning. After a scene in which most of the company make their farewells, Charles, Mrs. Cheyney and Lord Dilling are left alone on the stage. Charles announces his intention of going round the world, and, in spite of Mrs. Cheyney's pleas, insists on leaving her.

Dilling: Are you going round the world for pleasure, Charles?

Charles (imitating dealing cards): Mixed with business, my lord!

(He looks at Mrs. Cheyney, blows her a kiss.)
Exits.

Lord Dilling and Mrs. Cheyney then play a scene at the end of which they see the last of Mrs. Cheyney and the beginning of Lady Dilling.

Before it reached the stage of St. James's Theatre *The Last of Mrs. Cheyney* had had a very eventful history, and one that accounted for the fact that it was eventually performed by a cast consisting very largely of stars.

At this time Sir Gerald du Maurier was in management at Wyndham's Theatre. He had had a run of only moderately successful luck and he was looking for a play. Freddy offered him *The Last of Mrs. Cheyney*, and he went one night to dine with the du Mauriers at their house, Cannon Hall, in Hampstead, in order to read it to him. There were present at dinner Freddy himself, Gerald and his wife Muriel. After the meal was over the three of them settled down and Freddy began to read the play. All went well for some time, but as Freddy began to read the early scenes of the second act he looked up from his script, to see Gerald reclining in his chair in the position of a man who is asleep, his eyes shut and his breathing deep and steady.

Freddy rose to his feet, gathered up his manuscript, and strode out of the room. This room in which they were sitting was on the first floor of the house, which was connected with the ground floor by a broad central staircase. Freddy raced down this staircase with Lady du Maurier after him.

"Please, Freddy," she cried, "please come back. He's so terribly tired. He couldn't help it. Please, Freddy, come back."

But Freddy, as furious as he had ever been in his life, ignored her appeals, and, jumping into his car, which stood in the courtyard outside the front door, drove away back to London.

There is one thing in this story which will never be known for certain. Lady du Maurier obviously and genuinely believed that Gerald was asleep—that he was over-tired and that the steady sound of the voice reading had acted as a soporific. Freddy never believed this for one instant, either at that time or ever afterwards. He knew his Gerald, who had never either understood or especially cared for the success of his favourite 'muck-writer', and he believed he had deliberately staged this insulting scene. The truth probably lies between the views of these two people. It is most likely that Gerald did genuinely fall asleep, but that, when he was awoken—as he inevitably would have been—by Freddy leaving the room, and he realised what had happened, he decided that, rather than have a humiliating scene of apology, he would continue to play it as though he was still asleep.

Freddy arrived back in Lowndes Street in a towering rage, and he there and then took several oaths on my life: one that he would never speak to Gerald again, another that he would never have anything to do with him in the theatre. We, all of us who adored Freddy, were extremely incensed.

There was no difficulty in disposing of the play to other people, and Freddy began the next day to make other negotiations. Gerald, however, having had either his sleep or his fun, was by no means finished with it. He had on his hands a theatre that had to be filled and no other satisfactory play. The first thing he did was to send Viola Tree (Mrs. Alan Parsons) as an emissary.

Viola Tree, an exceptionally tall woman, amusing and intelligent, worshipped Gerald. I was there on the occasion when she came to try to placate Freddy. We dined at the Embassy Club and Michael Arlen was also of the party. Viola had rather a rough time, because Michael ranged himself with Freddy, and neither of them, from the beginning, was prepared to accept this olive branch at second hand. During the course of a rather heated conversation Viola tried to persuade Freddy that he ought to take the play once more to Gerald.

"Give me one good reason why I should do as you suggest," Freddy said to her.

Searching frantically in her mind for one of those unfamiliar phrases on which Christian charity is based, Viola hit on the wrong one.

"Wasn't it Christ," she said, "who said 'Suffer little children to come unto me'?"

Freddy was for once completely silenced, and it was Michael who replied to her.

"I take it," he said in a very calm voice, but actually spitting with rage, "that *we* are the little children."

Viola failed as an emissary.

After this Gerald made the next move himself. His manager at Wyndham's was a man well known in the theatre as Tommy Vaughan, and Vaughan also managed other theatres for Gilbert Miller. Cannon Hall, Gerald's house in Hampstead, stood on the top of a hill, and it was necessary to drive up a very steep road to get to it. One day Gerald was driving up to his house when he met Tommy Vaughan walking down towards him. He stopped the car.

"Tommy," he said, "I think I shall have to have that play of Freddy's."

"You're too late, old boy," Vaughan replied, "Gladys is going to do it with Gilbert Miller."

Gerald must have had his foot on the brake, because, when Vaughan said this, the car in which he sat slid gently backwards down the hill.

After this, Gerald apparently gave it up and went abroad, to Italy, I think, with the rest of his family. In London the work of casting the play began. It had always been Freddy's intention

The Author and Freddy

The Lonsdale daughters

On Approval. Left to right: Valerie Taylor, Ronald Squire, Edmond Breon and Ellis Jeffreys

A scene from *Never Come Back*

that Ronald Squire should play in it, and it was agreed that he should play Charles, the butler. Gladys Cooper was, of course, to play Mrs. Cheyney, and Miss Ellis Jeffreys, the most brilliant of all comédiennes in Freddy's plays, was engaged to play Lady Frinton. This left the part of Lord Dilling. Various names were suggested but no firm arrangement had been made, when a telegram arrived from Gerald in Italy, saying that he would like to play in the play. He had had an expensive sleep, because, without it, *The Last of Mrs. Cheyney* would have been done at Wyndham's Theatre under his management, whereas, as it was, he merely took a salary to play in it at the St. James's.

When he arrived back in London he was welcomed with open arms. The cast of *Cheyney* loved Gerald, and so did its author. They were all of them very glad, too, to have him for the production. It was decided that as there were two male parts in the play of about equal value, that of Charles and that of Lord Dilling, Gerald must be given the choice. Ronnie and Freddy looked at each other when he chose Lord Dilling. They both of them thought Charles the better part.

The Last of Mrs. Cheyney went into rehearsal with a third act that was never to see the light of production. All went well in the theatre for some time while the first and second acts were being rehearsed. Freddy was very easy in those days and he was quite happy to leave it all to Gerald. He used to arrive at rehearsals sometimes and sit in the stalls with a bag of boiled sweets in his pocket, but quite often, when he was wanted, he was not in the theatre. Then, one day when the rehearsals had been going on for about a week, Gerald and Ronnie Squire came down to the stalls to talk to Freddy just before luncheon.

"Freddy," Gerald said, "this third act is no good. We shall have a flop unless you can do something about it."

"I know," Freddy replied, "I know. You are perfectly right."

Gerald and Ronnie suggested that they should all three go out to luncheon together to discuss it. But Freddy refused.

"I'd rather go by myself," he said. "I must think about it."

When they returned after luncheon, Freddy was beaming.

"I've got it," he said.

He then told them of the device of the letter, on which the final third act was based, and which had occurred to him while away. The third act, as played at the St. James's Theatre and ever afterwards, was written while the company rehearsed the first and second.

The first night of this play was one of the most brilliant for years. All day people gathered on the pavement outside the theatre, and late at night they were still there hoping to catch a glimpse of the stars as they emerged. Amongst the famous people in the audience were Miss Ina Claire and Mr. A. E. Matthews, who were to leave on the morrow for America to play in the New York production. At the end of the play the audience called and called for Freddy, and refused to leave the theatre until he was dragged on to the stage. Faced once more with the necessity for a speech, he came down to the footlights.

"Ladies and gentlemen," he said, "this morning I composed a most brilliant little speech to make to you this evening, but this afternoon I read it to Sir Gerald du Maurier in his dressing-room. He liked it so much that he insists on making it himself."

He then left the stage, and Gerald, taken completely by surprise, as was, of course, the intention, was reduced to singing in, as far as I can remember, a not very notable tenor:

I want to be happy
But I can't be happy
Till I've made you happy too.

a song which had been used in the first act.

The Last of Mrs. Cheyney ran in London for 514 performances. The morning after its first night in London Freddy and I left for New York on the same boat as Miss Ina Claire and Mr. A. E. Matthews—Matty—who were to play the parts of the butler and Mrs. Cheyney in New York. With us too was Miss Nancy Ryan, who was to play a small part. Mr. Roland Young, who was to play Dilling, was I think already there awaiting our arrival.

The play was produced at the Fulton Theatre by Charles B. Dillingham on November 9th, 1925. Here the critics were full of praise for the production, but, although they liked the play better on the whole than had their London colleagues, they were not unduly excited by it. The best notice, I think, was by Frank Vreeland in the *New York Telegram*:

"It is full of Lonsdale's typically deft and witty lines, making mock of anything that comes to hand. . . . Perhaps the airy Mr. Lonsdale is taking a sly poke at English high life of the free and easy sort when he makes it appear that a suave adventuress can so readily swim into their fish-pond. That, however, is a point which Mr. Lonsdale must settle with his conscience, if not with his Maker. He has balanced everything by an astonishing and delightful turn in the last act. . . . Here the capricious play was at its best, with the paradoxical insouciance which has not been drained off from Lonsdale even by writing *Aren't We All?* and *Spring Cleaning*. He can still shake out the topsy-turvy jocosity by the half hour. . . . But what does the prankish Lonsdale mean by calling one choice spirit Charles and another Dilling? Has the man no respect for anything?"

Gilbert W. Gabriel in the *New York Sun* said:

"Of its three acts one is quite swift, the rest fair and often funny. Except of rare and renowned successes nowadays, you do not ask much more."

But Percy Hammond in the *New York Herald Tribune* said:

"This is one of Mr. Lonsdale's minor transgressions, half play, half musical comedy libretto, but altogether a capital evening with him, Miss Ina Claire and a dozen other charming persons. . . . The characters, the conversation and the romance are blue-ribbon; the plot, I fear, came out of Mr. Lonsdale's bottom drawer."

And an unsigned review in the *New York Times* read:

"Ina Claire returned to town last night at the Fulton Theatre in *The Last of Mrs. Cheyney*, which calls itself a comedy but which is really a melodrama sugared with typical paradigms of the newer English school of epigrammatical writing."

Almost all the critics, however, raved about the acting. I have no wish to disagree with them on this point. One has only to see the names of the casts in London and New York to know that they must have been justified in their praise. But *The Last of Mrs. Cheyney*, having run for 514 performances in London and 282 performances in New York, ran in Berlin, with Elisabeth Bergner in the title role, for 119 performances (a long run for that city), was produced successfully in Paris by Louis Verneuil, drew large audiences when done as a film, made a great deal of money when revived by Jack Buchanan in London, and has been given literally thousands of performances in English, American and continental towns. In the year 1955 it was played in Frankfurt and in Hamburg as well as in several English towns. It can no longer be said to depend for success on an all-star cast.

CHAPTER ELEVEN

Witherslack

In the years 1925 and 1926 Freddy used to drive down the Fulham Road to a house behind Hurlingham which belonged to Lord Beaverbrook. Here he would pick up his host and the two of them would go to play golf, later returning to the house at Fulham for luncheon. Sometimes they would be alone together, sometimes there would be other people with them. On one occasion Lady Maureen Stanley was present at luncheon. When they were leaving for London in the afternoon, she spoke to Freddy as she got into the car.

"Will you come and dine one night?" she said, "I want to find out if the terrible things that Max says about you are true."

Thus began a friendship with the Oliver Stanleys that was to dominate Freddy's life for twelve or thirteen years.

Oliver Stanley was the younger son of Lord Derby. At that time he worked in the City as a stockbroker, and he was a backbencher of the Tory Party in the House of Commons. He fulfilled more nearly than anyone else I have ever met the ideal of the English aristocracy at its most worthy. His appearance was distinguished, although he had the rounded, slightly bucolic features of his family. He was very tall, with those attributes of quality, such as long hands and feet and a small head, and his hair turned silver early. His clothes, unremarkable amongst his class and generation, were wonderfully tailored and of beautiful cloth, but simple and often well-worn, both in London and in the country, and his manner, although extremely weighty, was quiet and even shy.

He had a quality of honour that was unlike anything I have ever found in anyone else. It was not merely that one felt him incorruptible, unbribable, but that he seemed to understand by instinct what honour is. One felt that, faced unexpectedly with any situation, he would know, without pause for reflection, where his only course of action lay. This was an impression he gave. One could never imagine Oliver finding it necessary to consult some friend before committing himself to any behaviour, nor would one easily choose him as a consultant oneself, since any advice of his might proceed from a plane of thought and principle too difficult to rise to. From time to time he also gave an interesting demonstration of the quality which caused this impression.

In those days in London one of the leading motor-car manufacturers considered that it was a good advertisement for his cars to have them driven by people of fame and distinction. He was always anxious therefore to achieve a sale to anyone who would grace the car by his presence in it and drive it to the right places, and, in order to effect this, he was ready to forgo the normal profit on it and sell it at a very cut price. This was, from his point of view, a business transaction, as often as not carried out by his salesmen on a general instruction, not through his personal intervention, and demanding no further *quid pro quo*. In general, people scrambled to take advantage of this opportunity, and, where the point of honour arose, it was usually in a desire to make certain that there was no price differential that put the value of one's person low. I know of no one except Oliver who ever refused to accept a reduction on the retail price of his car, but Oliver did so with a wave of his hand and a grimace of distaste. The obligation was almost intangible, consisting of doing no more than using the car for the purpose for which it would be bought, but Oliver would no more have thought of accepting it than he would of lending his face to the advertisement of Pond's Cold Cream or a shaving soap. Reduced to these terms, his action seems not so unusual; I can only say that I never knew of anyone else to whom the matter occurred in this light.

Again when, in the 1939 War the Chamberlain Government fell and Winston Churchill took over, Oliver, who had been Minister of War in the old Cabinet, was not included in the new one; yet, although by then a man well over forty, one who could certainly be felt to have much to contribute to some civilian post, and still a Member of Parliament, he appeared within a matter of days in the uniform of a lieutenant of the regiment in which he had served in the 1914 War. He had not stopped to think.

He had a very good brain and a humorous and scholarly wit. Both in office and in opposition in the House of Commons this was used with point and flavour, but never merely with the intention to wound. As a result he had many friends on both sides of the House.

He was only about thirty-two when I first met him, but he already had the personality and the place in life of a much older man—the head of the house, liked and respected, but deferred to by his friends. Conscious of his manner, and unable to feel at ease in circles where brilliant and sophisticated small talk formed the bulk of the conversation, he often seemed cold and unapproachable. He was unapproachable through vulgarity, triviality or pretension, but he was also shy. Yet no one ever thought him simply a prig. His qualities were too luminous, his standpoint too unaffected, and his position too strong for him ever to be the subject of mean misunderstanding or gossip.

It is true, of course, that no one not brought up in an atmosphere of wealth so considerable as almost to eliminate money as one of the factors of life could have matured as Oliver did; no one not conscious from birth of the need for superior behaviour to justify superior breeding could so seldom have been betrayed by his instincts. But he was what his environment should have made him; and he was a very rare man.

Maureen Stanley was the eldest daughter of Lord Londonderry, and it required defiance on her part to marry a younger son. She had many of the qualities that Oliver had, but she had a natural recklessness that had been highly developed in the strong, supporting arm of her birth and upbringing; and this, I think, although it led her into many mistakes, and, when she became ill, caused her early death, was her finest as well as her most attractive quality. She never whined or cried in the night, never cared for spilt milk, never did anything by half and never blamed other people. She was not, in any sense of the word, a beauty, but she was so attractive she was often mistaken for one. She had very fair hair that hung too smoothly round her head, achieving an artificial, almost sculptured appearance; blue eyes, and a prominent, aristocratic nose. She was strongly built, but not gracefully, and, in her clothes, she constantly gave rein to a natural flamboyance. She was not, in fact, very sensitive, but this was more than made up for by her courage and high spirits, which were so infectious that she could inspire confidence and gaiety in any gathering of people. Her character was strong, almost masculine, and forceful; her recklessness never degenerated into that kind of irresponsibility and shamelessness which, although it can also be very attractive, is quite common in youthful or trivial societies; and her courage was real and did not consist in a twittering and uninhibited candour. She had no quality of tenderness, but she inspired in other people a reflection of her own

Never Come Back, with Athole Stewart, P. Kynaston Reeves and Viola Tree

But for the Grace of God. Michael Gough and Hugh McDermott

The Way Things Go. Glynis Johns and Ronald Squire

intrepidity and her enjoyment of life, and this caused her
to be much beloved and much sought after.

She was an enormously successful hostess. In London she
entertained, chiefly at six o'clock in the evening, a company that
was largely political in flavour, but which included any person
from any world whom Maureen happened to think amusing.
A great many of her closer friends went to the house in Dean
Trench Street every evening when the Stanleys were in London,
and the word *salon* springs to one's mind when one thinks of
the society which nightly met there. But the flow into and out
of the house was informal—although it included most of the
'great' of London, as well as foreigners from most of the
embassies and visiting Americans—and really notable quantities
of gin were drunk. The conversation was often political, and it
was aggressive, intelligent and pointed, and broken at times by
Maureen's high-pitched and unexpectedly schoolgirlish giggle as
she punctured the pomposity of some attitudinising great man
or some fledgling stranger. This was one of her great qualities;
she was no respecter of persons, and she could, with one debunking phrase, humanise the most ponderous conceit or the
frosted solemnity which covers shyness. Her victims loved it.

She was always assumed to be highly intelligent, and, since
she fulfilled all the duties which her position required of her, of
considerable executive power. The first of these things was
probably not true; the quality of her thought was not high or
original, nor had her mind any staying power. Nothing in her
character left place for contemplation, rumination or imagination. But, because of her vigour and her extraordinary lack of
respect for the outward forms of success, she was often
brilliantly effective. In committees she could raise the dust of
thirty years with her high-pitched giggle, while arming old
ladies and timid clerks with her own light-hearted joy in battle
and her really outrageous conviction of superiority.

G

Ridicule was a weapon much used in those days by the upper classes in their almost unconscious struggle to hold their place; and with this weapon Maureen was supreme. Most of the company who attended regularly at Dean Trench Street were the youthful members of the Tory Party, but other young men came there, too, representing other shades of opinion, and these Maureen held in an uneasy thrall. She was an influence among the younger ranks of politicians, even if not a power.

She had many friends, too, amongst the leaders of the governing party, who enjoyed her company, and felt their masculinity titillated by this high-spirited young woman's impertinent disregard of their authority. Prime ministers, viceroys, judges and even bishops lost their dignity in Dean Trench Street.

But at this time Maureen spent only a small part of her life in London. She lived for months at a stretch at Witherslack, the Stanleys' country house. Here she exercised that talent, which most Englishwomen have, for being eternally occupied within the confines of her house and garden, with the Women's Institute and with the local Conservative Party. At the week-ends Oliver would come up from London, and he would exercise that talent, which most Englishmen have, for being supremely happy pottering for hours in his rock garden, walking round his land with a gun and a couple of dogs, or playing a game of golf. On wet days he would read detective stories or P. G. Wodehouse, and in the evenings, if there was anyone staying, they would play bridge. Oliver loved this house set among the fells of Westmorland so much that, even when he was tired and overworked, he would travel to Carlisle by night on the Friday and back to London by night on the Sunday for the pleasure of spending two days there.

Witherslack was built on high ground, surrounded by the steep, stony hills called fells. As one drove towards it in the car that had been sent twenty miles or so to the station to meet one, one travelled on roads which ran between these fells and, turning at last into the lanes which lay beneath the house, one would see it some miles off. It was a Victorian house built in an L shape in a rather ugly grey stone with mullions and quoins of a different pinkish stone. It was not beautiful or even fantastic; it reminded one a little of some massive institutional building. When one entered the front door one came into a large hall which, with the staircase climbing round three sides of it, formed the well of this part of the house. Immediately in front of one, hanging over the fireplace, was a painting of a small child with a greyhound dog. The staircase, which formed such a large part of the furnishing of the hall, had a banister of a yellow-grained wood, probably fumed oak, and, when one mounted to one's bedroom, the cupboards and the dressing-table were of the same yellow-coloured wood. Here there would be a large double bed and a fire burning brightly in the grate.

It was a big house, although, because some of the bedrooms ran over the out-house, there were not so many rooms on the ground floor as there were above. On the ground floor Maureen had her own sitting-room and Oliver a library, and, for their guests, there was a large drawing-room, seldom used, and a sitting-room. In this room, which was oblong in shape, peat always burned on an open fire, and, on a red and blue Turkish carpet, two sofas and several armchairs were covered in a red and blue cretonne, which had acquired a soft and homely beauty with age. Prints were hung on the walls, so closely as almost to touch one another, and, in this room as in every other, hot-house plants were banked in one corner by a gardener with green fingers but a massive taste.

So it was when Lord Derby gave it to Oliver, and so it was when I first went there. Later Maureen made some changes, the worst of which was when Lord Derby gave her a present with which to re-decorate a bedroom for an expected visit of the Prince of Wales, and she spent almost the whole of this on a brassy-coloured kind of canvas material, which was stretched and nailed to the walls of the chosen room, always afterwards referred to as the Gold Room.

But this house had an exquisite charm. One would wake in the great bed in the morning, the touch of fine linen under one's cheek, to watch the young housemaid fold away the clothes one had worn the night before and put out the things for the day. When she left the room to run the bath in the bath-room next door, and one turned to the breakfast tray, which held fruit from the hot-houses and cream and the food on a covered and heated plate and the morning paper, it was not simply opulence which inspired the languorous enjoyment. I have been in other bedrooms where the opulence was as great or greater, and which only oppressed me with a sense of my own unimportance, reminded me of the freakish chance which had brought me there, and where I have reflected with an inexplicable feeling of loss that in any case I should probably never be there again. In these rooms I have wondered uneasily how long I could reasonably stay in bed to delay the terrible efforts of the day. But at Witherslack there was a reassuring unworldliness about the innocent ugliness of the great Victorian bedroom and furniture, and a small flourish in the neat movements of the maid as she laid out the clothes, which made one think she enjoyed doing her work so well, and which was very pleasant to watch. And later, when one got out of bed, one could see from the window, across the green fields and the dripping woods, the mist that hung over the fell; or, from the other side of the house and at a different season, the sun shining palely on the lawn which, beyond the wall of the terrace and the dark shadow of the house, fell steeply away to flatten out a

hundred yards or so before the shrubs and the lake. On the
right, on this side of the house, the greenhouses also descended
the bank, and on the left was Oliver's rock garden, formed in
an outcrop of the natural stone. A gardener might move
quietly across the lawn or a voice sound on the staircase, but
otherwise everything was very still. In this house wealth and
privilege were used to ensure everyone's privacy and the right
to solitude.

The opportunity for anything else was usually offered by the
butler.

"Shall I order you a caddy for this afternoon, miss?" or
"Her Ladyship asked me to tell you that if you want to play
tennis they have all gone on to the court," or, to those of
greater consequence: "Will you be going to the races, my
lord? Shall I have your car sent round?"

No greater pressure was ever brought on anyone to do
anything.

We used to play golf at Bowness, a short and mountainous
course with a springy turf. And we used sometimes to go duck-
shooting or to the local races. On these occasions there would
be a picnic lunch, of which the mutton pies were memorable.
The food in English country houses was so good. It was based
on French cooking, but it included such things as game pies
and Irish stew, beefsteak and kidney pudding, hams cured
locally and grouse; plum cake, gingerbread, treacle tart and
burbage pudding; and the cheeses of two or three counties.
The cold sideboard alone at Witherslack made it worth a visit.

Sometimes, for months at a stretch, there would be few
people in the house. At other times Maureen felt the urge to
entertain and there would be ten or twelve people every week-
end for weeks. Either way, everyone met in the sitting-room at
seven o'clock in the evening, and, as in London, martinis would
be drunk. I never understood how the kitchen staff timed their

arrangements. Dinner would always be ordered for 8.30; but night after night the effect of the gin was to make the whole party sit on talking and rush late upstairs to dress for dinner. Since no one Oliver or Maureen knew had ever learned to hurry in the bath, the company would actually be ready for dinner at about 9.15. The fact that it was then properly served would have been understandable if the servants could have counted on this behaviour. But every now and then, for some unforeseeable reason, everyone would appear at 8.30, when the food would still be served without a hitch.

Freddy settled down in this house as though he had been born there. He tried every bedroom until he found the one he preferred. Then he insisted it should be kept for him since he did not like rooms that had been used by other people, and even when he was away some of his clothes remained in the cupboards as sentinels against intruders. He also tried all the sitting-rooms, and finally decided on Maureen's in which to work. He spent a great deal of time at Witherslack, and for years it was the only place in which he could be expected to remain for more than two or three days at a time. Day settled equally comfortably into the housekeeper's quarters, and between them they gradually trained the whole household to understand their requirements.

Maureen took a bit of training. She had, as well as a school-girlish giggle, a rather schoolgirlish humour, and, although she was prepared to allow Freddy the run of the house, she was, at first, unable to take his absurdities seriously. Once, by way of a practical joke, she placed in his bedroom an exceptionally realistic-looking toy rat. When he went to bed she waited on the landing to enjoy the results of this joke, but, being met with silence, she thought it had misfired and went off to bed. Next morning Freddy appeared with a granite face and explained that he had not slept all night. He said he thought he had better go back to London, since he would now be unable to work until his nerves had recovered from this terrible upset. He did not go to London, but he did not set pen to paper for at least three weeks, and Maureen, who no better than anyone else in such circumstances could resist the role of Mæcenas, either believed that it was the rat that had upset him, or realised that, one could not afford to give him such ready made excuses. So, although she found this irresistibly funny, she afterwards confined herself to less broad jokes.

Freddy did, in fact, do a great deal of work at Witherslack. He must have written *On Approval* there, and *The High Road*, and *Canaries Sometimes Sing*. But largely he lived the life of a country gentleman of those rich and thoughtless days. Both he and Maureen had fast cars and they did not lack entertainment. They used to go racing a great deal and they betted in prodigious sums. Freddy always appeared to win a lot, but at the end of his life he told me that one way and another he had lost much more than he had won. Then he and Maureen used to drive round the country to political meetings where Maureen would be speaking, and stay a night in some other great country house. Freddy became interested in politics at this time, and Maureen's meetings were often amusing. As a speaker she was not very impressive, but she could always be counted on in a crisis, or to enliven a dull occasion.

I was with her once when Lord Derby came to Kendal to speak for Oliver, and the hall was filled with discontented and organised rebels. This was a surprise to the old man, who was used to affection and almost to reverence in the North of England, and when faced with constant interruption was at a loss. He faltered in what he was saying, and, unaware of the strength of the opposition, offered the audience racing tips. The clamour grew stronger and nastier until Maureen rose to her feet and simply berated these men, who had at the time the most genuine of grievances, for what she regarded as bad manners to an old man who had earned their respect. Her sincerity and candour carried conviction and her rather curious point of view was accepted, so that, when Oliver rose to speak, it was in a silent hall.

Another time Maureen and Freddy were standing by her car along with some members of the local party, when Sir Oswald Mosley, amidst a bodyguard of blackshirts, came out of a hall where they had been holding a meeting, and they all flowed down the street.

"Tom, Tom," Maureen called out as they passed, "why not come over to luncheon tomorrow?"

And the great Leader was forced to decide between leaving his thugs for social dalliance with an obviously social lady, or marching with grotesque sternness past an old and previously valued friend. I forget which choice he made, but the point was taken and delighted in by all the bystanders.

Freddy enjoyed all this. "This ass . . ." he said to me when he told me the Mosley story, but he was struck by the drama of local political life. During elections he even spoke on the platform for Oliver. I was amazed that Oliver took this risk, but, in the event, Freddy seemed always to behave himself, making short and witty speeches without much serious content, while they waited for Oliver to come on from some other meeting.

He tired quite quickly of this life or else the soft west-country air affected his liver, and then he and Day would pack up and be gone to London or to the South of France or to Hollywood. But soon he would be back at Witherslack, which, during all those years, called him as other men are called to their homes.

CHAPTER TWELVE

High Tide

Freddy had now reached his heyday. Few people, I suppose, remember exactly how successful he was during the years from 1923 until the early 'thirties. In December 1925 a writer in the *Daily Express*, reviewing *The Last of Mrs. Cheyney* when it appeared in book form, began his article:

"What is the secret of Mr. Frederick Lonsdale's popularity as a dramatist? I asked him the other day whether it was true that his royalties amount to the staggering total of £1,000 a week. He smiled that undecipherable Lonsdale smile and retorted, "I won't tell you what I make, but Michael Arlen is saving £1,000 a week.""

In December 1930, after the productions of *On Approval*, *The High Road* and *Canaries Sometimes Sing*, it was possible for a writer in the *Daily Telegraph* to write as follows:

"My reference yesterday to the loss the English theatre will suffer in the event of Mr. Lonsdale making good his threat to forsake it for the screen has inspired a statistically-minded colleague to research. The results are rather interesting. Mr. Lonsdale, he points out, is not merely the most popular playwright of the day; he is almost certainly the most popular who ever lived. Other men—Barrie, Maugham, Shaw, Pinero and Coward, for instance—have had many successes, but is any one of them quite immune to failure? Sir James Barrie comes nearest this blissful state. I believe that in his long and prolific career he has had only one full length play that failed to pass the 100 mark.

"That was his tragedy, *The Will*, and even this exception enjoyed a run of 225 nights when revived at the St. Martin's Theatre in 1923.

"Mr. Lonsdale has written seven or eight straight plays, and the book, or part of the book, of about half a dozen musical comedies. The shortest run he has ever had is the 110 nights of *Aren't We All?*—a total with which most authors would be satisfied. His record for straight and musical plays respectively are 514 nights for *The Last of Mrs. Cheyney* and 1,352 for *The Maid of the Mountains*, and his average run has been well over a year. No wonder Mr. Goldwyn finds him the most uniformly successful writer for the screen."

He was a much publicised figure, a gift to newspaper reporters, and anyone reading the files of newspapers of the time can trace much of his history and gain a surprisingly accurate impression of his personality. The reason why he lives so vividly in the columns of newspapers is, I think, because he was, in the word used at the Garrick Club, 'authentic'. In the first place he disliked and avoided publicity, so that reports of his movements or his opinions are never given in the form of set interviews, where calculated questions are asked and artificial responses made. On the other hand, he was genial and friendly in manner, so that a reporter who caught him on his way into a theatre and asked him a question got a spontaneous answer. Secondly, from a newspaperman's point of view, he was so splendidly eccentric. His eccentricities too were authentic. They sprang from a nature that was abnormally egotistic, but instinctively eager and enthusiastic; not, as is sometimes the case, from a position or an approach to life which, although it has grown to be genuine, has in youth been consciously and deliberately adopted. As a result, he wore his extraordinary success with confidence and authority, but without either vanity or superiority. He had a biting tongue, and an indifference to other people's opinions, he was bad-tempered, even violent; and, for emotional and unthought-out reasons, he adopted strongly unsympathetic views towards people and things. All these qualities made him, later in life, disliked by as many people as liked him. But in the nineteen-twenties the tide of his affairs ran so much in his favour that these characteristics were submerged, when he appeared in public, by his enjoyment of his success and his consequent geniality.

One supposes that this was the happiest period of his life; but it is difficult to say. He may have been happiest when as a youth he was kept engrossed by the simple struggle for bread and a belief in the glories that lay ahead; or in Birchington, where he lived an unassuming family life. The truth is that he reacted so strongly to outside stimulus that he had two distinct personalities. I remember him as a man who was never at any time very happy; restless, violently volatile in mood, un-satisfied, often bad-tempered and always incalculable; a man who at the end of his life was lonely, bored and disappointed; disappointed, not with what the world had done to him, because he knew that it had treated him generously, but with the world—which had not been so amusing as he had expected it to be. Nevertheless, and this remained true to the end of his days, two people gathered together could spark him into eagerness, gaiety and brilliance. So that, even among his greatest friends, I find that many people remember him as someone quite different from the man I knew myself. If I say: "Of course, he was so awfully lonely," people who knew him well look at me in amazement, since this view of one who seemed so convivial, so amusing and so light-hearted has never occurred to them—which shows a lack of understanding, because every single action he took, from the time that he had money and the freedom to spend it, made it more and more certain that he would suffer from boredom, loneliness and dissatisfaction with life. But in the nineteen-twenties the sap was still rising, the outside stimuli so great that the picture one finds of him in the newspapers of the day is close to reality and surprisingly like life, seen from the only view the reporters got of him.

Thus:

"Mr. 'Freddie' Lonsdale wandered from guest to guest indulging in his irresistible habit of making each of them believe that it was he or she alone with whom Mr. Lonsdale had longed for years to converse. . . . What a salesman was lost when Mr. Lonsdale became a playwright—though drama has of course, become in his hands a highly marketable commodity."

And Hannen Swaffer:

"He is a charming companion. He tells me lovely stories about marquises and earls—and Michael Arlen. He talks most engagingly about what some knighted actor said about some knighted manager. They love him at the Garrick Club. He always looks so expectant and so surprised. He really enjoys success. Yet it has not made him cocky or superior."

This is a good description of Freddy. He did look expectant and he did look surprised—except when he looked dejected. At this time he and Michael Arlen seem as a pair to have caught the public fancy. They were, of course, great friends, but the newspaper reporters gave their relationship a twist that made them serve almost as a pair of public entertainers, and if one wanted in those days to introduce a note of sophistication, wealth or worldliness into any description or narration, all it was necessary to do was to mention the names of Mr. Lonsdale and Mr. Arlen. Michael Arlen had a gift for self-depreciation and self-accusation which made him very quotable. Writing from Como in 1927, he said:

"There were three people in my hotel who had never heard of me. I saw to it."

And to Freddy after a first night:

"You and I are very good for each other. I convince you that you are not a muck-writer, and you convince me that I am."

They quarrelled a good deal too, and Sir Patrick Hastings quotes an occasion when, having sat up most of one night together drinking and gossiping, they met on the following morning.

"Well, how are you, Michael?" Freddy asked.

"I decline to tell you," Michael replied and stumped away without further speech.

All Freddy's minor eccentricities and most of his business were grist to the newspaper mill. "A mania for changing houses . . ." "Once he begins a play no manager can be certain when he will finish it, though the contracts stipulate delivery time." ". . . understood to have received offer of £10,000 for the film rights of *The Last of Mrs. Cheyney* . . ." "understood to have received offer of £15,000 for film rights of *The Last of Mrs. Cheyney* . . ." "understood to have received offer of £20,000 for film rights of *The Last of Mrs Cheyney* . . ." "dislikes publicity . . ." "has gone to the South of France . . ." "has returned from the South of France . . ." "has gone to Hollywood for six months . . ." "has returned to England after two weeks . . ." "is writing play called *Most of Us Are* . . ." "is writing play called *The Original Profiteers* . . ." "wears white socks . . ." "wears white socks . . ." "wears white socks. . . ." The white socks were a joy to the reporters, but none of them ever realised that they were worn not as an affectation, but from hypochondria. Freddy believed that if one wore a dye next the skin it was bound one day to end in blood-poisoning, gangrene, death. When he wore black socks in the evening he usually had white socks underneath them.

His witticisms were given much space in the newspapers, too. The best of these seems to me to have been his comment, in the days of prohibition in America, on 'near-beer'. Asked his opinion of it, he replied:

"America, if you will allow me to say so, sir, has lost her sense of distance."

And his work was constantly discussed and evaluated. The writer in the *Daily Express* already mentioned as reviewing *The Last of Mrs. Cheyney* in book form continued:

"In the first place Mr. Lonsdale is a master of the dramatic form. He spent two years on this play. There is not a superflous line in the three acts. The lightning speed of the action deprives boredom of any chance to breathe. Not one of the three acts limps or halts. There is dramatic movement and surprise in each of them. But the pace of the action does not kill the characterisation and the dialogue. The dialogue is not only witty, cynical and satirical, but it develops both the characterisation and the action."

He was spoken of as "belonging to the English school that ranges from Sheridan to Wilde," and one of his comedies was referred to as "the most entertaining since *The School for Scandal*". He was not always taken completely seriously and Hannen Swaffer, with some enjoyment, quotes him as saying: "I wrote it to save our daughters", but he was regarded as having great dramatic skill and a miraculous wit.

Then one day in January 1926 the *Daily Express* carried a headline:

LONSDALE PLAY ON PROFITEERS WRITTEN TO
HELP YOUNG ACTOR. NO MORE MANAGERS NEED
APPLY

and continued:

"Mr. Frederick Lonsdale, the most sought-after dramatist in
England, ignoring the offers of half the managers in this
country and America, has written his next play for a young
London actor, so that he can set up in actor-management for
himself."

The young London actor was Ronald Squire and the play *On
Approval*, and I am delighted to be able to reproduce this
quotation at this late date, because it was never absolutely
settled between Freddy and Ronnie who pulled whom out of
the gutter.

The relationship between these two was based on an interesting mixture of appreciation, affection and antagonism. When
they first met, Ronnie was playing small parts with Gerald du
Maurier at Wyndham's Theatre, and playing them with an easy
distinction and natural sense of comedy that immediately
attracted Freddy's attention. Freddy was determined to have
him in *Spring Cleaning*, and both the performance which Ronnie
gave in that play and the reception given him by the public and
the critics justified his judgment. Lonsdale plays were never
easy to cast, and, while one can think of two or three actors who
excelled in parts such as Lord Grenham in *Aren't We All?*,
where what is required is a combination of easy charm and
imperturbable timing, Ronnie has one other quality which
makes him, in my opinion, supreme in such parts as the Duke of
Bristol in *On Approval*, where the comedy arises from the
egotism and impenetrable self-righteousness of the character
played. After the 1933 revival of *On Approval* a critic on the
Sunday Times wrote as follows of Ronnie's performance in the
part of the Duke of Bristol:

"He possesses, too, a quality very rare on the stage—the sense of enormity. He will say something unpardonable with the air of an artist achieving a master stroke, and when he has finished saying it will relapse into the artist's condition of contented exhaustion."

Rarely does a critic hit off so exactly the essence of an actor's art, because Ronnie does, in fact, swoop like a hawk on certain lines, and then relax into a complacent self-satisfaction which is irresistibly funny.

All his life Freddy understood and appreciated all this, and, in return, Ronnie probably had the greatest admiration for Freddy's work of any actor living. He delighted in him. Ronnie is a pessimistic character, never entirely happy, and in after years, when one went to see him in his dressing-room after watching him in some play, one always knew in advance what he would say in reply to congratulations.

"Oh! my dear . . ." with a deprecatory shrug. And then, giving a burlesqued version of some line he had spoken in the play, "Not like Fred's lines. The trouble with Fred's lines is they spoil one for anything else."

He understood Freddy's character, too, to an extent that was given to few people, and he has always had the same joy in observing his acts and tracking down his motives that I have. At the same time he was, even in the early days, insufficiently robust to stand too much of Freddy himself, and his feeling for him has always been a compound of affection, admiration, and heartfelt irritation.

After the success of *The Last of Mrs. Cheyney*, Freddy and Ronnie decided to do *On Approval* together. What this meant was that Freddy himself would put up some of the money for the production, but for the rest it was up to Ronnie to find it. In order therefore to go into actor-management, Ronnie had to find a backer. This he naturally had no difficulty in doing, and it was soon arranged that two brothers who were financiers named Thornton-Smith would put up the money for Ronnie's share of the production. Freddy then began to write the play.

All went smoothly until the play was finished and taken to the Thornton-Smiths. I must now explain that it requires talent to judge a play on a reading. I think it is true to say that all good plays read badly, comedies read worse than other types of play, and that, of all comedies, few give so little idea of their possibilities on the stage as do Lonsdale comedies. Time and again in his plays actors and actresses have been bitterly unhappy in their parts at rehearsal, spoilt the performance on the first night because they had no idea where to wait for the laughs, and then been charmed into an appreciation of the play by the brilliance of the notices they have received for their acting of a part they had believed gave them no scope whatsoever. Ronnie never had to wait for the audiences or the critics to tell him, nor, I think, did A. E. Matthews. But on the first night of *On Approval* the Thornton-Smiths were not there to be told.

They were horrified when they read it. They thought it an unentertaining play about a lot of disagreeable people in whom no audience could be interested, and, since they were splendid business men, they immediately withdrew their offer of backing.

Ronnie arrived at Lowndes Street, and, with a mixture of amusement and despair, told us what had happened.

"They can't see that it's funny!" he said. "That's the trouble with Fred's lines. People don't understand that they're funny. There's the Judas line . . ."

On Approval is a play in which there are only four characters. Of these Richard and Helen, who are sweet and gentle, are in love with Maria and George, Duke of Bristol, who are egotistical and insensitive. The four go together to Maria's house in Scotland, in order that Maria and George may decide whether they care enough for Richard and Helen to marry them. During the time they are there the servants in the house all leave, and it is Richard's job to do the shopping. In order to do this he has to go to the village at the bottom of a long steep hill, and then walk back up it. In the second act he struggles in from the hill, laden with parcels—but he has forgotten to send a telegram for Maria and to bring *The Times* for George. Maria is exceedingly unpleasant to him and then leaves the room.

Duke: If I walked up that hill twice and a woman spoke to me like that, I——

Richard (moving down r.): Well, as you haven't walked up once, mind your own business. She asked me particularly to telegraph for her books and I realise it's most disappointing and I'm terribly sorry.

Duke: You make me sick.

Richard (turns to him): I will make you sick if you're not careful, George. (He goes up back of settee where George is sitting.)

Duke: Helen, I would like you to walk with me. I am anxious to read you my letter to the *Morning Post*.

Richard: If you have any decency you'll go and send that telegram for Maria.

Duke: I? Walk up that hill because Maria wants to read? Don't be funny. There's a book in this house she should read. Do you know what it is?

Richard: No.

Duke: The Bible.

Richard: What do you know about the Bible?

Duke: More than you think I do. It's full of examples of selfish women.

Richard: Any for selfish men?

Duke: Yes. Read about Judas and you'll find he was the type of fellow who was too lazy to bring his friend *The Times*.

This was the line that Ronnie spoke of.

"The type of a fellow . . ." he said, on a rising tone, "they can't see that it's funny." And he gave that inimitable chuckle which endears him to his friends. But on the first night in London he did not chuckle. He spoke the line with petulant and self-congratulatory righteousness, and he stopped the play.

Ronnie, having failed with the Thornton-Smiths, was not finished. He now took the play to Sir Bronson Albery. Sir Bronson, however, also thought it unentertaining, about disagreeable people and unlikely to attract audiences. He refused to touch it.

As far as I can remember, although both Freddy and Ronnie were naturally annoyed at what had happened, particularly as gossip about plays flies round the whole of the theatre world, and none of this made it easy to arrange production, neither of them was in the least shaken in their original opinion of the play. I do remember being in a slight difficulty myself when the matter was discussed, because I had read the play and secretly agreed with the Thornton-Smiths and Sir Bronson Albery. I did not find it unamusing, as they did, but my judgment on a reading of a play has always been bad, and I believed that a play with so trivial and so unreal a plot had very little chance of success. I was of a solemn turn of mind and I did not realise that Freddy's plays never had any merit except in dialogue and construction, by which they stand or fall, and that this, of all his plays, probably showed him at his best and neatest.

At this time Tom Walls had just taken over the Fortune Theatre in Drury Lane. This is a very small theatre, off the beaten track, and not very easy to fill. Tom Walls, a more experienced judge of a play, leapt at the chance of doing *On Approval* when Freddy offered it to him, and poor Ronnie lost his opportunity to set up as an actor-manager.

On Approval was produced at the Fortune Theatre on April 19th, 1927, with Ronald Squire, Ellis Jeffreys, Valerie Taylor and Edmund Breon in the four parts. This theatre, as I have already said, holds comparatively small money. They played to capacity in the first week, and for considerably more than a year the figure for the takings never varied. The play ran for 469 performances.

The critics at this production were nearly unanimous in their praise of the wit and the construction of this play. "It sparkles with brilliant dialogue." "It is the wittiest piece of writing I have listened to for many a long day." "Brilliantly constructed and admirably acted." But *On Approval* did more than please the public and the critics while it was spiced with the spirit of to-day. After a revival in 1933 Mr. James Agate wrote of it in the *Sunday Times* as follows:

"The piece was extremely witty and diverting on its first production six years ago, and it is much too late in the day and too low down in this column to begin proving that time is powerless against true wit and true diversion. But nitwittery is unalterable and it is an authentic sign of nitwittery in playgoers to pretend that sallets have lost their savour because they were salted yesterday. Therefore let all who go to the Strand Theatre laugh with a clear conscience. They will be in better company than mere fashion because this always was and still is a thoroughly good and amusing comedy."

And in 1944, Hugh Beaumont, of H. M. Tennent, Ltd., speaking of the production at the Aldwych with Barry K. Barnes and Diana Churchill which afterwards went on tour, was able to say to a *Daily Sketch* reporter:

"One of the best theatrical money makers of this war is Frederick Lonsdale's fifteen-year-old comedy *On Approval*. On a forty-seven-week tour of the provinces it has taken £50,000."

In New York it was played at the Gaiety Theatre with

Kathleen MacDonell, Violet Kemble Cooper and Hugh Wakefield. Here too it received great praise from the critics. Later it was filmed with Clive Brook, Beatrice Lillie, Roland Culver and Googie Withers. In this film someone other than Freddy seems to be responsible for a dream sequence of great hilarity, but the film as a whole has a high reputation amongst serious film critics. Altogether, this play, for which at first it seemed impossible to find a backer, was one of the two or three most successful Freddy ever wrote.

As a result of Tom Walls's unflinching judgment and fearless behaviour in putting on *On Approval* after its previous history, Freddy gave him his next play, *The High Road*. *The High Road* is a play I never greatly cared for. The situation is the old one of the scion of a noble family who becomes engaged to marry an actress, and the twist on this situation is when the actress's father, sent for by the members of the young man's family in order that they may find out what bribe will induce the girl to call the marriage off, and innocently unaware of their intentions, begs them to do what they can to induce the young man to sacrifice his future happiness in order that his daughter's great career as an actress may not be sacrificed instead. Later the play develops more seriously, and greater and more noble sacrifices are made both by the girl and by the head of the family, the Duke of Warrington, originally sent for to take part in the family councils, but who falls in love with the girl himself. In London this play was acted competently but dully, and this may be the reason why it did not appeal much to me. In any case, the critics gave Freddy almost the best notices of his career, and, produced at the Shaftesbury Theatre in September 1927, the same year as the first production of *On Approval*, *The High Road* ran for 237 performances. It was also very successful in New York, where it was produced a year later by Charles B. Dillingham, and where Mr. Lonsdale remarked at the opening performance that it was better played than it had been in London. In New York it ran for 144 performances.

In these years Freddy spent much of his life on the Atlantic, crossing back and forth to America. The pursers and stewards on the Cunard liners were at least as well known to him as the head waiters of his favourite restaurants. A great deal of this travelling was necessary for the production of plays which appeared almost simultaneously in London and New York, and in 1927 he went for the first time to Hollywood, where he did the film version of *The Last of Mrs. Cheyney*. John Rumsey, his agent in America, who had quickly become very fond of him, but who remarks that at this time he developed "what I considered some bad habits", tells an amusing story of his return from Hollywood on this occasion. Freddy got off the train in New York about ten o'clock in the morning, and handed John, who had gone to meet him, a cheque for $75,000. This was a cheque of Metro-Goldwyn-Mayer drawn on a Hollywood bank.

"I'm leaving on the *Mauretania* at three o'clock this afternoon," Freddy said. "Will you meet me at the boat with $12,500 worth of English money, $12,500 in French money and a draft on London for the other $50,000?"

It takes sixteen days in New York to clear a cheque drawn on a Hollywood bank. John Rumsey, who took rather a pride in accomplishing smoothly the intricacies of Freddy's requests, hesitated to tell him that his own firm was not in a position to advance the sum of $75,000 for sixteen days, and almost immediately found himself alone on the platform with six hours in which to fulfil Freddy's airy behest. When he did, in fact, arrive at the *Mauretania* with the exact sums of money requested, this was received without either comment or approval.

In addition to these necessary journeys across the Atlantic, many more were made as a result of the perpetual momentum by which Freddy escaped through life. John Rumsey, who, it has been seen, complained of the bad habits Freddy developed, used to receive cables from him which read: "Arriving *Mauretania* (or *Majestic*—or *Olympic*). Please meet me."

Sending then for the list of shipping arrivals and consulting his watch, John would often find that he had only about half an hour in which to reach the docks, because Freddy always waited to send off these cables until the boat was in sight of land. On one of these occasions, having arrived in a white heat and only just in time to catch Freddy, he asked him:

"What have you come over for?"

"I'm damned if I know," Freddy replied. "I think I shall go back again."

And he did, in fact return to England on the first boat which left New York harbour.

On another occasion John Rumsey was spared his journey to the docks, because Freddy, having left Southampton with the intention of travelling to Hollywood, got off the boat at Cherbourg and returned to London. This incident caused much excitement in the press.

" 'Why did you come back from Cherbourg instead of going right on to New York?' I asked Freddy Lonsdale yesterday.

" 'Consenting to go was an act of cowardice,' he replied. 'My sudden decision to return was the bravest act of my life. I was going to Hollywood to make money. I came home to find peace.' "

However, questioned a second time, he gave up these histrionics.

"There is nothing more to it than this," he said: "when I set out I fully intended to go to Hollywood, but when I got to Cherbourg I thought I would not."

The second was, I think, the true answer, because at this time Freddy was not really looking for peace. He was simply ex-

tremely spoilt, and one second's tedium would cause him to feel
he would go somewhere more amusing. In his desire to avoid
boredom he subjected himself to none of the ordinary
disciplines which most people never question. Once he asked
me to go with him from London to Liverpool and back by
train in one day, in order to see the Grand National. As I was
living in the country at the time, I stayed the night before the
race at Claridge's, in order to be ready for the early start. In the
morning, as Freddy and I were walking down the platform
towards the carriage in which our seats were booked, he
suddenly stopped and turned to me.

"Do you want to see this race?" he asked.

I scanned his face. I had never really wanted to go and was
there only to please him.

"No," I replied.

"Nor do I," he said. "We'll go back to Claridge's and have a
decent breakfast."

"When I booked the seats," he would have said, if questioned,
"I thought I would like to see the Grand National. As we
walked down the platform, I thought I would not. There was
nothing more to it than that."

And at this time in his life there was very little more to it than
that. When he started on the journey to Hollywood which he
abandoned at Cherbourg, he was probably suffering from an
attack of boredom or liver at Witherslack, and so he and Day
had packed up at a moment's notice and torn off to Southampton. By the time he reached Cherbourg, weighing the charms
of Hollywood against those of Witherslack, he decided in
favour of the latter and simply returned there.

He seemed convinced that it was possible to avoid those
periods when life drops into the doldrums and there is nothing
to do but wait for the breeze to spring up, but he never felt
committed even to his own avoiding action. At the same time

he did have, and this distinguished him from a lunatic, a perfectly sound sense of responsibility in certain directions, he did shoulder these responsibilities, and, when life, which made no exceptions in his case, unexpectedly cornered him, he did behave with reticence and an uncriticisable courage. In the nineteen-twenties, when he was rushing about giving this world-wide exhibition of a charming but spoilt child, he did the only thing that it would have been unforgivable not to do, and only his manner of doing it was characteristically unusual.

Some time in 1927 he wrote to John Rumsey in New York and told him that he wanted the money that was accumulating there to be invested in a trust for my mother. He explained that the income from this trust was to go to her during her lifetime, after which the capital should be equally divided between her three children. He told John that he was to make it absolutely certain that the trust could never be broken either by himself or by my mother. He then said that he would be passing through New York in about two weeks, and that he was most anxious that the deed should be ready for him to sign.

John, out of the kindness of his heart, always performed miracles in order to comply with Freddy's immediate wishes, and he did, in fact, have the deed ready in the specified time. He then heard nothing further from Freddy for nine months.

At the end of this time Freddy cabled his arrival from the boat and the two men later lunched together at the Ritz-Carlton.

"Have you got that trust arranged for me to sign?" Freddy asked at lunch.

John regarded him, as always, with affectionate good humour, and replied that it had been ready for some time.

"Well, that's all right then," Freddy said, "we'll go this afternoon and sign it."

On their way in the taxi to the Guaranty Trust Company of

New York he spoke with happiness of what he was about to do. He had given my mother a house, he told John, and so, now that she would always have an assured income, she would be all right.

Arrived at their destination, he took out a pen.

"Where do I sign?" he asked.

"What!" John said, "aren't you going to read it?"

"No," he replied, "why should I? You've read it, haven't you?"

He then signed on the dotted line, and, as far as I know, never at any time knew the exact provisions of the trust.

When these two men walked out of the office and on to the busy New York street, Freddy turned to John Rumsey and smiled at him. Then he took his hat off his head and dashed it on to the pavement with all the strength of his arm.

"King Lonsdale!" he said, "that's me."

John says that, although this gesture was made as an expression of pleasure, it looked far more like a preliminary to his coat coming off too. In a matter of seconds they were inside a circle of eager New Yorkers waiting for the fight to begin. John seized Freddy's hat and clapped it on to his head. Then, taking his arm, he broke a way through the crowd and hustled King Lonsdale into the nearest taxi.

Two years after this Freddy made another and smaller trust, the income from which was to go to himself during his lifetime and pass on his death to his three children. He also during these years took out a life insurance for a very large sum to be paid on his death or in twenty years.

CHAPTER THIRTEEN

'Foreigners'

Some time in 1926 John Rumsey came to London. He went one evening, soon after his arrival, to Lowndes Street to call on Freddy. He says he was met at the door by Miss Chesher, who, looking rather solemn and moving with ostentatious quiet, showed him into one of the rooms on the ground floor.

"Mr. Lonsdale would like to see you," she said, "but would you mind waiting a little? The doctor is with him."

"But what is the matter?" John asked.

Miss Chesher's reply was a little mysterious.

"We shall know more," she said, "when the doctor has gone."

John waited some time in the downstairs room, and then Miss Chesher re-appeared and conducted him up to the bedroom to visit Freddy. She seemed to know no more of his illness than she had before, and John went quietly and nervously up the stairs, unsure what he would find in the bedroom.

Freddy was sitting straight up in bed, propped by pillows. He was smoking a cigarette, and he greeted John with a quite creditable imitation of Al Woods.

"What is the matter with you?" John asked.

Freddy waved his hand.

"These bloody doctors don't know anything. A specialist is coming at six. Where," he proceeded, "is Archie Selwyn?"

Freddy had a contract with Selwyn for the production of a play, at this time entitled *The League of Nations*. John Rumsey said that he thought Selwyn was in Paris.

"Get hold of him," Freddy said, "and tell him to get a theatre. I'm not going to hang about for the production of this play. It's the best I've ever written. Do you want to hear the story?"

John says, and it is a view that many people share, that Freddy told the story of a play better than anyone he had ever known.

"The play opens," he said, "on board a ship in mid-ocean. A German steward is wiping glasses at a bar. Ronnie Squire will play this German . . ."

He then went on to tell the story of the play. On board the ship at sea there is one representative of each of the great nations of the world and also a Jew. All these people are men, on their way to attend some conference, but later a girl is found who is a stowaway. At the end of the first act the ship is wrecked and the whole company is landed on a desert island. As a result of the actions of the captain of the ship in the first act, there is on the island only one gun; there is also, of course, only one girl. The gun changes hands occasionally, and with it passes complete power and the allegiance of the girl. The play was to be a satire on human folly—on the futility of war and of the human behaviour which leads to it. It was to show also the force of the gun—how all nobility, all intelligence and all rights go down before it. The girl was a dramatic invention designed to keep the audience in their seats, and one which would provide a great part for some actress. In the nineteen-twenties the idea for this play was pointed, but not too pointed; of moment, but not too great moment. Freddy told the story, interpolating much dialogue, and John Rumsey was much excited by it. He went away promising to get hold of Selwyn immediately and saying that he would call on Freddy the next day to enquire after his health.

His mother was with him when he came the next day, and she asked if she might come in to see Freddy, of whom she was very fond.

"You'd better wait," her son replied, "until I find out whether he's fit to see us."

And he left her in the car while he went to ring the doorbell of the house.

The door was opened by Freddy himself, wearing country clothes and carrying a bag of golf clubs over his arm.

"Hello!" he said. "I was expecting my car. I'm just going to Cornwall to stay with Leslie and the children, and to work."

"Don't let me delay you then," John replied, and, after a few minutes conversation between the two of them and Mrs. Rumsey, Freddy drove off in the car, accompanied, John says, by myself.

About a week later Freddy telephoned to the Rumseys' hotel to say that he was back in London and to ask John to go round to see him.

"Did you get some work done?" John asked him when he got there.

Freddy looked surprised.

"Yes, as a matter of fact I did," he said, "I've been working on my new play. You'll like this play very much. Would you like to see what I've done?" And he handed him a pile of paper that lay on a side table.

John Rumsey says that when he first saw this bundle of papers he thought it was a manuscript, but, on closer examination, he saw that the first three or four pages were written on, but that underneath there was simply a stack of blank paper. He looked at the top sheet and he read as follows:

"Act 1

The play opens on board a ship at sea. A German steward is wiping glasses at a bar."

Freddy had completely forgotten that a week before he had told John that the play was nearing completion and had asked him to tell the Selwyns to get a theatre.

During the course of the next six or seven years this play was described and promised to a great many people. Ronnie Squire, who had lived much in Germany in his youth, was under a permanent verbal contract to play the German, and, in spite of his knowledge of Freddy's character, was from time to time induced to believe that the play was ready for production. Gladys Cooper, in management at the Playhouse, had a verbal contract to give it production, although, knowing Freddy very well, she made no actual arrangements. The press referred to the play a great deal under the title *Most of Us Are*.

Then in January 1928 it made the headlines. Sir Alfred Butt had engaged Miss Tallulah Bankhead at a salary of £300 a week to play in Mr. Lonsdale's new play *Foreigners*, and he had spent £12,000 on re-decorating the Globe Theatre for this production. Mr. Lonsdale, however, had not delivered the play.

"Mr. Lonsdale," Sir Alfred Butt told a *Daily Express* reporter, "contracted in writing to deliver the play on or before January 1st. He now writes stating that after working on it for days and weeks he cannot write the play. The consequences are, of course, very serious from a financial point of view, very serious to myself. Here I am left with a theatre and a leading lady on my hands, but no play. In the circumstances, I am now obliged to consider what steps I shall take."

In spite of the ominous note in the last sentence of Sir Alfred Butt's statement, the playwright appeared in London in what seemed a cheerful frame of mind.

"If I can't finish it properly, it's better to say so," he is reported as saying. "It saves them money."

He was to find Sir Alfred in a more truculent mood than his experience had led him to expect, however. The impresario refused to see him or to speak to him.

There is a story told of how Freddy overcame this difficulty and it is supposed to illustrate his cleverness and his charm. Arrived at Sir Alfred's office, he made short work of the posse of secretaries whose duty was to stop him, and walked into Butt's own office. Being met there with angry silence, he picked up a piece of paper and, writing on it, handed it across the desk to Butt.

"You are a gentleman," this paper read, "I am not."

I have never been able to understand why these simple words should so much have charmed Sir Alfred that he decided to forget his anger and forgive the whole thing. I think it more probable that, during the time it took Freddy to write this message, he was reflecting that, in spite of everything, this was still the most successful playwright in England, and that there are easier ways to make money than by suing the bird that lays the golden eggs. In any case, as a result of this interview he came to an agreement with Freddy which resulted soon after in the production of a play called *Canaries Sometimes Sing*.

In America, at about this date, a Mr. Charles Bennett was being congratulated on having a play accepted by Mr. A. Woods after the latter had been forced to abandon the production of Mr. Lonsdale's *Foreigners*. In both countries the excitement very quickly died down and the incident was forgotten, except when it was needed as an illustration of Freddy's careless ways and eccentric temperament. What no one in either country seems to have realised is that when Freddy said that he had worked for days and weeks on the play and he was unable to write it, he spoke the simple truth. The theme of this play interested and excited him more than anything he had ever attempted. He committed himself to managements in the glow of this excitement, but, when faced with the enormous difficulties of giving life to a dozen characters of different nationality, and of writing sustained satirical dialogue on one of the great tragic subjects of the world, he was unable to do it. On this occasion, after much expenditure of spirit, he had succeeded in changing the title to *Foreigners*, but this, apart from a dustbinful of torn paper, was all he had to show for weeks of work. He abandoned *Foreigners* now to write *Canaries Sometimes Sing*.

In *Canaries Sometimes Sing* he repeated the feat of *On Approval* and wrote a play with only four characters. It is not as good a play as *On Approval*, but it is in places extremely funny, and, in the part of Elma, Freddy created his ideal character. Two married couples are thrown together in a country house. Each of the four characters is bored and disillusioned with marriage, and in Ernest (Athole Stewart), the conventional heir to a peerage, married to Elma (Yvonne Arnaud), it seems at first that Anne (Mabel Sealby), the highbrow and pretentious wife of Geoffrey (Ronald Squire), a commercial playwright, has found her ideal partner; while Geoffrey and Elma, both in rebellion against the artificiality of the lives they are forced to live, seem made for each other. Through three acts and many characteristic Lonsdale twists, the two marriages are endangered, first by one pair and then by the other; but in the third act it becomes clear that Geoffrey, though less obviously than Ernest and Anne, is influenced more by convention, hypocrisy and fear than by any nobler or even more attractive emotion. Only Elma, who from the opening of the play has shown herself eccentrically free from regard for the mere rules of manners or morals, proves to be wholly without the meaner virtues, and at the fall of the curtain she leaves the other three on the stage, to

Aren't We All? Ronald Howard and Ronald Squire

FREDDY

go, as she says, in search of another 'co-respondent'. The truth
is that Elma is a tramp, and, as such, she was the darling of Mr.
Lonsdale. She represented all that he cared for in life against a
background of all he disliked. The timbre of Miss Arnaud's
seemingly uncontrollable French squeak, as well as her relish of
the outrageous, added a great deal to this part.

When Freddy arranged with Sir Alfred Butt to do this play,
he reserved a share in it for Ronnie, and this time, in partnership with Butt, Ronnie went into management.

The course of the production was not without incident. Sir
Alfred seems to have been a man who could rather easily be
teased, and at this time Mr. Hannen Swaffer, the famous critic
of the *Daily Express*, had succeeded in teasing him to a point
where he refused him the right of entry to his theatre. Freddy,
on the other hand, was fond of 'Swaff', and, quite apart from
this, he counted, I think, on his approval of his plays. After
Freddy's death in 1953, Mr. Swaffer described how he came to
be present at the first production of *Canaries Sometimes Sing*.

"Lonsdale insisted," he said, "as Sir Alfred Butt, the producing manager, was barring me from the Globe, that I should
attend the 'try-out' of *Canaries Sometimes Sing* in the Theatre
Royal, Birmingham.

" 'That's not Butt's theatre, and so he can't keep you out . . .'
said Freddy, stressing that he wanted my view and no one
else's.

"To oblige him I went to Birmingham, stood by while a
heated argument went on in the lobby between Butt and
Lonsdale as to whether or not I could go in, and then, after the
play, supped with the author and the cast in the Midland
dining-room, while Sir Alfred, who refused to join us, sat all
alone in a corner."

My own recollection of this scene is that, towards the end of
the evening, Sir Alfred did join the group at the author's table

H

in spite of Mr. Swaffer's presence, but whether I am right or wrong, on looking back to the occasion, it does seem to have been a high-spot for Freddy. To have accomplished at one and the same time the pleasures of annoying Sir Alfred, persuading Mr. Swaffer that he could not do without his opinion, and arranging for the finest advance publicity for his play before it reached London must have been a hat-trick such as seldom occurred even to him. Mr. Swaffer wrote as follows:

"Frederick Lonsdale has achieved in *Canaries Sometimes Sing*, produced last night at the Theatre Royal, Birmingham, the distinction of repeating his *On Approval* feat. He has written around four characters a sparkling comedy which has at least twenty witty remarks and a plot the next move in which you could never guess two minutes before. *Canaries Sometimes Sing* is one long surprise . . . will be a great success unless I am more wrong than usual."

Canaries Sometimes Sing was a success. Produced at the Globe Theatre in October 1929, it had a run of 144 performances, and, revived at the Garrick Theatre eighteen years later in 1947, it ran again for over 100 performances. In America, however, it was not successful, and, in spite of Miss Arnaud's presence in the cast, when produced at the Fulton Theatre on October 20th, 1930, it closed after twenty-four performances.

Although this could not have been apparent at the time, *Canaries Sometimes Sing* marked the end of an epoch. In the whole of his life Freddy wrote only one play that had to be counted a failure, and to the end of his life he remained a dramatist who had to be reckoned with, but the enchanted period of enormous output and fabulous success in the theatre was now over. It was to be three years before his next play was produced in London, and this play, *Never Come Back*, was his only London production of a new play in fourteen years. It seems almost unnecessary to seek the reasons for this. The tide which had born him so easily and flung him so far was bound, in the normal course of events, to ebb. In seven years he had written as many comedies, almost as many musical comedies. It would hardly have been surprising if he should have written himself out. In all these plays he had had only one kind of thing to say. It would not have been unexpected if the public, who all this time had listened so rapturously, had got tired of hearing him say it. Both these things may have been in some degree true, but the course of his life after this was affected by the complexities of his nature and his manner of living, and contributed to by many different factors, some external, some internal. In his interior life *Foreigners* was always to loom very large. For ten or twelve years more he wrestled with this play, constantly thinking of it, often speaking of it. During this time when someone asked: "Is Freddy doing any work?" the answer would most often be: "Well . . . he's working on *Foreigners*." It began to be regarded as a stock expression, meaning that he was not working. He was always extremely reticent in failure, and no one during all these years understood that he was frustrated by something other than laziness. From time to time he put the play aside to work more fruitfully on other things, but he always returned to it. It would be wrong to speak of it tragically or to suggest that he was tormented by it. He never understood sufficiently well what he was trying to do or why he found it so difficult to realise that this play lay outside the sphere of his talents. He continued to believe that he had the idea for a very great play, and that in a matter of weeks he would finish it.

CHAPTER FOURTEEN

The Nineteen-Thirties

The nineteen-thirties opened well for Freddy. For some years now the American Motion Picture Studios had been making him offers to go to Hollywood to work on films. Several times he had been on the point of accepting, but, except on the occasion when he went to work on the film of *The Last of Mrs. Cheyney*, he had always backed out at the last moment. In 1930 he signed a contract with Metro-Goldwyn-Mayer, although the London *Evening Standard* reported him as saying: "I shall voluntarily give up my contract if I find my services unsatisfactory." At this time Metro-Goldwyn-Mayer also signed a contract with Maureen Stanley, by which she was to work as a screen adviser on matters pertaining to English life.

This was in the very early days of the talking picture. The technique of this new medium, which could be seen to have a great future, was not yet clearly defined, and no film of much interest had as yet been made. Al Jolson had been well received by certain sections of the public, but no film had been shown that made it quite certain that here was a powerful rival to the live theatre. When it was known that Frederick Lonsdale, renowned for his dialogue and his tight construction in the theatre, but not for themes of wide appeal or strong action, was at work on a film in which the Englishman, Ronald Colman, was to star, much interest was aroused.

182

"If this film," wrote the New York correspondent of *The Times*, "with its extensive use of dialogue, proves popular, it may have an effect on the future of talking films, since the prevailing opinion at the moment is that the trend of the future will be away from dialogue in the direction of increased action."

In *The Devil to Pay* Freddy wrote a light-hearted comedy of two young lovers. He seemed to take easily to the new medium, and he produced a script which was simpler and less sophisticated than his comedies for the theatre, but dramatically stronger and of a higher quality of wit than anything he had written for the musical comedy stage. He worked quite happily in the studio during the shooting of the film, and it owed a good deal to his presence there during production. Ronald Colman gave a fine comedy performance in the leading role, and Loretta Young, previously unknown to the public, made her name in this film. Miss Myrna Loy also played a small part, and this is a fact of interest, because *The Devil to Pay* was the precursor of many light comedies in which she was later to please the public all over the world.

The Devil to Pay deserved a place in history. It had a great success both in New York and in London, and in both cities the period of its showing was extended again and again. The press took it seriously, and in London I can remember that leading members of the theatrical profession were for the first time seriously apprehensive of the effect the talking picture might have on the future of the theatre. It would be too much to say that *The Devil to Pay* was the first film to demonstrate the possibilities of this new medium, but it was the first of a long line of comedies which did much to consolidate the popularity of the talking picture.

Following this success Freddy returned to Hollywood and repeated his achievement with a film called *Lovers Courageous*.

The story of this film was, slightly dramatised, what he believed
to be the story of his own life. In one scene the young man
stole meat from a butcher to take home to his starving wife in
exactly the manner of Herne Hill.

It seemed now that Freddy was financially a made man. The
money that can be made in the theatre by even the most successful of dramatists is a mere pittance compared to what can be
made by a successful writer in Hollywood. By staying in the
film studios Freddy could have earned a princely salary in any of
the following ways. He could have continued to write original
films. He could have worked as a kind of consultant on other
people's films, altering a scene here, interpolating dialogue
there. Thirdly, provided that he had stayed in Hollywood, it
seems probable that he could have continued to earn enormous
sums without writing a line. Many were the great names
which at this time appeared on the pay-roll of the American
film studios in consequence of their owners putting in a weekly
appearance to draw a cheque.

Freddy returned to England.

"I could never live in a film city," he went on record as
saying, "because there is no conversation."

In London in 1932 he produced the last comedy which was to
appear under his name for many years to come, *Never Come
Back*. This play, starring Raymond Massey and Adrianne
Allen, was only moderately successful, and is, I think, one of the
least good of his plays. For me its chief interest in retrospect is
that it was at this time that Freddy and I made friends with
Adrianne Allen. Adrianne is extraordinarily gregarious and
loves to entertain on a large scale, but she remains devotedly
loyal to her friends. In New York and London for the rest of
his life Freddy was at home in her house.

After the production of *Never Come Back*, in terms both of his
potentiality as a film writer or as a writer for the theatre, the

first of which was very great although the second may have
been diminishing, and in terms of any settled order which might
have made for happiness, Freddy threw his life away. It is
necessary to consider why he should have done this.

In the first place he was much too rich. During the whole of
his life he was said to dislike work. This was not entirely true,
because it can never be true for someone with a gift which
needs expression, but he could be distracted from working by
almost anything under the sun. His great output during the
nineteen-twenties can only be accounted for by assuming that
every writer has a period of maximum productivity and that
this coincided in his case with his period of maximum
popularity, so that he was constantly under the pressure of
outside stimulation. Now, having passed out of the phase
where his talent flowed unaided, he could only have continued
to work by the discipline of the grindstone; and this was a
discipline which, unless whetted by the scourge of poverty, was
not for him.

This is the simple explanation of why at this time Freddy
almost ceased to write altogether. I think in fact his situation
was more complex. In youth people write as best they may.
They write for money, or for fame, but chiefly because they
must. When in middle age the candid vigour of youth begins
to fail, there is great danger from a kind of scrupulosity which,
to a lightweight talent, can be lethal. "The more books we
read, the sooner we perceive that the only function of a writer
is to produce a masterpiece. No other task is of any consequence." The more I consider it, the more I believe that the
only chance most writers have to produce a masterpiece is to
pray for deliverance from this vanity of vanities, this self-
conscious and ungodly squeamishness.

The meticulous mood was one that was almost certain to
have occurred to Freddy in the exhaustion which must inevit-

ably have followed his great productive phase, but it impinged on his mind, or so I think, with added sharpness because of his external circumstances.

When Freddy first made friends with the Stanleys, he moved into a circle of people who were basically serious in principle and serious in thought. The two families of Stanley and Stewart had for generations appeared at the centre and peak of English public life. Holding positions amongst the highest in the land, they had for centuries counted it their duty as well as their main interest to partake in the government of the country and, while from time to time they showed themselves as fallible as most men, they believed in the honour of their position and the obligations of their privileges. Their interests lay in the circumstances and the manipulation of power, and this still remained true in a generation which scoffed at too open an avowal of lofty intentions or professions.

It happens to many people to move into a circle of new acquaintance who appear to exist on a plane of thought or morals higher than that previously encountered; and it is normally counted as good. Whether it was so in the case of a little Jersey playwright is uncertain.

In the theatre the business of entertainment is taken seriously. It is regarded both as an honourable vocation and as the proper occupation by which both the more and the less talented members of this profession earn their daily bread. Its value is seldom questioned. At any dinner table for members of the theatrical profession the topic of conversation will be the theatre. At Knowsley, Mount Stewart, even at Witherslack, where Freddy dined, a topic of conversation quite usually and quite unpretentiously discussed was nothing less than the administration of the world. From these Olympian heights the business of entertainment can seem a trivial affair, belonging essentially to the lighter side of life. Only as a vehicle for great art, for a masterpiece, does it assume a place among the higher activities of mankind. If Freddy had continued to live in the theatre he might or might not have found themes for his plays from the circumstances of his daily life, but he would certainly have remained convinced of the importance of the gifts with which he had been born. If he was corrupted at this time, and I think he was, it was not by money, rank or power, but, in all innocence, by precept and example, to serious-mindedness.

In any case, the only play he tried to write at that time was *Foreigners*. Only in this play, which took for its theme the great tragedy of modern life, and, for the subject of satire, the wilful futility of the human race, which quarrels its way to annihilation while covered by a gun, could he find a subject which matched his present mood. And although, one day in the future, he was to finish with *Foreigners*, he never lost the passionate interest in international politics which, because of his distorted views, was so much to alter his life, and which he acquired at this time.

In 1933 he took a house in Wilton Place in London and I shared it with him. He seemed very unhappy at this time. I was not sufficiently in his confidence to know why this should be so, but I am convinced it had nothing to do with his inability to write or his career as a playwright. Some other, more strongly felt disturbance of his inner life kept him tense and nervous, and this may have been the greatest barrier of all to creative work. In any case, his despair was such that his impatience, never well controlled, exploded two or three times every day like a bombshell and nothing I or Miss Chesher or Day could do was ever right. The house we had was very charming and ideally suited to two people living separate lives, because it was tall and narrow with a suite of rooms on every floor. Soon after we moved into it someone told him that it had a history of short tenancies, and was believed to be haunted, not by any explicit ghost, but by unhappiness. I knew then that it

H*

was only a matter of time before we all moved out again, and, this, after spending without restriction on the house we meant to make our home, we duly did within the year.

And now his eccentricities, in particular his wanderings round the globe, began to take on a quality of desperation. Undisciplined and unstable, he had until now appeared to be chasing happiness around the world in an artless but perfectly harmless fashion. Nowadays it began to be apparent that he himself was chased. He used, right through the nineteen-thirties, to go frequently to visit Jersey. These trips would be planned with the intention of working there, and he would travel with Day and his car and with all arrangements made for a six-weeks stay. He had a great friend, Reginald Biddle, a fellow Jerseyman, who held a high position on the Southampton Docks, and his travels were usually arranged through him. Mr. Biddle says that Miss Chesher would telephone to him, always on the actual day that Freddy wanted to travel, and in an apologetic voice would say:

"Mr. Biddle, you will know what I am going to say. Mr. Lonsdale has just decided to go to Jersey tonight. He wants a *cabin de luxe* for himself, a cabin for Day and space for his car on tonight's boat. He also hopes that you and your wife will dine with him at the South-Western, before he sails."

Freddy would drive to Southampton, dine with the Biddles, when he would be in excellent form and most amusing, depart for Jersey, and be back in Southampton within three days. On one of these occasions the Biddles were unable to dine with him, in spite of much pressure from him to do so. The following morning Mr. Biddle asked his assistant whether Freddy had gone off all right.

"No," the man replied, "he didn't."

"He didn't? What happened?"

Freddy had embarked his car late in the evening, gone to his cabin, and Day had started to unpack. Then, shortly before the boat sailed, he had given orders to Day to re-pack, had his car disembarked and driven back to London. One dinner in his own company had sent him tearing through the night away from solitude.

He had always suffered from the peculiarity that he could not be alone. In the days when he lived at home, it was not at all unusual to come in in the evening and find him talking to the cook, to a housemaid or to anyone else who had passed his door. Later in life his great popularity with the servants in the hotels in which he stayed was partly accounted for by the fact that late at night, his guests having departed, rather than go to bed alone he would sit up talking to the hall porter, the liftman or the waiter on his floor. He knew the lives of almost everyone he came in contact with, because the most ordinary little history, the most commonplace views, could be for him a shield against the boredom of his own thoughts. The most important part of Day's job, of Miss Chesher's work, was to talk to Freddy. If Day could have replaced the Biddles in the dining-room of the South-Western Hotel, Freddy might have gone to Jersey that night. Having dined alone, he had provoked the mood which in any case would have come upon him within two days in Jersey.

But the inability to be alone was not the only thing that caused this perpetual motion, for which it is impossible adequately to account, and which now became a mania. One of the things that I have always found it difficult to explain is, given that he did not keep yachts or racehorses or gamble on the Stock Exchange, how he managed to get through the enormous sums he had earned in all these years in what seems now such a comparatively short space of time. He had, it is true, expenses which, given the present level of income tax, no writer could nowadays sustain. Having made my mother a permanent settlement, he never expected her to live on the income from it, and he kept up a big house with many servants for her and her children, providing cars for us to drive, horses when we wanted to ride, and everything else my mother convinced him was necessary to our welfare. But when one comes to try in earnest to account for his expenditure, it is apparent that he spent in unnecessary travel the equivalent of several thousand pounds a year.

John Rumsey told me once that in 1936 he received one of Freddy's laconic cables: "Meet me *Olympic*." Arrived on the docks, he asked him the usual question:

"What has brought you over here?"

"I'm going to Hollywood," Freddy replied, "to write a motion-picture treatment of Melchior Lengyel's story *Angel* for Ernst Lubitsch. Marlene Dietrich is to play in it. What are the fees?"

"What are the fees?" John Rumsey said in amazement. "You mean to tell me you've come all this way without an agreement?"

"I've left it to you," he replied, and he then went on to say that he was leaving for Hollywood the next afternoon at two-thirty.

John agreed to see him off at the station the following afternoon, and in the meantime to get something arranged. He then got in touch with Paramount, for whom Mr. Lubitsch was making the picture, to be informed that, while Paramount was financing the cost of the picture, the employment of actors, writers, etc., was entirely in the hands of Mr. Lubitsch. He tried to find Mr. Lubitsch in California, but he was told that he was out on location and inaccessible. Finding it impossible to make the arrangement himself, he now telephoned to Mr. Leland Hayward, an agent who worked in Los Angeles, and asked him to conduct negotiations out there.

The next afternoon, when he arrived at the station, Freddy came striding down the platform to meet him.

"Is there a good doctor in Chicago?" he asked, without preliminary greeting. Chicago was the first stop of the train, sixteen hours hence. He said later that he disliked living in hotels, and asked John to get hold of Mr. or Mrs. Walter Wanger and ask if he could stay with them.

John afterwards learned that Freddy had been met at Pasadena by Mr. Lubitsch, Mr. Hayward, the agent, and Mr. Walter Wanger. He also heard from Mr. Hayward that Mr. Lubitsch had agreed to pay Freddy $5,000 a week, with a guarantee of seven weeks or a total of $35,000. Mr. Rumsey's office subsequently received a cheque for $250, his share of the commission, two weeks running.

In the third week his accountant came in to him and said:

"There is something odd about the cheque from Mr. Hayward for Mr. Lonsdale's fees. This week's is only half the usual amount."

John told him not to worry; Mr. Hayward would certainly have an explanation.

Three or four days later John Rumsey was lunching at the '21' Restaurant in New York, when Mr. Hayward walked in. Seeing John sitting in a corner, Hayward went over to him.

"What did he say to you when he went through?" he asked.

"What did who say to who?"

"Freddy."

John Rumsey started.

"Is Freddy in New York?" he asked.

"Freddy went through New York on his way to London more than a week ago."

The two men looked at each other for a moment.

"What happened?" John asked.

"Nobody knows. After a couple of weeks he asked Lubitsch

if he could move over to his house. Lubitsch said: 'Yes, of course,' and he moved over there. On the Wednesday of the third week Lubitsch came into his house about six-thirty in the evening to find a note from Freddy saying he was very sorry he had been forced to return to London."

No more detailed explanation of Freddy's reasons for throwing up $5,000 a week was ever given to anyone.

It would be wrong, however, to suggest that at this time in his life he was a harassed or unhappy man. After we moved out of Wilton Place he recovered his spirits, he had an enormous number of friends, plenty of money, and he lived in a world in which it was still possible to pass the day amusingly without working. It was only that it began to be apparent that the exceptional measures he had always taken against boredom might now be producing something worse. Like an old and indulged roué, it seemed he might have missed the recipe for happiness, while finding pleasure ever and ever more difficult to achieve.

He is reported all over the world: sitting beside Lord Castlerosse on a terrace at Cannes, while the latter wrote his Sunday article, and asking: "What the devil can you find to write about?"; in the Garrick Club, replying convincingly to the question when he would produce another play: "September 9th"; in Phœnix with Lord Castlerosse and Lord Beaverbrook, refusing to dress as a cowboy, and with them again in Palm Springs; on the racecourse, winning an enormous fortune on Windsor Lad; again and again in London, giving an early date for the production of his next play.

The only productive work he did was on the film *Don Juan* for Alexander Korda, and the fact that he delivered this script and worked on the production of the film was probably a tribute to the personality of Korda himself. Freddy was always enchanted by Korda. During the course of his life he

met only two or three people in whom characteristics he
delighted in had been exaggerated by success until they were so
extreme as to be almost artificial—like a stage rather than a real-
life conception of a quality. Korda was one of these. As other
people enjoy this kind of presentation on the stage, Freddy
enjoyed it in real life; and he became adept in artlessly feeding
the conversation to produce the kind of rejoinder he was
angling for. He admired, for instance, ruthlessness—although
he was never merely ruthless himself—but above all he found it
endlessly, exquisitely funny. What tickled his humour was not,
of course, the results of ruthlessness, but the arrogance in the
assumption of it, and the amusement he got from this was
immeasurably heightened when the quality was masked by an
innocent, bewildered self-righteousness. To Korda belonged,
in addition to his many other endearing qualities, an accented
rendering of English; so that Freddy, who had no ear and was a
bad mimic, had the extra pleasure of delivering his account of
the latest Kordaism in an unlikely but not unpleasing imitation
of what he took to be Korda's voice. People who have great
power, the rulers of an empire, do not always receive the
normal meed of genuine affection. Freddy, whose vagrant and
thoughtless nature prevented him from having calculated hopes
of anyone, loved Korda, and, in return, I have always understood that Korda was extremely fond of him. The film of *Don
Juan* was the only work they did together, but their friendship
survived this one occasion unscathed.

During the production of this film, the B.B.C. broadcast a
half-hour programme that was intended to allow the public to
participate in the actual shooting of it. A press correspondent's
report of this broadcast is interesting for the light it throws on
Freddy.

"Frederick Lonsdale, author of the scenario, was the only
subject of an interview who made no attempt to be casually

conversational, but delivered his very witty speech without pretence, in the best Lonsdale manner—than which there is no better. His contribution was easily the high-spot. He was alone, too, in giving the plain unaffected English pronunciation to the name Don Juan. For that I salute him. The others all tried unsuccessfully to pronounce the name in Spanish."

And so the nineteen-thirties passed, largely spent in pleasure and in travelling about. And life, which takes a very exact revenge, wore on. Most of us pay as we go; Freddy, like some famous, spoiled beauty, defaulted constantly; so that only perennial youth, untarnished success, or early death could have saved him from the inevitable loneliness, the disappointment, and the bewildered sense of the futility of all things with which he finally paid. Unannounced, the preliminary moves were already being made, and the debts would now be levied.

Freddy had for years sacrificed everything to independence, to the right to do as he liked. Not being entirely inhuman, he had, however, felt the need for some sphere which was more than any other his own, where he felt and was a familiar, some place which, if only a shadowed representation, had the atmosphere of what other men call home. This he had found not in any one place, but amongst the circle of people who were the friends of the Stanleys. For years and years all his journeys had ended here. Maureen was the undoubted leader of this circle, the person who had given what was in reality a group of overlapping entities a definition. At this time she began, unknown to anyone, to suffer from a tearing, galloping tuberculosis which, in only a few years, was to cause her tragic death. She became exceedingly difficult—restless, feverish, destructive and inconsiderate. For a long time Freddy behaved exceedingly well, summoning up reserves of patience and affection which one could not have believed he had. But it was soon apparent that these two temperaments now could only

harm each other, and when he realised that neither he nor
anyone else could help her, he threw off this whole life that for
so many years had meant so much to him, as though it had
never existed. This left him very much alone.

During the last months of this tortured friendship something also happened in the theatre, something about which few
details have ever been told by the circle of people concerned
with it, but which I have always believed to be important. The
facts which were generally known were these. In 1937 Hugh
Beaumont of H. M. Tennent Ltd. put a play of Freddy's into
rehearsal. The cast he engaged included Laurence Olivier,
Hugh Williams and Harry Andrews, Edna Best, Irene Browne
and Ann Todd; a cast, one would imagine, which might have
ensured the success of any play. Two or three days after
rehearsals began it was announced through the newspapers that
the play had been withdrawn and would not now be performed.
No reason was given. It was rumoured that there had been a
row between Freddy and one of the leading actors. Hugh
Beaumont was reputed to have said: "Freddy behaved
marvellously." Years later in a letter Freddy said of Beaumont:
"He once behaved with great understanding when he need not
have." At the time he said almost nothing, was very quiet and
very smooth, but he told my mother that one of the leading
actors had thought the play old-fashioned, and soon afterwards
he announced his intention of going to live in America.

"There is nothing here for me," he said, "I have no friends.
Most of the people I cared for have died. [There was some
truth in this; one or two of his greatest friends had died
recently.] The theatre is finished. There are people I like in
America and it's the place of the future. I shall go and live
there."

All this might have happened in any case. His great friendship with the Stanleys had ended, he had long given up going

regularly to the Garrick Club, and it was true he had many friends in America. But, although he was a natural escaper, he was also a natural fighter, and I do not believe he would have withdrawn this play so quickly or so easily except in response to some humiliation, nor do I think it possible to understand his character or his behaviour in later life without some discussion of what happened then.

There was only one thing that could have affected him deeply. He would not have been easily disturbed by critical opinions of the construction or the dialogue of the play. He had the certainty of the artist, and he would either have agreed with criticisms and made the necessary alterations, or disagreed with and ignored them. The only thing that could explain his complete and unexpected withdrawal of the play was the sudden surfacing, as the result of hot temper, of the word 'old-fashioned'.

This word vibrates in the world of entertainment as much with romantic horror as with any certain meaning or actual peril. (An old star, an aged beauty, an old-fashioned playwright —these are themes for tragedy.) No one could, nevertheless, at this point of his career have expected Freddy to be morbidly responsive to it. He still stood at the head of his profession. He had had no play produced for some years, but his success was legendary. He was at that time the most formidable of all the personalities concerned with this production. The criticism must have seemed then to be both relatively unimportant and fair comment.

Nor do I think that professionally he ever was unduly sensitive. He knew that one cannot please everyone and he preferred to please himself. But personally this word touched him very deeply, for he would not accept old age. He was at this time in his late fifties, but he looked years younger, vivid and debonair. He had friends and acquaintances of every age, but the circle of his intimates and particularly of his women friends consisted largely of people twenty years younger than himself. The life that he had chosen to lead depended on energy, talent, and really in the last resort on an up-to-date smartness, on being in the swim.

Some people do miraculously remain youthful long after their time, and this encourages them to think of themselves as exceptional, able to defy the laws of nature. Freddy was one of these; and he was never going to accept deference in place of equality, or prefer maturity to vitality. The word old-fashioned as applied to himself was to him not admissible, not something he was prepared publicly to discuss. Rather than discuss it, he withdrew the play.

In his private life he was able, in some measure, to maintain this attitude until he died, although I do not think it necessarily added to his happiness to do so. He was, in fact, completely individual—not conditioned by any particular generation or environment. Those people who loved him did so for his oddities, his natural charm, his affectionate generosity, and his extraordinarily vivid personality; while those people who loved him very much did so because he combined these qualities with a touching vulnerability, a doomed expectancy. No one ever took him very seriously, regarded his views as important, or his lead as one to follow; but to the very end, when his mood was spontaneous and unaffected, he could still enchant the very young with the very old.

But from now on in his professional life he was to be shadowed a little by this word; and this, I think, was bad luck, because, as with his personality, so with his plays, the concept of fashion had so little to do with him.

Few people, I suppose, are likely to give much weight to anything I have to say about Freddy's plays. Nevertheless, I have done something recently which probably no one else has

ever done. I have read with great care every comedy he ever
wrote. From beginning to end, I can see no sign of
deterioration, nor any sign of fashion, new or old. Of the last
three plays he wrote, *The Way Things Go* seems to me a better
play than *Spring Cleaning*, *But for the Grace of God* far better than
The Fake, and *Another Love Story*, although as a play I never
cared for it much, is infinitely funnier to read to-day than is *The
High Road*. None of these plays suggest to me any trend of
thought or ideal of behaviour sufficiently alive to become dated,
except in the sense that everything written almost throughout
history has suddenly dated in the last twenty years. Freddy's
style was the same in 1908 as it was in 1923 and as it remained
until 1950.

As a playwright he had only one talent, the talent for comedy.
In general there are only two kinds of comedy, the comedy that
arises out of poking fun at the superior being, and its opposite,
the comedy that arises out of the disability and absurdity of the
ordinary man. In the great tradition of English dramatic
comedy, Freddy poked fun at the superior being. This, of
course, he had to do. For him the comic concept was always
'this ass', never the pathetic figure of fun, battling unavailingly
against the winds of chance. He was not moved to smile at a
man who slipped on a banana skin, because, although he had
great wit, he had no sense of humour. And so, like almost
every writer of his kind of comedy before him, he dressed his
characters as members of the aristocratic classes, not because he
loved a lord, but because he wished them to be recognised for
what they were. In the nineteen-twenties the actual superiority
of the well-born was, almost for the first time in history, being
seriously questioned, and in poking fun at these Freddy was,
quite accidentally, perfectly up to date. In every other sense his
comedy—I do not refer here to its quality but to its kind—was
timeless. But in the nineteen-thirties the critics, who, it should

always be remembered, have to say something, began to say, in effect, that if Freddy was going to continue to poke fun at superior beings, he ought to dress them as commissars. And this was disconcerting, for there was this much truth in the reiterated suggestion that Mr. Lonsdale, who had been new-fashioned in the style of the previous five hundred years, was now old-fashioned: he did not know anything at all about commissars and he had no idea how they were dressed. The public, who at this time began to love royalty as never before in history, and who do not give up easily their ingrained pre-ferences, continued to enjoy the fun, and it was in the early nineteen-forties that Hugh Beaumont said that *On Approval* was one of the greatest of the war-time moneymakers, while *The Last of Mrs. Cheyney* drew audiences in London; and it was in the late 'forties and early 'fifties that *Another Love Story, But for the Grace of God*, and *The Way Things Go* played successfully in England. But the box-office, although it sustains and nourishes, can never quite offset the effect of the written word, and in every Lonsdale production from now on not merely the author but the management and the actors waited appre-hensively for the expected malediction.

When Freddy went to America he was immediately reported as "back at work" with Sam Goldwyn. But I can find no evidence that he did any work in the film studios at this time. It was also said that he was going to do a play called *Once Is Enough* with Gilbert Miller, and from time to time it was rumoured that Miller was having great difficulty in getting a third act. This was true. It took him nearly a year to induce Freddy to finish the play, and there is a story told of the two of them which may be apocryphal but is very characteristic. Freddy complained to Gilbert Miller that he was unable to work in New York, and so it was arranged that he should go and stay on the Millers' farm in the country. Gilbert took him there himself, and, as he was busy, left him there for a week or so by himself. When Gilbert returned he was met by Freddy, wreathed in smiles and with a manuscript in his hands.

"Gilbert," he said, "I have news for you. I have finished the third act."

Mr. Miller, immensely pleased, stepped forward to take the manuscript from him, but Freddy drew back.

"The only difficulty is," he said, "that you can't have it, because it's no good."

And with a quick gesture he tore the manuscript in two and threw it into the wastepaper-basket. Later, after Miller had left the room in despair and disgust, Freddy retrieved this pile of paper from the basket and joined the pieces together again in his hand. Only one sheet, the top one, had been written on. The rest was simply blank paper.

Freddy did in the end finish the play, however, and he must have been in London at this time, because he is reported in the *Evening Standard* as follows:

"As successive attempts to complete *Half a Loaf* (*Once Is Enough*) have failed, his manner has become increasingly effacing, his gestures increasingly subdued.

"Last night, however, there was a bold light in his eyes, a tendency to histrionic effect in the movement of his hands, the angle of his cigar; a faint but unmistakable suggestion of the old star about to make his entrance, after long absence, on a familiar stage.

"And when I later met Mr. Gilbert Miller he supplied the solution. Miller believes that *Half a Loaf*, which is about the married life of a duchess, is the best play Lonsdale has ever written. He says the lines will still be thought models of polished wit fifty years hence. If that means that Lonsdale need not trouble to write another play for fifty years the eminent but reluctant dramatist will be a happy man."

The play, which is indeed about the married life of a duchess, is, in my opinion, amongst Freddy's best. It opened in Washington, where Mrs. Eleanor Roosevelt wrote of it as follows:

"Last night I went to see Ina Claire in *Once Is Enough*. Sometimes we are fortunate enough to see plays in Washington before they are given in New York. While the first few performances of a new play are not as a rule the best, still I enjoyed every minute of the show last night. I thought the acting excellent and the show most entertaining.

"Yesterday the immaculate playwright enjoyed the signal honour of being received by President Roosevelt."

But, after the first night in New York, Richard Watts, jr., seems to have summed up the opinion of the critics in the *New York Herald Tribune*:

"It is consoling," he wrote, "to know that in a changing, chaotic world, England and Frederick Lonsdale stand undismayed and unaltered. House parties given by the Duke and Duchess of Hampshire are still attended by Reggie, Archie, Hugo and Johnny and their wives, who talk amusingly about adultery and practice it a bit. . . . There is, as I have suggested, something comforting about a play like *Once Is Enough*. Mr. Lonsdale may be surprised to hear it but his work possesses a certain lavender charm."

In spite of this notice and others in the same vein, it appeared that the American public still had some interest in duchesses, and *Once Is Enough* ran at the Henry Miller Theatre for 105 performances.

CHAPTER FIFTEEN

America

Freddy spent the whole of the Second World War in America, and before one can describe his life there it is necessary to discuss his attitude to war. In America it was believed, and in England it was rumoured, that he was hostile to Britain and pro-German. To anyone who knew him at all well this is the most absurd idea. Apart from any other consideration, the few people that he loved best in the world were in England, and, in spite of all his oddities and his lonely, lunatic travelling, Freddy was not inhuman. In moments of crisis he had the same feelings of affection and protection for his family as any other man; he never, in the whole course of his life, shirked his responsibilities towards them nor was he indifferent to any circumstances which might affect them. How could he, then, be hostile to Britain when his whole family resided there, and when their very lives must be endangered by anything that endangered England?

At the outbreak of war he wrote me the most agonised letter, at the end of which he said:

"As for Jack, I dare not even ask after him. I am so afraid he is now a bloody soldier."

And all through the war he wrote regularly to all of us letters that were filled with his misery and unhappiness and his tortured thoughts for us.

"I get worried about Jack," he wrote my mother, "I hope that he is all right. Poor Frankie, she must be out of her mind. And there is nothing that one can do, and I wish so much there was.

"If you remember, I was always a first-class worrier, I have an obsession about the damn thing, and no power to stop it, and in addition despair comes so easily to me, consequently I am never happy."

And again:

"I have a feeling our way to the grave is decided for us. . . . I live only because I haven't the courage to die, but, if in my sleep I were to leave you all, don't fuss because there cannot be more unhappiness in Heaven or Hell than there is here. Miserable as one would have been I wish I had not been here when it all started. Obviously one would not have had the courage to leave and I should have been miserable, but I don't believe to this extent. . . . All the time I think of you all, how you are and whether I will ever see you again. By the time you receive this you will know whether Russia has beaten Germany or the opposite. If those German bastards beat the Russians oh what a lovely long war it might easily be. But my hourly prayer is that it won't be, and the God damned thing will soon be over and you will be happy again."

And:

"I have given up reading the papers and listening to the wireless, both drive one insane, so it is better to hear the news from some damn talkative person, and there are many who are quick to tell it to you."

He worried hysterically over letters from England. It was impossible to find out whether the letters we wrote him never reached him or whether he noticed only the days when he received nothing, forgetting the letters that had arrived. My mother wrote continuously, although my sisters and I found it difficult, and did not write often enough. He continually complained that Miss Chesher did not write to him, and this was hard to believe, since she was here in England with little else to do for him.

"I write to Miss Chesher and ask her things that are worrying me, but under no circumstances will she answer. If she is unable to write, perhaps you will get from her what I want and write it to me yourself, but it is very important for me to know."

And:

"Chesher writes me very kindly once in six months, and I asked her particularly to be certain to write regularly. It may be that she put on that flying cap she used to wear and they seized her for the Air Force and she is now a prisoner in Germany. She might be a prisoner anywhere for all the use she is to me."

Miss Chesher, questioned by us, said she wrote to him regularly every week, when she had news and when she had not, but all through the war his sad complaints went on, and it was impossible to know what to believe.

He himself wrote with surprising regularity, although he always bewailed that he had nothing to say.

"How very dull I have become. In a letter I wrote to Frankie I complained bitterly about myself, but there seems to be little to be done about it. I spend my life in the same sort of condition that a man is when Joe Louis has knocked his damned head off."

"Now what shall I say? It is awfully difficult to know what to say. You can't, if you have a grain of humour, say I hope you are having a good time and don't overeat because it's bad for you.

"In the next room there is a bloody woman playing the wireless so loudly that they can hear it in Chicago. I hope she doesn't fall down and break her blasted neck. It would be so sad. And if she did, I expect the next woman would play it louder. Life is like that. . . . To you only I confess that I am the dullest of them all. And it seems only a few days ago that I was a jolly boy, the life and soul of the party."

And yet he managed to convince people who did not know him well that he was pro-German.

Freddy's attitude could be summed up by saying that he hated war and believed it to be unnecessary. This statement could never pass unchallenged, because it suggests that his feeling was unusual or that he hated war more than other people do. I believe this to be the truth. Freddy's hatred of war was greater and more intensely felt than is the hatred of the sane; and I think it is necessary to understand this if one is to understand how he came to adopt the views he held and to behave as he did throughout the whole course of the war.

Why then did he hate it so much? It would be absurd to pretend that he had that kind of suffering nature that feels the pain of mankind as though it were his own, and it is quite clear that in inconvenience he suffered less than most Englishmen, while, although he lived in fear of tragedy amongst the few people he loved, he did not actually experience it.

Freddy in war was a misfit—there was no place for him, nothing he could do. He was nearly sixty at this time, and I do not refer to the fact that during the whole of his life he would have been only a liability as a fighting man. There was nothing else he could do instead, and, much worse than this, he could not, except hysterically, even feel the proper things. He was not inspired to hatred of the enemy by the thought of other men's sufferings, nor sufficiently to pity for other people's sorrows. He was aware of these limitations of his nature, and they made him very uncomfortable, much more uncomfortable than did the restrictions on his movements, from which he suffered very much, or the loss of self-importance, which he disliked extremely.

One further thing contributed to his misery. He believed himself to be a coward. This was very curious, because I knew him very well and I do not believe he was. If I had been forced to go into some situation knowing in advance that some physical danger might present itself, I would just as soon have had Freddy for my companion as anyone else I ever knew. His immediate reactions were always steady and, as far as I could ever see, quick and courageous. In anticipation of any event, however, his imagination proved him to himself a coward, and his life was such that he had never received full reassurance on this matter by having it put to the test. This should never be forgotten in any judgment of his angry attitude to war.

He was always quite open about his fears, and it was from him one knew of them. Lord Grantley, in his book of memoirs, tells a story of Freddy at this time.

"Are you going back to England?" someone asked him.

"No," he replied, "I'm going to Japan."

"To Japan! But why Japan?"

"Because," he is said to have replied, "they're so yellow they'll never notice me."

Freddy was without the ordinary resignation of most men. All his life he had been accustomed to doing what he liked, and he had shown the most extraordinary tenacity in avoiding what he disliked. Since he most particularly disliked war, he thought that with a little good will and the most moderate intelligence it could have been averted.

It might be thought that, feeling as he did, his hatred would have been directed against Germany, who provoked the war, but this was too simple a reaction for him. He was constitutionally incapable of joining with the majority opinion at any moment, and, in any case, he reserved his greatest contempt

not for villains, but for fools. He believed that Hitler was a
very evil man, but he believed, and his long personal acquaintance with the politicians of England only strengthened him in
his opinions, that the Allied statesmen were fools.

This opinion led him one stage further. If they were fools,
they were in terrible danger of losing the war. What criminal
incompetence, then, what arrogance, what complacent folly not
to have somehow staved the whole thing off. He was greatly
sustained in these views by his friendship with Mr. Joseph
Kennedy and Mr. Lindbergh, both of whom sincerely believed
that Germany was too strong and would not be beaten. The
only English statesman for whom he had any regard was Mr.
Chamberlain, his greatest hatred he reserved for Mr. Churchill.
I do not think he ever did Mr. Churchill the injustice of
believing that he would have lifted one finger to achieve his
great position through war, but he believed him to be a warrior
by nature, and that consequently, the great position having
been achieved, it brought many satisfactions with it. And this,
in the circumstances, having regard to the folly, the "damned
stupidity" of the whole thing, was too much.

So that, while it is absolutely untrue to say that Freddy was
hostile to Britain, it is unfortunately only too true that he was
bitterly, insanely hostile to Britain's leaders. He began to
believe, too, that for years and years he had warned them in
private where their actions were leading, and that they had
wilfully, contemptuously, ignored his advice.

"Poor Frankie," he wrote to my mother, "and so damned
undeserved. I can see that fatuous S—— complacently ridicul-
ing me when I ventured to tell him these things would happen."

In England my sisters and I knew all these things about him,
but for a long time we were unable to attach any importance to
them. We expected him to make himself very unpopular,
because in war-time people cannot stand this kind of thing. We

were very glad ourselves that he was not in England with us, and we could well have understood it if his friends had found him simply too tiresome to be borne. What we found impossible to believe was that anyone could take his rantings seriously.

"There is a belief here," he wrote my mother once, "that the Pope and the President are having one more try for peace. But that will only inflame Mr. Churchill and Mr. Duff Cooper to further rage. Mr. Churchill is the boy who told the world that not a German would be allowed to remain in Norway. Mr. Cooper is the gent who informed the world that the Germans would not be left alone until they had had their what-you-call-its cut out. I hope to God he doesn't find his own missing one morning. A bright lot of boys, I am thinking. And just the type to fight cads like Hitler and Goering. We are very lucky to have them. . . . I wish, of course, they knew P——. He would tell them about the days when men fought like gentlemen, and they would have a grand time and ignore that bounder Hitler even more than they are doing already."

Used all our lives to this kind of thing, we only thanked God we did not have to listen to it most of the day; then we passed an hour that might otherwise have been tedious wondering what Mr. Duff Cooper could possibly have said that could be construed in this way. The only thing that never occurred to us was that anyone living could possibly see poor Freddy as a menace. We were wrong.

One thing we overlooked was the tenacity with which he continued to shout his opinions long after even he must have realised they could achieve nothing but his unpopularity. He conceived that he had a duty to urge the world to a saner view, continually to challenge the universally-held opinion that we fought because we must, and to press on all occasions his own distorted but long-considered belief that we fought because we were wholly and viciously misled.

There were two reasons why he would not change his behaviour. In the first place, he had a genuine toughness, in relation to public opinion, of the kind that is almost necessary in a politician. This quality is well illustrated by a story told to me by another Englishman who was in America at the same time. This man, who was in America through circumstances not in his control, received one day a letter from England signed by several of his friends which accused him in bitter terms of a cowardly evasion of his duty in not returning home. Very much upset, he took the letter with him and called on Freddy.

Freddy, dressed in a dressing-gown, with his white scarf tucked into it, read the letter.

"Achh!" he said, when he had finished it, "you don't want to bother with this kind of thing."

"But I do, Freddy," his friend replied, "that's just what I do want to do. And I want you to read the letter I've written in reply."

Freddy took the second letter and read this carefully too.

"Brilliant," he remarked, "ab-so-lutely brilliant." And he threw both letters into the fire. "Never bother with that kind of thing," he repeated.

The second motive for his behaviour is more obscure. I was talking to Binkie (Hugh) Beaumont about it once.

"It's obstinacy," he said, "obstinacy and pride. These kind of characters are always the same. They wake up one morning and find that, quite unintentionally, they have dug a little pit for themselves. Then they can't *rest* till they've turned it into a grave."

Freddy never rested until he had made himself very much disliked.

Lord Beaverbrook told me that once, when he was in America during the war, he was lunching at the Colony Restaurant with Mrs. Harriman and Mrs. Robert Sherwood, when Freddy walked in.

"I rose," he said, "and I greeted him with all that enthusiasm I felt in my heart for him."

As he returned to his table he noticed that both his companions had their heads turned away.

"You are wrong to speak to that man," they said to him, "he is seriously hostile to England."

What was even more surprising was the rage of a famous fellow-countryman. Freddy and Noël Coward had never been very close friends, but they had for long been on perfectly good terms both in the theatre and elsewhere. Freddy had a respectful jealousy of Noël which kept his tongue wagging, but this is not unusual in the theatre, and is unlikely to have been very much misunderstood. But Noël was enormously patriotic, and no one who has read Clare Luce's account of her meeting with him at Lisbon when, in the late summer of 1940, she was on her way to America from an isolated, defenceless and apparently finished England, and Noël was journeying in the opposite direction, could ever doubt the sincerity of his feeling at this time. And so, to him, one Englishman in any part of the globe behaving badly was an outrage, an injury to everything he held most dear. If he had given one second's objective thought to Freddy, he must have realised that his views on politics or war were without interest or importance, and were derived from a pathetic emotional disturbance. But he was unable to do this. And so Noël, who had been on friendly terms with Freddy most of his life, and who almost certainly knows something about turning little pits into graves, viewed him with an unwavering and unforgiving hatred which persisted long after the war.

As a result of his feeling, and, of course, of the tales of other Englishmen who travelled between the two countries during the war, Freddy was believed here as well as in America, by people who knew and understood him as well as by those who did not know him, to be hostile to England and pro-German, and he was disliked accordingly.

I have dealt with this matter at some length, because it was for so long taken seriously, and I have quoted from his letters in the hope of showing what his real feelings were. It is necessary to say now that the letters give a wholly untrue picture of his life at this time. Freddy, in spite of all this, had plenty of friends in America and was, as always, much beloved by a large circle of intimates. I think none of his friends, reading these letters that give a picture of despair, of a man "when Joe Louis has knocked his damned head off", could possibly recognise Freddy in them. They were written in moments of solitude when his volatile nature sank to its depths and they were not insincere. But when Freddy emerged from his flat to go and visit Simon Elwes or Andrea Behrens, soon to become Andrea Cowdin, to call on Dr. Devol or to lunch in a party at the Colony Restaurant, his spirits shot up vertically, and no one could then have thought that he believed "there cannot be more unhappiness in Heaven or Hell than there is here."

During all of his life Freddy had only about half a dozen friends who thoroughly understood him, and who, understanding, doted on him. Of these were Simon Elwes and Andrea Cowdin. Freddy, aware of their approval, and elated by their response to his eccentricities, was always at his best with them. Simon had a studio in New York, and here Freddy used to appear on most mornings. As Simon painted the portrait of some reserved and dignified patron, he would hear Freddy's voice outside the door.

"Mr. Walker," it said to Simon's man, "some black velvet."

I

And then, oblivious of the personality of the sitter, Freddy would appear, followed by the man with his drink, and discourse to Simon on whatever occupied his mind at the moment.

In Andrea they both took a protective interest which showed itself in unexpected ways. Soon after this she married Cheever Cowdin, but at this time she had not yet made up her mind, and Freddy and Simon had not made theirs up either. Everywhere that Andrea went with Cheever, she would hear their booming voices, and presently they would appear, to take up a watching position at a table on the other side of the restaurant. When Cheever married Andrea he must have felt that he had married these two clowns as well. At any rate he accepted them as part of his life, and in no time had entered the brotherhood, so that Andrea found herself with three impossible companions.

Freddy stayed constantly with the Cowdins at their house in California, on their farm in the country, and he visited them regularly at their flat in New York. He had for years had no home of his own, but he had a facility for settling down in other people's houses. The servants always adored him, connived with him in treating certain rooms in the house as though they were his own, and treated his wishes almost as though they were the instructions of his hosts. When he went too far, which he often did, he had his own methods of making peace with his friends. The following story, which Andrea told me once, is typical.

Andrea asked him one day to go to the theatre with herself and Cheever and another woman on the following evening, and Freddy said he would. The following morning Cheever told Andrea that he had a very important speech to make the next day and no time to work on it until the evening, so that he would not after all be able to go to the theatre. At the same time the telephone rang, and Freddy's voice said that he also would be unable to go to the theatre.

"I shall come to dinner with you, though," he said.

"Oh no, you won't!" Andrea replied. "We shall have to have dinner early, and if you can't come to the theatre you can't come to dinner."

She then invited two other men to accompany her, and ordered dinner for four.

That evening when Andrea and her guests were halfway through dinner, she heard Freddy's voice in the hall of her flat.

"Lay an extra place, like a good chap," he said to the butler, "I shall be dining here."

Then he pranced in, kissed Andrea and her woman friend, and sat down to dinner, and, although Andrea gave him black looks, she could not easily have turned him out. When she was leaving for the theatre, however, she spoke to Freddy.

"You're to go now," she said, "Cheever has some very important work to do, and you're not to hang around here talking to him."

That night, when she returned from the theatre, she walked into her drawing-room. Cheever sat on a sofa at one end of the room, Freddy on another sofa at the other end. It was evident that they had passed the evening well.

"You had better go to bed now," Andrea said to Cheever coldly, but controlling her anger, "you have got this long day to-morrow. And you, Freddy, you'd better go at once."

She then went into her own bedroom.

"After half an hour," she said to me when she told me the story, "it was obvious that no one was going to go anywhere. So I went back to the sitting-room. And by now I was furious."

When Cheever rose from the sofa to make some dignified reply to Andrea's attack, he tripped over a low table directly in front of him and he fell flat on his face. He picked himself up again immediately, but the heart had gone out of him, and Freddy was left to face Andrea's wrath alone. He rose quickly and slid by Andrea to the door. As he passed her he ducked a little. He thought she was going to hit him.

The next morning Cheever telephoned Freddy from his office.

"You'd better stay away for a while," he said. "Andrea says she won't have you in the flat—and she means it."

"I'll be in there before you are," Freddy replied.

Just before luncheon that morning, Andrea, who had been out, returned to the flat. In the hall there was a very small chair, a purely decorative piece of furniture, never meant for use. Sitting on this was Freddy, his hat on his head and his white scarf tucked into a bulky overcoat. He looked wistful and dejected and very uncomfortable, and he said nothing. Andrea burst out laughing.

*   *   *   *

Freddy had two plays produced in New York during the war. The first of these was *Foreigners*, produced at the Belasco Theatre on December 5th, 1939. When we heard in England that Freddy had at last really finished this play and that it was in rehearsal it seemed too good to be true. I had been certain he could never write it, and it seemed that, now that the tragedy was on, he could hardly have chosen a more unpropitious moment to finish it. But I believed so much in his magic that I thought he had probably done by instinct what he could never have achieved by thought.

On the morning of December 6th, 1939, John Anderson wrote in the New York *Journal-American*:

"When Mr. Lonsdale turned up season before last, after seven years of absence, with one of those gay nothing comedies called *Once Is Enough*, most of us asked rudely in the reviews the next day where on earth he had been all that time, old boy, old boy. . . . So what has Mr. Lonsdale done? He has written a little play, I hope as a sly joke on the critics, called *Foreigners*, which opened at the Belasco last night, and I wish to be among the first to beg Mr. Lonsdale to give us another comedy about the sex life of the Duke and Duchess of Hampshire. The Critics' Circle, which doesn't know when it is well off, is probably a bad collaborator for any playwright, and I trust that Mr. L. pays no further attention to it."

Richard Lockeridge in the *New York Sun* wrote more soberly:

"The dialogue is smooth and expert, and Mr. Lonsdale says several wise things in jest. Now and then he turns an epigram with admirable dexterity, and laughter ripples through the play. But I am afraid *Foreigners* is a little ineffectual in face of the problems which seem to have called it forth."

On this occasion, too, the public deserted Freddy. On December 9th, after seven performances, the play was withdrawn. *Foreigners*, which had occupied Freddy's mind for the best part of fourteen years, was the only resounding flop he ever had.

How great a blow this was to him, no one will ever know. He was completely reticent when things went wrong for him, and he never mentioned this play again, until, in the last two years of his life, he began to believe that he should re-write it.

On October 12th, 1943, Louis Lotito produced *Another Love Story* at the Fulton Theatre with a cast which included Roland Young. On October 13th, 1943, the New York papers did what they could to kill it.

"The bad news this morning from 46th Street," wrote Lewis Nichols in the *New York Times*, "is that Mr. (Roland) Young still does not have a play that fits him like a glove, and there is further bad news in that Mr. Lonsdale has not, himself, been up to his higher standard."

And Robert Coleman in the New York *Daily Mirror*:

"*Another Love Story* is as thin as the roast beef in a drug-store sandwich, and about as filling."

Having read these and other bad notices, Freddy was found wandering that afternoon in Central Park by someone connected with the Fulton Theatre. Asked what he was doing, he replied:

"I am considering my future. This makes things very difficult for me."

"What makes things difficult for you?"

Freddy looked at his friend in silence.

"Haven't you heard," the other man asked, "we are nearly sold out for tonight and the advance booking is good?"

And in fact *Another Love Story*, although it was never a smashing success, picked up and ran for 103 performances.

It was at this time that a rumour began to circulate about Freddy, which was repeated on and off until his death, and which is believed by many people until this day. It was that he was completely broke, in debt and living, by his wits and his charm, on his friends. Since this was at all times completely untrue, and since it throws a light on his character and on his life which distorts it entirely, I am going to deal with it at some length here.

As from the time that he wrote *The Maid of the Mountains* he was never at any time in his life short of ready money or unable to pay his way. In his early life he had been careless about money, but, as from the time that he cleared the debt he owed to Mr. Conran and settled his debts in Jersey, he developed an integrity about money which is quite unusual. He was extremely generous and, in the ordinary affairs of life, he paid with a great deal more alacrity than do most people, he lent to his friends or even acquaintances enormous sums, many of which were not paid back, and when he died suddenly and unexpectedly he owed only current debts, and these were under £200. Not only this, he developed a stickling kind of character about money. He never owed money himself, he never artlessly forgot to pay his way, and he never forgave other people who did.

In 1937 he settled £30,000 on my mother and he gave her a house. Until about a year before his death he never expected her to live on the income from this trust, and he regularly settled the debts of his family and paid unexpected expenses, such as illness.

In 1939 he invested a further £14,000 on himself, and, with the income from this and the fees he received from repertory and amateur rights, he could never in any circumstances have had less than about £1,200 a year. If he had ever been forced to live on this, he would, in any sense that was relevant to his manner of living, indeed have been broke. But he earned an enormous fortune in the 'twenties and 'thirties, and some time in the 'forties a life insurance matured to the value of £50,000. If he had invested this sum when he received it, he could never have had less than about £3,000 a year. But he did not. He simply put it in the bank and drew from it, and, at the rate at which he used it, it was good for only about ten years. Nevertheless, there was no time at which he did not earn some new money, and when he died he left behind him, some of it in banks, but most of it in traveller's cheques in a safe in Paris, £7,000. The rub at the end of his life, the thing that worried both him and his friends, was this. By the standard on which he lived, he had at the time of his death only about another eighteen months to go. Since no one could imagine how he could live on £1,200 a year, since he appeared to have lost the capacity to do so, what could his future possibly hold if he lived to a great old age? His luck held out, and this question was never answered.

There were several reasons why people who did not know him well might have believed in all seriousness and without

malice that Freddy was short of money. The most important of
these was that he constantly said he was. This is a thing I cannot
account for. Since he had no intention of borrowing money, or
even of taking advantage in small ways of the generosity of his
friends, I can think of no reason why he should so often have
spoken as though he was in serious difficulties. The only thing I
can suggest is this. Freddy's careless attitude to money in his
youth may have been the result of a conviction that he could
always make it. Consequently it was without importance. At
this time in his life he could no longer write a play that could
certainly satisfy the critics, and in spite of the fact that no play of
his, except *Foreigners*, failed to make money, he seldom had the
satisfaction of a smash hit. All his plays were a little uneasy—at
rehearsals the management and cast were a trifle apprehensive,
the critics were, at the best, divided, and the play usually
trembled between success and failure for the first few weeks,
until, by word of mouth, it built up into a success. Perhaps, to
Freddy, the concrete feel of money lay in his ability to earn it.
When this became insecure, he felt destitute.

In any case, there is no doubt that he constantly spoke as
though he was immediately worried about money. When he
told the story of the meeting in Central Park, after the critics
had reviled *Another Love Story*, he always said that at this time he
had no money in the world, and that his thoughts had been of
how he was going to live.

Given that he himself provided such a reasonable basis for
the rumour that he was in serious trouble, there were several
things about his method of living that supported it. In all his
life Freddy always gravitated towards the very rich. When
people own sums so vast that money becomes one of the
irrelevancies of life, they live rather differently from other
people. People with eighteen bedrooms in their house do not
consider who is sleeping in them; nor, if there are regularly a

dozen people for meals, do they in their minds' eye present each
of these with the bill. If hospitality of this kind is to be
repaid, it must be done in other ways at other times. There was
something a little feudal in Freddy's attitude to money, and this
was enhanced by the fact that he was so generous by nature he
never needed to fear himself in other people's debt. Nor was
his accounting strictly done. Freddy did more than his fair
share of entertaining all through his life, but he did not
necessarily entertain exactly those people who entertained him.
As I have said before, where money is so overwhelming as to be
unimportant, meticulous rules of payment are not kept.

In addition to the fact that Freddy's behaviour in relation to
money was always the behaviour of the very rich, his own
pecularities, once some misunderstanding had arisen, lent much
colour to a picture that he was living on his friends. When he
spoke to the butler in some rich house in Los Angeles as though
he himself employed him, to a casual onlooker it often appeared
that he was a more or less permanent inmate of the house. No
one who did not know him well could be expected to guess that
he had arrived from New York only a few days before, would
leave again soon and unexpectedly, at a cost in travel which
would have supported a large household for weeks, while in
New York the expenses of his own flat and servant were
permanently maintained.

I have dealt with this matter at so much length because there is
no doubt that it was often misunderstood, both by people who
did not know Freddy well and even by his friends. More than
one rich man drew Freddy aside at this time and said to him:

"Look, Freddy, if you are in trouble, you can draw on me for
any sum you want."

And in order to understand the latter part of Freddy's life it is
absolutely essential to know that Freddy had such a savage
independence that he could never have been beholden to anyone

for anything. It was this which made one so unhappy about
him towards the end of his life when one feared that he was
nearing the time when he would indeed be short of money.
There were very many people who would willingly have looked
after him, should this ever have become necessary, but I have no
hesitation in saying that he would have died rather than accept
charity from anyone once it was outside his power to pay it
back. And there is no doubt at all that in his last years he
worried feverishly and constantly about money, and in this
way contributed to the belief that he was without it. He had
every reason to worry, but the reason was at no time immediate.

During the whole of the war and for some years afterwards
he had a flat in New York and a servant who looked after him,
and I think he spent most of his time in New York. He was,
however, often in Los Angeles, and there seem to have been
periods when he stayed there for months at a time. He stayed
much of the time with the Cowdins in their house in Tortuoso
Way; he also stayed at times with Cary Grant. On April 7th,
1943, he wrote from Hollywood to his great friend, Dr. Devol,
as follows:

"Mr. Lonsdale presents his compliments to Dr. Edmond
Devol, and would like to inform him that Mr. L. is feeling very
old but behaving very young. Mr. L. would be very grateful if
the eminent physician would send him a few Vitamin Z tablets
which might make him feel very young and behave very old.
Mr. L. also has much pleasure in informing the eminent
physician that he has sold his play, and although the medical
profession are not concerned with money, but only the
happiness of their patients, it will be fun for the doctor to
receive a cheque from Mr. L. one morning soon.

"Mr. L. has pains round the heart, and when out of bed
cannot keep awake, but when in bed cannot sleep. The whole
thing Mr. L. feels is very queer."

Edmond though English and correct should have read Edmund.

And in December 1943 he wrote to him again from the same address.

"It has rained ever since I arrived. It is a noisy and un-attractive place when the rain is with us. The shining sun makes one forget. The only comfort I can offer myself is—we all have to be somewhere. I still wonder always why I am in the place I am . . .

"You may have gathered from this letter that I am not quite the man you visit occasionally. And you are right. I am not. I am, it is my firm belief, in greater need of His Eminence (Samuel Trexler) than I am of you. And I wonder if he can really be of any service to me."

Between the writing of these two letters Freddy had been for a long time in New York. At this time if he would have stayed in Hollywood, and if he would have made the smallest attempt at disciplined work, he could still have made a great deal of money in the film studios. It is said that he often went to Hollywood on contract, but that these contracts were always broken by his hasty return to New York.

"You know what Freddy was," people say, "no one ever seemed to mind when he broke his contract."

In 1947, after he had been again in England but returned to Hollywood, I received the following letter from Mr. Paul Hollister, whom, unfortunately, I have never met:

"RKO RADIO PICTURES INC.
"R.K.O. Building,
New York.
October 13th, 1947.

"DEAR FRANKIE,
"Probably before this note reaches you it will have been

anticipated by a badgered outrider of our acquaintance. I did not know that he was going to England. I never know where he is going. All I know is that he was raving about you, that he said you were coming to America in January. I said I would write to you to tell you about the customs of our country, and he said Do That.

"I don't know why I ever undertook the task. I know almost none of the customs of our country. Lonsdale knows them all, and he has a great gift of distortion, so you require no poor power of guidance from me . . .

"Lonsdale then gave me your address. That was great fun. Wotton-Under-Edge, indeed. Sharehold-on-Margin. Want to know how to make expenses? Just collect fifty or a hundred such addresses right off the notepaper of your friends, bring them here and place them with a publisher for a book. Maybe somebody draws pictures for it, maybe not. Intrinsically they are funny. Wotton-under-Edge, Peek-over-Transom. Truman-under-Pressure. Lonsdale-under-Cloud.

"For that, indeed, is where Lonsdale sits, for not telling that he was going abroad. He sits there most of the time as a mettrafekt. Under a cloud surrounded by little dog-eared volumes of Wilde, Winter, Pinero, Shaw from which he nibbles and nibbles. Washed down in Ovaltine, diluted with J. Cheever Gilbey's Best Gin.

"Believe it or not, we shall miss Lonsdale. We love Lonsdale, and I will be damned if I know why. Perhaps it is his stubborn uniformity in a changing world. Perhaps it is because he is a Black Republican disguised as a Commie. Never mind why. He is habit forming. You can't pass Lonsdale without dropping in for just one more—and usually emerging with an abraded shinbone.

"But there is a consolation in his absence. For the calendar indicates that he will probably be bringing you back with him.

That is good. We shall have a crimson carpet unrolled for you. Carol will receive you with good food, drink, talk and affection. Andrea will provide you with all this and pomp as well—and will no doubt assemble the Lords and Ladies Eric, Cedric, Waffle, Muffle, Mewee, Mimi, Kits, Gloria, Shirley and Card-sharp so as to offset your nostalgia. Cheever will tell you stories, and a buck gets you a grand that you will never hear the last of them. The January weather will stink. But the Old Gal down the harbour will flourish her torch to you with a special signal of welcome.

"That's all I intended to say, anyhow, except to tell Lonsdale that he ought to be more taciturn about his plans.

"Yours faithfully,

"Paul Hollister."

I approved of the "Black Republican disguised as a Com-mie". It always seemed to me that Freddy was most at home in America. The Americans had a sharp understanding of his character combined with a rich enjoyment of his eccentricities which few people in England ever had.

CHAPTER SIXTEEN

The Last Years

When Freddy came over to England after the war, we thought at first that he had hardly changed at all. His face was a little thicker, but his hair was as fair and plentiful as ever, and he himself as gay and as odd as before. He stayed only a short time and then went back to America. It was when he returned again and I saw more of him that I realised that he had in fact changed a good deal.

The first thing that I noticed was that he seemed to have developed a manner, a kind of front for himself. This was never used when one was alone with him, or when he was with people he knew well and who amused him, but it appeared very often in ordinary life.

In his book *Stage by Stage*, Peter Daubeny gives the following description of Freddy, whom he met for the first time in 1945.

"He is a difficult, paradoxical fellow—almost the embodiment of his own paradoxical dialogue. His great friend, Cary Grant, once described him to me as 'maddening but irresistible.' He is both cynical and sentimental, states of emotion which are, I suppose, complementary to each other. He is of course witty, yet it is generally wit of a rather old-fashioned, considered, and contrived and rehearsed kind: he is not often addicted to the spontaneous sally, as when one day I asked him if he liked New York. He turned to observe some

workmen, glorying in the infernal racket of their pneumatic
drills: 'I would,' he said, 'if they'd finish it.' "

To anyone who knew Freddy as a young man, or to anyone
who knew him very well and met him only in the intimacy of
his own room, this would not seem a good description of him.
He was much more spontaneous than this, often cross and
cranky, but never mannered, witty when he felt like it, but in an
inconsequent, unexpected, and not a considered way. But it
was a very good description of him as he now appeared in
public, or even alone with us, when he was trying to amuse. I
was interested immediately in this manner, and I wondered
what it was there to hide. Before attempting to account for it, I
must, however, record two other changes. With his intimates
he was much sweeter-tempered, much less intolerant, and much
more anxious to please. He seemed even a little dependent on
one, an entirely new conception. With other people, and most
particularly in the theatre, he was much worse-tempered, much
more intolerant, almost impossible to please.

As he drew older, the 'manner' appeared more and more
often, until it was, except on rare occasions, Freddy himself. I
believe it to have covered boredom; a detached and almost
complete disappointment with life. People no longer amused
him, no longer struck sparks off his wit, neither interested nor
entertained him. He could never be alone, and he had arranged
his life so that he depended entirely on people; he could not
avoid them. But I believe that when he said in one breath:
"There are so few people I care for," and in the next: "My dear
fellow! My dear fellow!" that there was no real inconsistency.
The tragedy of his later years was that he could not do without
people, but, with very few exceptions, he got no satisfaction
from them. The manner was a method of keeping going, a
contrived response to situations which induced no real response.

His sweeter temper with his family was, I think, because, the world having disappointed him, he turned now to love, to the homely things that keep men anchored in the world. It was difficult for us to adjust to this new mood. My sisters and I had always been frightened of Freddy, frightened a little of his quick temper, but frightened much more of his quick tongue. We had been brought up not to be bores, to be corrected by wounding witticisms, to be very unsure of today's reception of any conduct or remark. We did not easily realise that now he was much less critical, quite easily pleased, and above all anxious for equality in his relationship with us. My sister, Mavis Bennet, was living in London, and when he came there he liked her to be permanently at his beck and call.

In the theatre Freddy developed a reputation for an unpredictable and senseless temper. He had three new plays produced in London towards the end of the war and after it. *Another Love Story* was done during the war and he was not here for the rehearsals. *But for the Grace of God* was done by Peter Daubeny, and Mr. Daubeny had the grace to hero-worship him, and, as a consequence, managed him much better than anyone else. But during the production of *The Way Things Go*, and again with the revival of *Aren't We All?*, he was like a tormenting wind blowing through the theatre, driving people hither and thither for no apparent reason, scorching the skin of contentment, and tumbling the production to pieces with blasts of motiveless rage. It was very difficult to understand.

When he came back to the English theatre he found it altered considerably. Gone were the nonchalant, airy manners, the Garrick Club procedure. Everything was much more serious, much less debonair, and suspiciously intelligent. It was not utterly unreasonable to be critical of some of the changes. England had developed during the war some of the finest acting ever to be seen on the stage, but it was true to say that her leading actors seldom appeared in a dinner jacket or a tweed suit, that they seemed uneasy outside a costume. And it was not certainly wrong to infer that, because of this peculiarity, they were killing the contemporary genius stone dead. During his later years Freddy only found two new things to admire in the London theatre: one was the plays of William Douglas-Home, the other, when he came to rehearse *The Way Things Go*, was the acting of Miss Glynis Johns.

So when he went into a theatre, he went in a suspicious and slightly apprehensive mood. He circled round young actors, his new manner well to the fore—who knew which of them might be a potential genius, which, given the opportunity, would put the black words on him, before departing to render Shakespeare?—and every now and then he let out screams of rage. His temper was partly a result of his natural reactions, but partly, I think, deliberate. Freddy knew that on the whole people loathe the humiliation of a row, and will not provoke someone who is fearlessly willing to cause one. And so he built for himself a terrifying personality, one far better never scratched.

Another Love Story was done in November 1944 by Linnitt and Dunfee in conjunction with H.M. Tennent, and, in fact, Hugh Beaumont was responsible for the production. At this time in the war it was not easy to cast plays, and *Another Love Story* suffered a little, not from bad acting, but from personalities who were miscast. It opened in Manchester and Liverpool before London and in both these cities it was extremely well received, breaking all records at the Manchester Opera House by playing to £4,000 for eight performances. In London the critics were divided in their opinion.

"Several performances of brilliance and charm," one critic wrote "and dialogue rich in sparkling and stinging wit adorn *Another Love Story*, Frederick Lonsdale's new comedy at the Phœnix Theatre."

And the critic of the *Manchester Guardian* wrote:

". . . and all with the deftest sense of the theatre and to our constant merriment and sustained interest. And all, it may be added without grossness or offence, and that in spite of a bedroom scene of quite unusual implications and comic subtlety. Peace to the ancients, but our new Restoration comedy has prettier manners than the old—even, perhaps, a hint that, if the social deluge should follow, it would not be undeserved."

But the *Daily Telegraph* said:

"At his best Mr. Frederick Lonsdale is a dramatist with a magic touch. He has a superb sense of the theatre which gives his dialogue—even when it is merely tricky and smart—the iridescence of wit. *The Last of Mrs. Cheyney* showed him and is still showing him at his best. *Another Love Story* at the Phœnix shows him far below that standard."

And *The Times'* judgment of the play was given in much the same terms.

Another Love Story was successful, however, and, after its record-breaking start in the provinces, ran for 173 performances at the Phœnix Theatre in London.

So when Freddy came to London, he came as a still successful playwright, and when Mr. Daubeny went to New York to try to get a play from him, he went in a hero-worshipping mood. This succeeded very well with Freddy, who wrote a play for him, a play he might otherwise not have written.

"He was, I think," Mr. Daubeny says in his book "vaguely flattered by the directness of my approach, perhaps even touched by my having travelled so far to seek a play from him. At all events, far from snubbing me, he later confessed that indeed he did have an embryonic idea in his mind. If necessary, he added, warming to the thought, he could begin to work upon it straight away.

" 'I never work out anything in advance!' (untrue) 'I just write a couple of pages every day, and see what happens. If you really want me to write a play why not drop in every morning at ten o'clock, and I will read you what I've written. And now, let's talk about something else . . .'

"And, for the rest of luncheon, he talked evocatively of the great days, in the London of the 'twenties, when the opening of a new Lonsdale comedy was an event of far greater importance than for instance an unsuccessful *putsch* in Munich by the ridiculous band of cranks who called themselves National Socialists. He conjured up for me the ghosts of Maureen Stanley and of Jean Norton, of Valentine Castlerosse and of Evelyn FitzGerald. He asked with nostalgic affection for news of such friends of his as Helen FitzGerald and Max Beaverbrook; did I know how Hugh and Foxie Sefton were prospering?

"I called upon him the next morning at ten o'clock, and continued to do so for many mornings. He would talk, talk brilliantly of anything but the work on hand, of plans for the future, and how he would never again write about Dukes. His *Last of Mrs. Cheyney*, his *On Approval*, his *High Road* had surfeited the public with Dukes. As the public had never met a Duke, he said, they once had thought that Dukes really talked like that in real life. Now they didn't care any longer how Dukes talked. Dukes, he added, are finished, as finished as infidelity; in future he would write about ordinary people or about perverts. A page or two at a time, he delivered to me the script of what subsequently came to be played under the title *But for the Grace of God*. I found that a Duke, an infidelity and a pervert were alike present in it.

"Mr. Daubeny had the usual difficulty about the third act.

"I was compelled to sail home with one scene of it missing. 'Don't worry, old boy,' Freddie Lonsdale would say, brushing aside my fears: 'it will be on the next boat. I'll give it to Billy

Rootes to bring over. He's flying next week.' As it turned out, the lacking pages reached me by post some two months later."

When Mr. Daubeny got back to London he suffered some shocks.

"Lonsdale plays never read well"; he says, "there is a vast disparity between the effect of his lines when read and when spoken. This had mattered little in the great days; it was enough that they were lines by Lonsdale and that they would inevitably be spoken by a Gerald du Maurier or a Ronald Squire. But in 1946 it mattered a great deal. On every hand they said that Lonsdale was finished, belonging to a hopelessly outmoded past, and when anyone overcame his first prejudices enough to read the play he politely tore it to shreds."

Mr. Daubeny was probably not aware that even in the great days *On Approval* had been hawked all round London before a management had been found to put it on.

He then had difficulty with the casting.

"It was almost impossible," he says, "to find any young player with a sense of aristocratic style."

So he was very much pleased when Freddy arrived.

"I went down to Southampton to meet him; it was a great comfort to encounter again the red face, the inevitable white socks and white muffler, and the Olympian contempt for the theatre. He is an outstanding example of a man who despises the very medium where he excels. He makes one feel that dramatic success is merely an affair of hocus-pocus; and in the weeks that followed while the production of *But for the Grace of God* took shape, I began to suspect that he was right . . .

"In these days of meticulous directors, I look back with awe and pleasure to the Lonsdale method of conducting affairs. He would stroll in to rehearsals at any unpredictable time, sit down beside Matty, and start gossiping about the Good Old Days at the Garrick Club, without apparently bothering to notice what was happening on the stage. When he found time to, he directed by a fastidious process of elimination, rather like a connoisseur turning over and rejecting the trash in an antique shop and steadily moving towards the objects of real worth. Then suddenly he would pounce on something he did not like; and an admonitory finger would caress the fruity nose, and out would come a suggestion which, even if caustic, was always to the point."

Mr. Daubeny had, as I have said before, the secret of managing Freddy. This was the Lonsdale of *The Last of Mrs. Cheyney*, the Lonsdale never to be seen in the theatre again.

But for the Grace of God opened at the St. James's Theatre on September 3rd, 1946, after a successful try-out in the provinces. The critics were as usual divided in their reception of the play. The critic of *The Times* did not like it, the critic of the the *Daily Telegraph* did not like it either, but, nevertheless, remarked:

"But Mr. Lonsdale cannot fail to be entertaining even when he is straining our credulity to breaking point."

The *Daily Express* said: "A brilliant play in his best manner," and Ivor Brown, in *The Observer*, said:

"The play is rendered in a very simple fashion; the actors stand or sit facing the audience in a row and talk straight at us: the talk, however, is good enough to make the old and simple method work."

The play seems to have hung fire for a week or two, because there was some suggestion at the time of new money being found to keep it going until it had had a chance to build up. But it did build up, and it ran for 201 performances. Peter Daubeny says:

"What with the preliminary try-out, its seven-month run in London and a further provincial tour that followed it, *But for the Grace of God* played to crowded houses for all of a year."

Until 1950 Freddy continued to live mostly in New York,

but, the high seas now being open, he took advantage of this fact to resume his constant journeyings backwards and forwards to England. He never stayed for long in England. He found it cold and depressing, and he was quite unused to the degree of discomfort caused here by the aftermath of the war. He came in a wary mood. He knew that he had made himself very unpopular during the war and would be met with hostility. Once the cause of anger has been removed people are very forgiving, however. Soon they cannot recollect exactly what it was that made them so angry. In any case, it was not very long before Freddy was again surrounded by an enormous circle of friends and acquaintances.

"Ho, ho," he wrote to Andrea Cowdin, "Frederick is now greeted with delight by people I thought had forgotten me. The strangest voices are heard asking me to dine. It is a pity I am so busy."

He was, in fact, busy; dining or lunching constantly with all these voices. If one wanted to see him it was always most difficult to arrange. Nevertheless, he was not a fool and his memory was long for some things.

He wrote in 1951 to Andrea Cowdin as follows:

"In the year 1946 when I went to London I had very few friends, you will remember. I have many now. But, at that time, Billy Rootes was perhaps as good a friend as any man could have. His friendship and loyalty to me was very touching, and I shall never forget it. So I wish him only happiness . . ."

There were certain people to whom Freddy was genuinely devoted: the Cowdins, the Talbotts, Bob Rubin, Cary Grant, Dr. Devol in America; and here the Seftons, the Marriotts, Sir Alexander Korda, about whom he wrote: "He must be having a bad time, but he keeps his marvellous humour," and through whom he seems to have made great friends with Sir Laurence and Lady Olivier, both Billy and Reggie Rootes, and Ronnie

Squire, Lord Beaverbrook, later, Mr. Frank Goldsmith and his
wife, and certainly others of whom I do not know. But his life
was made up of constant meals with the merest acquaintances,
of continual scurrying to and fro. And:

"Boredom let me tell you is my master," he wrote to Andrea.

While Freddy had been in America, Ronnie Squire had
married a young and charming wife. Esyllt Squire tells me that
when she and Freddy first met they disliked each other intensely,
and she believes that this was, on his part, because she had
married Ronnie. I am sure she is wrong about this. I am not
convinced he did dislike her, but, if he did, I think it was not
because she had married Ronnie, but because of her name. He
would not have known how to pronounce this and he would
have felt it tiresome and affected of her to have it. In any case,
their dislike of each other was dissolved in the following way.
One night Freddy was dining with the Squires, and he had
spent the evening ribbing and riling Ronnie.

"Ah!" he said, late in the evening, "that's the trouble,
Ronnie, with marrying a young wife."

"The trouble with marrying an old husband," Esyllt
remarked, "is his old friends."

"Ho! Ho-o-o!" Freddy said, and pulled at his nose with
excitement. Here was the real Garrick touch. After this he was
extremely fond of her, and he solved the problem of her name
by calling her Fanny.

In 1949 Freddy wrote his last and my favourite of all his plays,
The Way Things Go. One has to be a little careful in a judgment
of this play, because there were two unusual things about it—the
first, Miss Glynis Johns, the second, Mr. Kenneth More. Freddy
had, all his playwrighting life, been lucky in Mr. Fred Kerr,
Mr. A. E. Matthews and Mr. Ronald Squire. Usually in his
plays there was a character of a woman of fifty, and again he had
been lucky in several old war-horses who could be counted on

to extract the last ounce from his humour and his wit. But never before in England (Miss Ina Claire played only in America) had he had a leading lady with a genius for light comedy. Miss Johns's performance in *The Way Things Go* was a pearl beyond all price, and only in a country which despises comedy would she fail to rank amongst the most talented actresses we have. Mr. Kenneth More made his first comedy appearance on the London stage, and he played a small but important part. One could only feel it was a pity he had not been born twenty years earlier, because here again was the real gift for comedy, that unsung, unloved gift, which is nevertheless denied to many actors of the greatest power and consequence, who can stop our hearts in tragedy. These two, in my extremely biased opinion, with Ronald Squire, made *The Way Things Go* one of the best acted plays I have ever seen.

I read it through the other day, and, even without these personalities, it still remains the comedy I like the best. It has a weak third act, and a poor solution—it could not have anything else—but, in spite of this defect, it is so amusing and so charming that it wins the heart. Freddy could never write a serious love scene, any more than Gerald du Maurier could ever play one, but he could write a scene which was very gentle, very charming, and wittily touching. In this play it seems to me he succeeded completely.

At rehearsal Freddy did everything in his power to ruin the production of this play. Directors followed each other in and out of the theatre at an unbelievable speed, actors were changed constantly, the rest of the cast was harassed to death. After Freddy had spent two or three weeks effecting this chaos, he spoke to Ronnie Squire.

"You're all terrible," he said, "simply terrible."

And with that he left for the South of France, leaving the company to get out of this situation as best they might.

The play was almost unanimously well received. 'Lonsdale Back With A Kick', said a headline in the *Daily Mail*, the morning after the first performance in London. "The wit of veteran playwright Frederick Lonsdale sparkles as freely and as gaily as ever," said the *Star*, and John Barber in the *Daily Express* reported:

"My eyes were pricking during her (Miss Glynis Johns's) love scene . . . Lonsdale's piece is no more than a trifle, but as such it is the work of a master-craftsman. It reaches no farther than the walls of the theatre: but how coolly and completely it fills the intermediate air."

The play was an immediate success and in the first week it played to capacity. With that part of the audience which fills the stalls it continued as great a success as anything he had ever written. I remember that when I spoke of it to Kitty Sackville, one of the most charming of that year's débutantes, she exclaimed:

"Oh! but that is our play."

"What do you mean?"

"My friends and I go to it regularly. We think it the most amusing play of the season."

So much for fashion. Nevertheless, that part of the public which is known in the theatre as the 'cheap parts' did not attend too enthusiastically. The salaries of the star cast were too high for the play to continue for long except at or near capacity, and so, while it ran for 155 performances and made money for the management, because of the defection of the 'cheap parts' it had then to be withdrawn.

Freddy was in New York by the time of the first night in London, and when he received the cables telling him of his great success, he was sitting with Gladys Cooper.

"There you are," he said, "like *The Last of Mrs. Cheyney*, I owe my success to my leading lady."

"Oh! pouf!" she replied.

"But," she said when she told me this, "on this occasion, he may have been right."

She referred to the subsequent history of the play in America, and she was suggesting that it was because Miss Johns did not play in it there that the play did not succeed. This may have been so, but there are two other possible reasons for the failure of the play in America.

There was one person in London who had not liked it. Mr. Harold Hobson found it shocking. The story of the play is of the efforts of a rich American girl to force a poor Englishman, whom she knows loves her, to marry her; and, because of her excessive fortune and his lack of one, of his attempts to refuse. I am amazed that, as played by Miss Johns, anyone could find this situation shocking, but it is easy to believe that, performed with less skill, some of the scenes might surprise. And in London there had seemed to be some fear amongst Americans that offence might be given in New York by the fact that the determined young lady was American, the recalcitrant young man English.

Whether these things were enough to spoil this charming comedy for New York will never be known. Freddy left nothing to chance. Ferociously and idiotically unreasonable, he rehearsed the cast himself. No one pleased him, no one understood him; and after three damaging weeks, he again left a situation bordering on the mental asylum for someone else to straighten out. Sir Cedric Hardwicke took over, but he had no time to begin again from the beginning and no opportunity of undoing all that Freddy had managed to do. The play was a complete failure.

After this Freddy lived mostly in France—at the Hotel Carlton at Cannes or the Hotel Lotti in Paris. I think he was very lonely and very unhappy. He had always hoped for too

much. The look of expectancy that he wore did not mean
nothing—he expected perpetual entertainment. And he was a
man without resources. For the last years of his life he lived in a
country of spires and towers and arches—Romanesque arches
and Gothic arches, pointed arches within the round, round
within the pointed; of rose windows and vaulting and tapestry;
of sculpture, of painting, of carving; a country where any little
inn might be capable of a talented meal; where the grape is
grown and made into wine. Freddy drove in a fast car from
Paris to Cannes, from Cannes to Paris, accomplishing the
journey in two days even when he was over seventy.

He took at this time to letter-writing, and, although all his
life he had resorted to extreme measures to avoid putting pen
to paper to write a play, he now spent his mornings with a
typewriter writing letters to his friends. The trouble with
these letters was that he hoped they would produce a reply,
and, like a little fawning dog, he resorted to all sorts of tricks to
get them answered.

"To get another letter from you I am writing this one," he
wrote to me once. "At my memorial service you will be heard
to say, I wish I had written to him more often, he so liked
hearing from me."

And another time:

"I am hard at work on my new play. It is an entirely
different play to any other play I have written. My liking for it
is the cause, and the only cause, of my not being at this moment
in a nonsense house. I have in the play a young clergyman, the
young clergyman is me. Through him I hand out all the things
that I think about everything, he is a splendid fellow, and were
he alive you would write to him often."

And again:

"It is evident that I have departed from your life. It is a long
while ago since I heard from you. You may wonder what I am

doing here. Should you discover the reason kindly let me know. Slowly and surely I am leading myself to a nonsense house."

Until the last two or three years of his life he still travelled like a maniac. Miss Chesher, his secretary, wrote to my husband once:

"The cost from his English banking a/c for his recent trip to France (and he paid *all hotel bills* and travel from Cannes to London out of American money) came to no less than £400, which included his return fare to New York. Nothing seems to make him realise that his own travelling expenses alone are out of all proportion to his income. In every letter I get he appears to be extremely 'money conscious'—he says he is very worried, fearful for his future, etc., and is always *going* to live economically somewhere. But in the present he is spending all he has on these everlasting trips across the Atlantic. Four and five times a year—ten trips at an average of £210 a trip for fares alone."

He was extremely worried about money. I have recorded elsewhere that he had a diminishing capital sum on which he was living, and that he knew quite well that, whether or not he had the ability to earn new money, too much of it, if earned, would nowadays go in income tax for him to be able to afford the millionaire's life he was accustomed to. But he always believed that each journey would be his last; that he would find peace at the end of it. After 1951 he did confine his journeyings to France, with occasional trips to England, but although he restricted his travel, he did not limit it. Binkie Beaumont told me once that he had gone to luncheon with Walter Crichton in a villa at Mougins and that Freddy had been there, obviously staying in the house. After luncheon, Freddy asked Binkie if he was going down to Cannes, and when Binkie replied that he was, he asked him to take him and his luggage to the Carlton Hotel at Cannes. Late that evening some member of Binkie's party remembered that he had left something at the villa at Mougins and on their way home they stopped there to pick it up. Freddy was there, again installed in the house, having hired a car to drive him back from Cannes.

"What is the purpose of all this journeying?" Binkie asked Walter Crichton.

"I think, you know," he replied, "that it is just a little madness."

It was at about this time that Freddy wrote to me:

"I have the greatest understanding of your wish to get away. You only run away from yourself for a fortnight every year. I run away from myself every hour of every day."

We used to go and stay with him every winter in Cannes. He looked forward very much to these visits, and was happy while we were with him. He liked our company, but what chiefly gave him pleasure was our enjoyment. It seemed to him a fascinating thing that two people could so genuinely enjoy life.

"I've booked your rooms at the Suisse," he wrote to me once, "and I have hired a photographer to take Mr. Donaldson eating."

I wrote to him once after one of these visits and told him I had tears in my eyes when I left.

"I am sorry that you cried," he wrote back; "the last time I saw that happen was after dining with Marie Tempest. Gerald was there. In the car as we left you cried, because, you said, 'Gerald is dying.' It may be you spotted that I was, and it would only be proper and conventional that under such conditions you should cry again. So please, under no circumstances, assuming that I resist the passing this time, mention that you have cried. You should both be flattered—when you left I was very sad, and I missed you very much. Like most people at the funeral of their beloved one—they think of all the nasty things they said and did to the loved one. My feelings were—I might have done more to make your holiday more exciting. I hope that I alone noticed it, but I was conscious there was a little meanness."

In the last two or three years of his life he began to fear that he could no longer write a play. He seldom admitted this even to himself, almost never to other people.

"My new play is *brilliant*," one would hear him say to some stranger. But: "The type of play I write certainly isn't wanted. You know that," he wrote to Andrea Cowdin. (His letters to the Cowdins are extraordinarily touching, they are so full of affection.) To Cheever he wrote: "Working under difficult conditions: still Carol (Reed) and others think well of my play." And: "I could not tell you if the story of my play will be liked, but this I can tell you, it is the best dialogue I have ever written." But in his diary he recorded: "Think at last have got story—but how can one be sure? I have thought so so many times."

His diary makes sad reading.

"A dull day."

"Another dull day."

Dull was a serious word for Freddy. "A dull dog" was the greatest condemnation he could make of any man.

The records of the days when he was more amused are hardly less pathetic.

"Lovely day. Frankie arrived! Most enjoyable talk!"

We sat in a garden, if I remember, and we discussed *The Strange Case of Alger Hiss*.

Nevertheless, he was a creature of many moods, and he still retained an enthusiastic hopefulness at times.

"I go to Max for a fortnight at Cap d'Ail."

"I am going to stay with Sheila—Freda will be there."

"Going to stay with Diana and Duff at Chantilly. Diana says the flowers will be out."

"I stayed some time with Hugh and Foxie which was very enjoyable."

"My twelve days' visit to London was pleasant. I saw Frankie . . . Momo, and John, a week-end with the Oliviers which could not have been nicer. The production of *Cæsar* will fascinate you. It is one of the most distinguished productions I have seen for many years."

"Do you think I am wrong," I asked Simon Elwes once, "to believe that the end of his life was very unhappy?"

"Oh no," he replied. "I think you are right. You see, the extraordinary thing about Freddy was that there was that vibrant personality which we all *loved*—or hated—and behind that there was nothing."

He reminded me of a little boy who has been badgering his mother for months to allow him to go to school. And now here at eleven o'clock on his first morning he stands in the playground, facing reality. The thing that was so touching about this little boy was that he took it bravely. He did not cry or flinch; on the contrary, he joined rather too boisterously in the games, and only his eyes suggested the shock he had received.

In August 1953, in the last year of Freddy's life, H. M. Tennent staged a revival of *Aren't We All?* Binkie turned the production over to John Perry, but between them they staged it lavishly. Cecil Beaton did the décor, and the cast included Ronnie Squire and Marie Löhr, Marjorie Fielding and Jane Baxter. Binkie, who had heard from afar the stifled noises that issued from the rehearsals of *The Ways Things Go*, had an arrangement with Freddy that he would not go to rehearsals. This agreement was not kept, because Roland Culver, the director, becoming worried about the casting, sent for the author. This production meant a great deal to Freddy. If it should be a great success, it might inspire him with the confidence to write a new play, or alternatively it might suggest to managements the revival of others of his plays. This did not make him easy or benevolent at rehearsals.

The play opened at Brighton, where it was very well received, both by the public and by the local critic, who was well-respected in the theatre. Then it went to the Haymarket Theatre on August 6th. August is a difficult month to open, and it was felt that much depended on the reception given the production by the critics.

The majority of the papers were on the next day favourable to the play. *The Times* gave it a good notice, so did the *Daily Mail* and the *Telegraph*. These critics were surprised at how well the thirty-year-old piece had worn, and generally they admired its wit and dexterity. "Lonsdale, whom I still prefer to Wilde . . ." one critic wrote. But the *Daily Express* and the *Evening Standard* were vicious. It seemed to me then and it seems to me now that the notices printed in these two papers were inspired by some emotion warmer than the critical spirit.

"Did they think," John Barber enquired in the *Express*, "that Cecil Beaton's sumptuous decoration would save it? Did they hope that the charm of Ronald Squire and Marie Löhr would give it the right aristocratic air? They hoped in vain . . .

"So the adroit little piece turns soggy and serious. And so it only answers one question. It does explain why poor triangle plays of this kind drove audiences into the cinema—just thirty years ago."

This is very sad, this picture of audiences being driven out of the theatre by triangle plays to take refuge—in the cinema.

The *Evening Standard* was even more virulent.

"*Aren't We All?* snappily inquire the posters outside the Haymarket Theatre. Well, we were: but are we still? Frederick Lonsdale's comedy, first produced thirty years ago, is what some would call gentle, others toothless: where Somerset

Maugham chews and digests his characters, Lonsdale merely mumbles them."

Mr. Tynan succeeds perfectly in his intention to denigrate without the unnecessary effort of giving his words a meaning.

"Tennent Productions," he continued, "who have presented this play, have had one sensible impulse: they did not trust it. Hence, they and their designer, Cecil Beaton, have decked it out in the costumes of 1914, nearly a decade before it was written. But of all unfortunate decades! Lonsdale's style was ever a sentimental hangover from Wilde's: and you do not help a man with a hangover by reminding him of the night before. The discrepancy between the bright, stately decor and the blunt, breezy wit is brutally wide.

"*Aren't We All?* in short resembles a dear old lady embarrassingly got up as Mistinguett."

A blunt and breezy dear old lady?

Freddy had left London before the first night of *Aren't We All?* and gone to stay with Lord Beaverbrook at Cap d'Ail. His arrival there coincided with a French railway strike and no English newspapers and no letters were delivered at Cap d'Ail except those in the *Daily Express* bag for Lord Beaverbrook, which travelled by extraordinary means. For two or three weeks Freddy heard no news of the play except that contained in the *Daily Express* and the *Evening Standard*. He made no complaint about this, either then or later. He never complained about this kind of thing.

Aren't We All? had an uneasy run. It was never entirely successful, never completely a failure. One week it would play to very good business, the next be unaccountably down. It had the distinction of being chosen for H.M. The Queen to attend for a gala performance in aid of The Actors' Benevolent Fund. In November the Haymarket Theatre was wanted for Sir John

K

Gielgud, and *Aren't We All?* was not sufficiently successful to be allowed to keep him waiting. So, after a run of three months, it was withdrawn.

A few months after this Freddy died. We visited him in Cannes in the February, and he seemed quite as usual, very affectionate and gay, and gambling like a madman at the Casino. In April he came to London. He had a cold which had affected his antrum, and he felt sorry for himself. On Sunday, April 4th, he telephoned me.

"We must be careful about money," were the last words he said to me, "but you can count on your holiday next winter. There will be enough for that."

That night he died in the street as he was walking home from Claridge's with Sir John Marriott, with whom he was staying. He left no debts except current ones, and a little less than £7,000; almost no possessions except his clothes; only the letters he had received in the last week or two. Two of these, at least, might have been received by him at any time in the last thirty years.

"Dearest Freddy," wrote Mrs. Cary Grant, "the fact that you had written two acts of a play to throw in the fire makes you far superior to most men. The thing that makes me superior to most women is that I don't believe you . . ."

The other was from Lady Marriott.

"Thank you, darling. I couldn't like this more. Definitely *no* cottage in England, no hotel in France. *Quoi faire?* Love, Momo."

When someone one loves dies unexpectedly, one feels, for the first day or two, very little emotion. Immediately after Freddy's death my only feeling was of relief. There had been so much to worry about. There was the terrifying question of his money. On my reckoning he had, when he died, about eighteen months to go before he was reduced to about £1,200 a year and a way of living which would have driven him insane. Many people would have been willing to rescue him from this, but rescue equally would have driven him insane. Walking in the gardens of the Tuileries one morning, when we were staying in Paris with him, I said to Jack:

"What is going to *happen* when his money has gone?"

"That is a thing," he replied, "that one cannot even contemplate until it happens."

I had been tortured, too, by the nightmare that one day I would take an aeroplane to a deathbed in a hotel in a foreign land—a hotel where the management, averse to death on the premises, were scarcely civil—where Freddy suffered unknown fears.

Even if the worst imaginings had proved unfounded, Freddy detested old age. The advantages of age we none of us would choose, but they are there for most of us. For most men there is a fire to sit by, books to read, an easing off of responsibility, some hobby; children, grandchildren—perhaps a belief in God. For Freddy there were only the fruits of egotism.

I often wished that he could read. He would have found consolations in Shakespeare.

"It is a tale Told by an idiot, full of sound and fury, Signifying nothing."

Two or three days after his death I began to remember how vital he had been, how charming, humorous and gay; how long and how devotedly he had loved me.

The Works of Frederick Lonsdale

(Listed in order of production)

The dates are of the first *London* performance (where the play was first produced in America, the New York date is also given).

The King of Cadonia. (Musical Play); (Music: Sidney Jones). Prince of Wales Theatre. September 3rd, 1908. 330 performances.

The Early Worm. Wyndham's Theatre. September 7th, 1908. 77 performances.

The Best People. Wyndham's Theatre. August 5th, 1909. 60 performances.

The Balkan Princess (Musical Play, with Frank Curzon); (Music: Paul Rubens). Prince of Wales Theatre. February 19th, 1910. 176 performances.

Betty (Musical Play, with Gladys Unger); (Music: Paul Rubens). Daly's Theatre. April 24th, 1915. 391 performances.

High Jinks (Musical Comedy. English Version of an American adaptation from the French); (Music: Rudolph Friml). Adelphi Theatre. August 24th, 1916. 383 performances.

The Maid of the Mountains (Musical Play); (Music: Harold Fraser-Simson). Daly's Theatre. February 10th, 1917. 1,352 performances.

Monsieur Beaucaire (Romantic Opera); (Music: André Messager). Prince's Theatre. April 19th, 1919. 221 performances.

The Lady of the Rose (Musical Play. Adaptation of a Viennese original); (Music: Jean Gilbert). Daly's Theatre. February 21st, 1922. 514 performances.

Aren't We All? Globe Theatre. April 10th, 1923. 58 performances.

Madame Pompadour (Musical Play, with Harry Graham. From a Viennese original); (Music: Leo Fall). Daly's Theatre. December 20th, 1923. 469 performances.

The Fake. Apollo Theatre. March 13th, 1924. 211 performances.

The Street Singer (Musical Play); (Music: Harold Fraser-Simson). Lyric Theatre. June 27th, 1924. 360 performances.

Spring Cleaning. St. Martin's Theatre. January 29th, 1925. 262 performances. First produced in America. Eltinge Theatre, New York. November 9th, 1923. 292 performances.

Katja the Dancer (Musical Play, with Harry Graham, from the German); (Music: Jean Gilbert). Gaiety Theatre. February 21st, 1925. (Transferred to Daly's, September 1925). 505 performances.

The Last of Mrs. Cheyney. St. James's Theatre. September 22nd, 1925. 514 performances.

On Approval. Fortune Theatre. April 19th, 1927. 469 performances.

The High Road. Shaftesbury Theatre. September 7th, 1927. 237 performances.

Lady Mary (Musical Comedy, with John Hastings Turner); (Music: Albert Sirmay and Philip Craig). Daly's Theatre. February 23rd. 1928. 181 performances.

Canaries Sometimes Sing. Globe Theatre. October 21st, 1929. 144 performances.

Never Come Back. Phœnix Theatre. October 28th, 1932. 58 performances.

Once Is Enough (Produced in America only). Henry Miller Theatre, New York. February 15th, 1938. 105 performances.

Foreigners (Produced in America only). Belasco Theatre, New York. December 5th, 1939. 7 performances.

Another Love Story. Phœnix Theatre. December 13th, 1944. 173 performances. Originally produced in America. Fulton Theatre, New York. October 12th, 1943. 103 performances.

But for the Grace of God. St. James's Theatre. September 3rd, 1946. 201 performances.

The Way Things Go. Phœnix Theatre. March 2nd, 1950. 155 performances.

Index